THE ART OF

CHARLES W. THWAITES

FREEDOM OF EXPRESSION

SUSAN HALLSTEN McGARRY

FRESCO FINE ART PUBLICATIONS
ALBUQUERQUE, NEW MEXICO

This book was issued on the occasion of the July 16 to September 7, 2008, exhibition of Charles W. Thwaites' paintings at the Museum of Wisconsin Art, West Bend, Wisconsin.

All dimensions are in inches, height preceding width. Painting dates are in most cases approximations. Artworks not identified as private or public collection are in the estate of CWT Art, LLC.

Photographs other than those identified by a photographer's name are by Gary Mankus, Santa Fe Editions, Santa Fe, New Mexico.

Design and Production
Fresco Fine Art Publications, llc
Albuquerque, New Mexico
www.frescobooks.com

Library of Congress Control Number: 2008921842
McGarry, Susan Hallsten

Freedom of Expression: The Art of Charles W. Thwaites / by Susan Hallsten McGarry.
ISBN: 978-1-934491-08-9

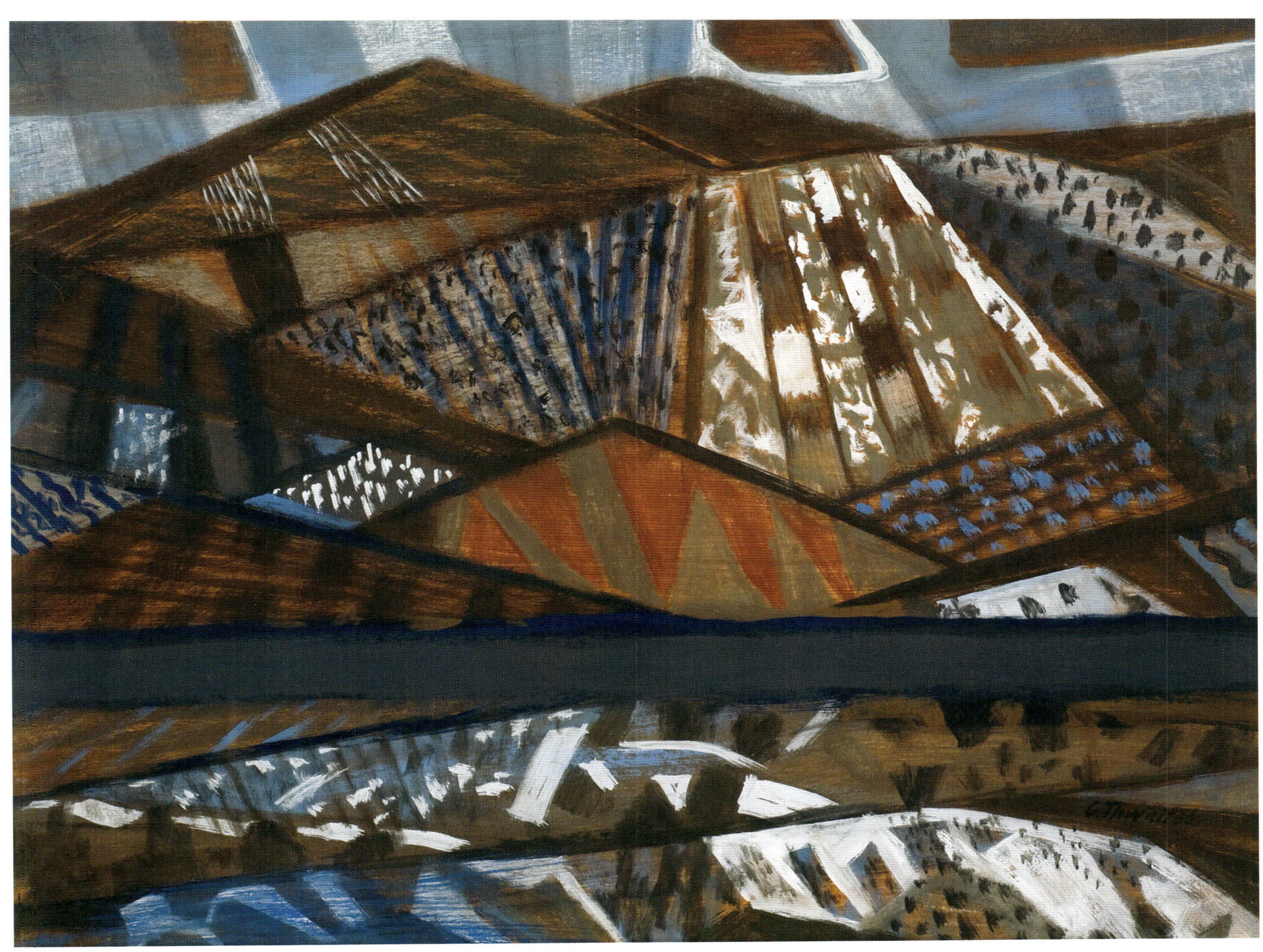

TAOS MOUNTAIN, 1964
acrylic on paper
17½ x 23
private collection

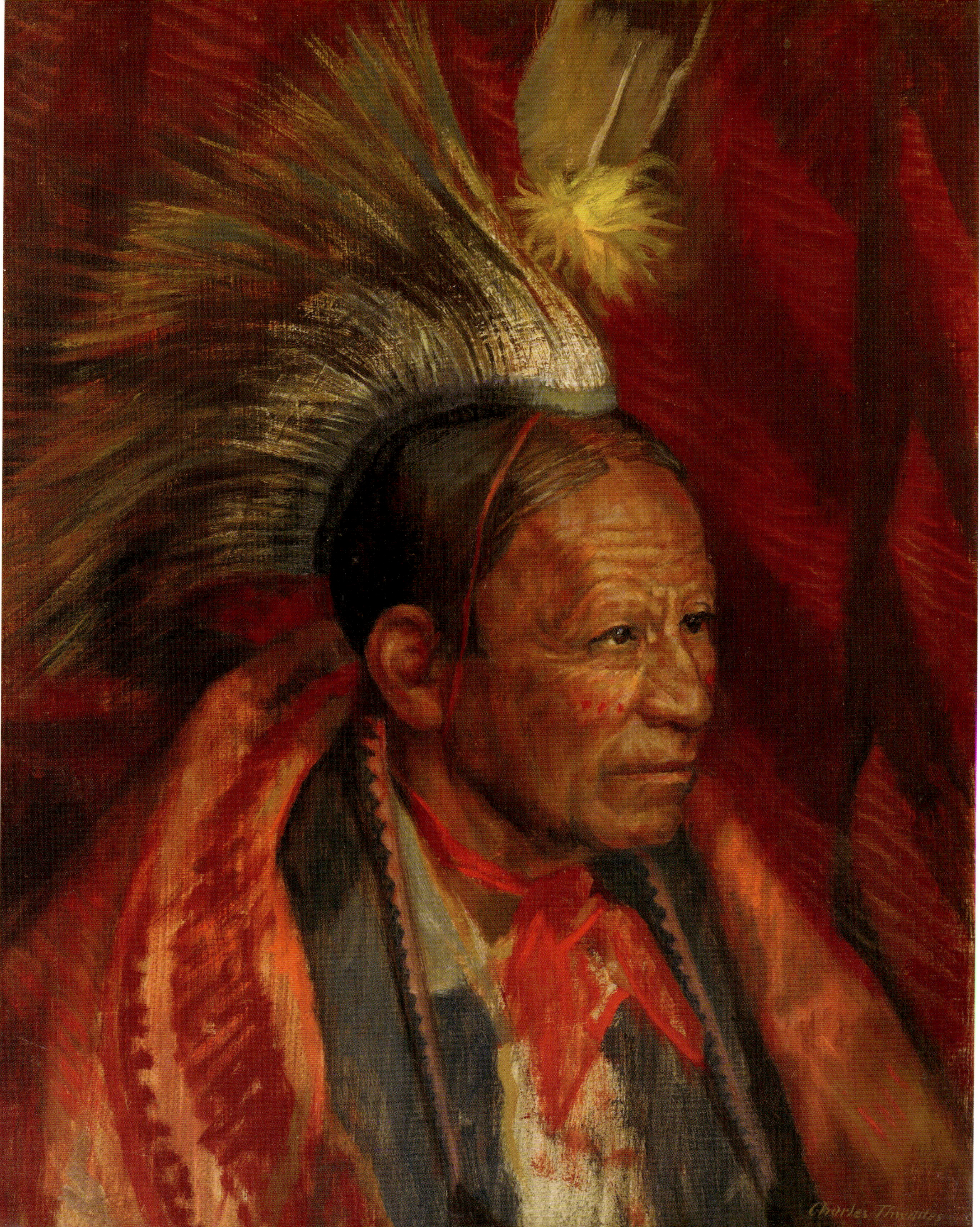
Charles Thwaites

CONTENTS

FRANK ZAMORA, 1955
oil on masonite
24 x 18
private collection
Philip Harsh Photography

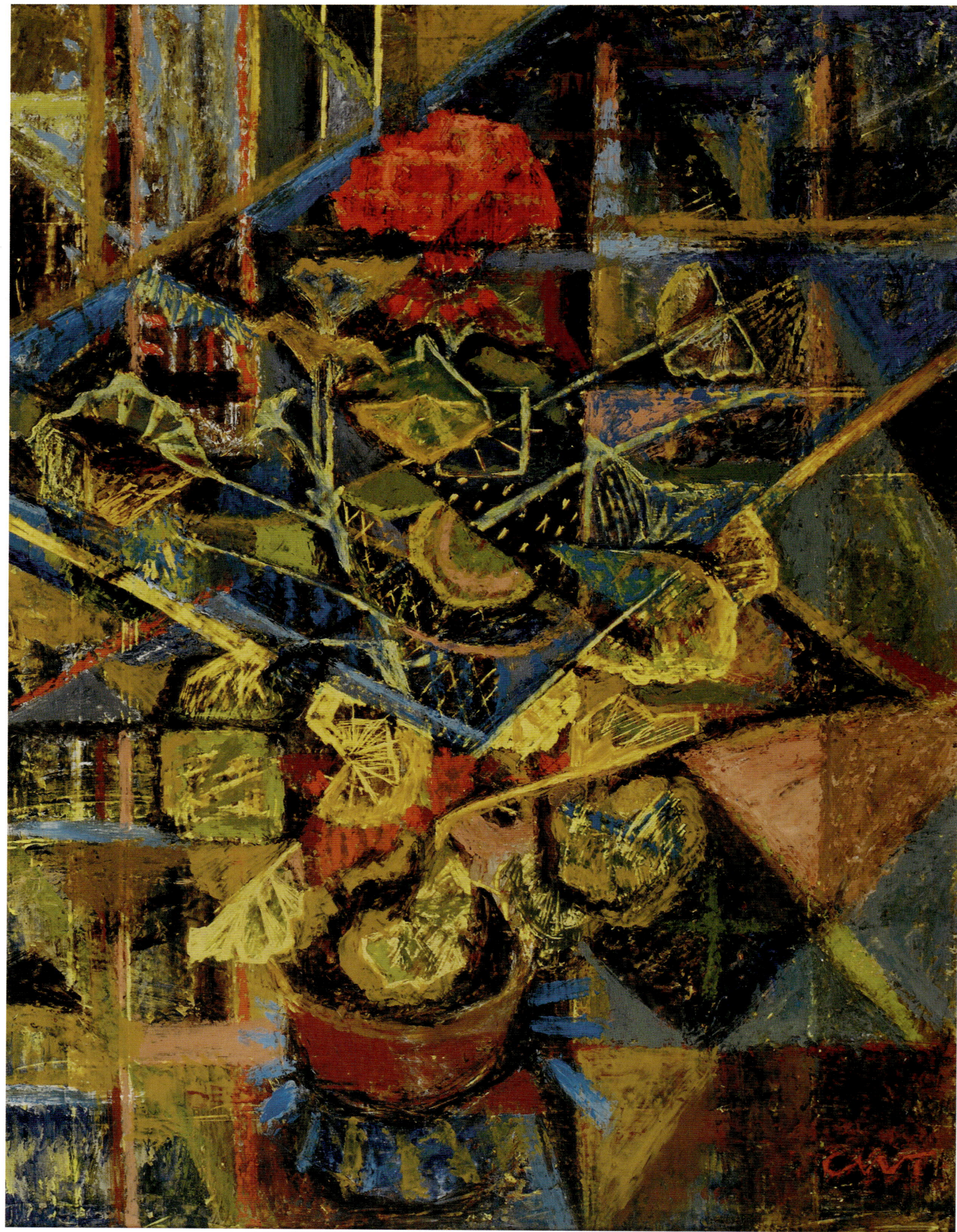

PREFACE

OLOF AND LUCIA THWAITS DAHLSTRAND

On a clear, bitter-cold day in late November 2002, with a touch of snow on the ground, a simple wood box containing Charles W. Thwaites' earthly remains was lowered into the ground next to the grave of his beloved wife Antoinette in Rosario Cemetery, Santa Fe, New Mexico. The ceremony was attended by a few old Santa Fe friends, including Charles' attorney William Federici, New Mexico Supreme Court judge from 1977 to 1985, and as he told us later, attorney for artist Georgia O'Keeffe.

At the burial, we represented the estate, which Charles, being childless, left to his nine nieces, nephews, and their descendents.* This unusually large number of heirs, contrary to many family situations, proved to be firmly of one mind as to the disposition of the estate. Before distribution of assets, the primary goal of the heirs was to re-establish Thwaites' position as an important twentieth-century artist. This philosophy dominated the thinking for the next several years, during which the heirs met with numerous frustrations, in large part because Charles had virtually disappeared from the art world during the last two decades of his life.

An idea that had floated among the heirs, though never seriously considered, was the possibility of a book. Unfamiliar with the path for such a project, it had been shelved until Susan Tarman of Santa Fe, who appraised the estate, recommended writer and art historian Susan Hallsten McGarry as a potential book author.

Our first discussion with Susan McGarry centered on a very modest project, but as more information was unearthed in the CWT Estate Archives, it became clear that an expanded exploration of Thwaites' career and philosophy was appropriate. The result is this book, which reproduces more than a hundred of Charles' paintings and chronicles his career. It also documents a selection of his penetrating thoughts on the creative process, which will undoubtedly inspire readers and particularly art students who sincerely desire synthesizing their personal responses with universal emotions.

Working with Susan McGarry, photographer Gary Mankus, Graeme Reid, associate director of the Museum of Wisconsin Art, and Kay Fowler and Nancy Stem of Fresco Fine Art Publications has been enjoyable and inspiring throughout the entire process. We thank all who have been so helpful.

*Charles W. Thwaites was the youngest of five siblings, in order of age: Frederick, Howard, Edmond, Mabel, and Charles. Their children are: Jean Thwaits Dahlstrand, Frederick Thwaits, Jr., Alan Thwaits, John Thwaits, Helen Thwaits Buttel, Priscilla Thwaits Garcia, Lucia Thwaits Dahlstrand, Charles Ogg, and William Ogg. Jean Thwaits Dahlstrand died, leaving her share to Peter Dahlstrand and Alan Dahlstrand. Priscilla Thwaits Garcia died, leaving her share to David Garcia, Tania Garcia Fowler, and Michelle Garcia Winner. The heirs formed CWT Art, LLC, to hold the assets of the estate and conduct business on their behalf.

GERANIUM, 1953
encaustic on paper
23 x 17 1/2
private collection
Dennis Wyszynski Photography

FOREWORD

*To understand yourself—to understand your personal philosophy—is to understand your likes and dislikes in an organized way.**

Charles W. Thwaites (1904-2002), although seventeen years her junior, shares many parallels in life and art with Georgia O'Keeffe (1887-1986). Both were born into large families and raised in southern Wisconsin. Both worked as teachers while establishing their fine arts careers. Both married artists, and neither felt compelled to study abroad nor seek out foreign subject matter, choosing instead to document their immediate surroundings. Each exhibited in New York and was invited to submit works to the 1941 and 1942 Art Institute of Chicago American Paintings and Sculpture Exhibitions. In the 1942 exhibition, which memorialized Grant Wood (1891-1942), O'Keeffe exhibited *Red Hills and Bones* and Thwaites exhibited one of his penetrating self-portraits.[1]

O'Keeffe stayed in the Pink House while visiting Mabel Dodge and Tony Luhan in Taos, New Mexico, and Thwaites lived in it for two years. Each found the American Southwest invigorating, settling in northern New Mexico—O'Keeffe in 1949 and Thwaites in 1952. Thwaites briefly encountered O'Keeffe during a 1950 camping trip and later crossed paths with her at social gatherings of Taos artists and patrons. By the early 1970s, O'Keeffe painted sporadically, moving to Santa Fe in 1984. In 1962 Thwaites moved to Santa Fe, and by the early 1980s painted sporadically. O'Keeffe died at age ninety-eight in 1986; Thwaites died at age ninety-eight in 2002.

O'Keeffe and Thwaites each left a legacy of unique, bold responses to the splendor of their environments; however, this is where the similarities end. O'Keeffe, who had numerous solo exhibitions, retrospectives, and monographs during and after her lifetime, went on to become an icon of American art. Thwaites, who had ten solo shows and enjoyed recognition in more than 150 juried and invitational exhibitions, died in relative obscurity. Unlike O'Keeffe's recognizable subjects and style, Thwaites thrived on an evolving variety of media and styles.

This examination of Thwaites' career is the first to put his art in context. It has been developed through archival materials, the majority of which have been supplied by Thwaites' niece Lucia and her husband Olof Dahlstrand, executors of the artist's estate, which includes more than 350 paintings and sketches. Hundreds of newspaper articles, correspondence, vintage exhibition catalogues, and the artist's personal writings, combined with research into the cultural atmosphere in which he lived, flesh out the name inscribed on a remarkable oeuvre. The Dahlstrands, who also provided recollections and anecdotes about their visits with Charles and his wife Antoinette, speculated on dating the artworks, many of which were neither dated nor titled by the artist. Where works were not titled, we have given them descriptive titles, and the vast majority of the dates are educated guesses.

The text is broken into two parts. The first part covers Thwaites' five decades based in Milwaukee, Wisconsin. The second part describes the ten years he and Antoinette (nicknamed Toni) lived in Taos, New Mexico (1952 to 1962) and their last years in Santa

*Later in his life, Thwaites compiled his handwritten notes on art into a bright-yellow three-ring notebook he called Notes to Myself. The quotes appended with CWT are from these essays and notes. Transcripts and additional notes are included in Appendix B.

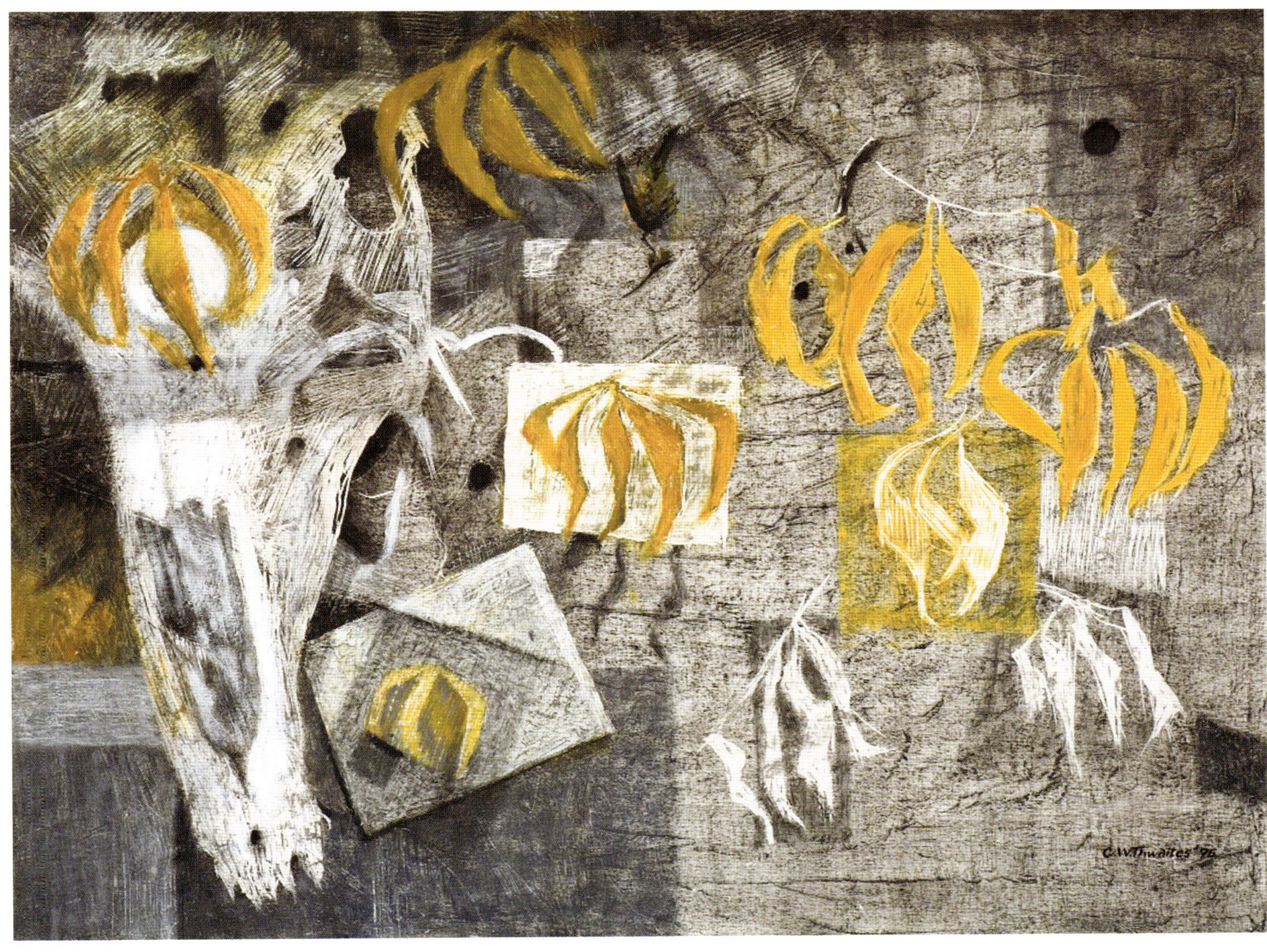

SKULL WITH LEAF MOTIF, 1976
mixed media on paper
17½ x 23
private collection

Fe. The appendices include transcriptions of articles and letters by Charles and Antoinette, and a selection of writings from Thwaites' journal, which he called Notes to Myself—excerpts from which are also included in the text.* The Chronology highlights significant events in Thwaites' life and career, and the exhibition list, which is prodigious, is annotated with artworks displayed, when they are known from catalogue records and/or identified in the estate.

It was a pleasure working with the Dahlstrands, whose enthusiasm for bringing Thwaites' art back into the limelight is infectious. I would like to acknowledge Susan Tarman, of Tarman Appraisals & Consulting, Santa Fe, for introducing me to the Dahlstrands, and art historian and former curator of the Harwood Museum David L. Witt for reading the manuscript with the eye of a specialist in the area of the Taos Moderns. Thanks also go to the librarians and researchers in Wisconsin and New Mexico who contributed time to verifying facts and locating paintings.

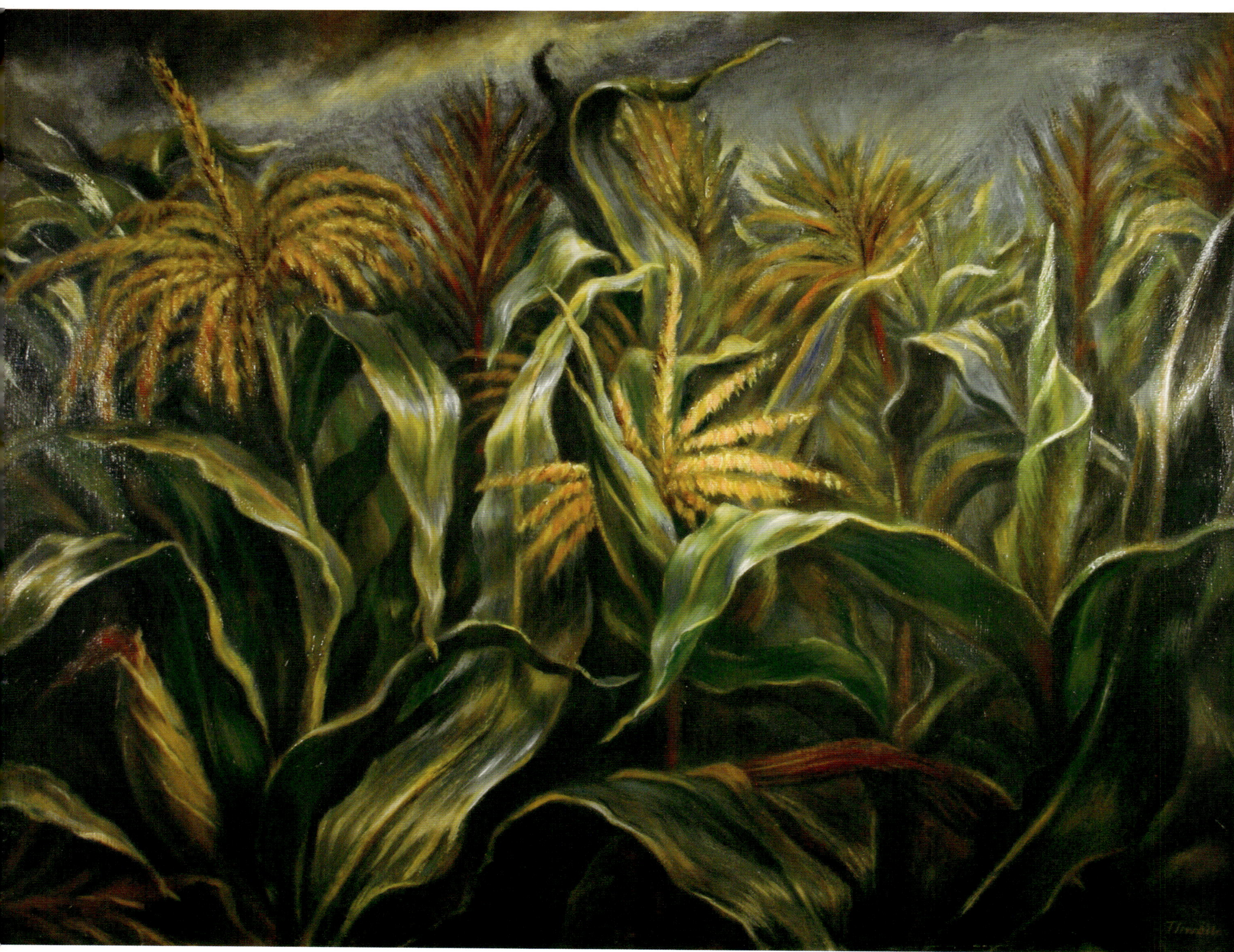

CORN, 1948
oil on masonite
24 x 32 1/8
Gift of Gimbel Brothers
Milwaukee Art Museum, Wisconsin

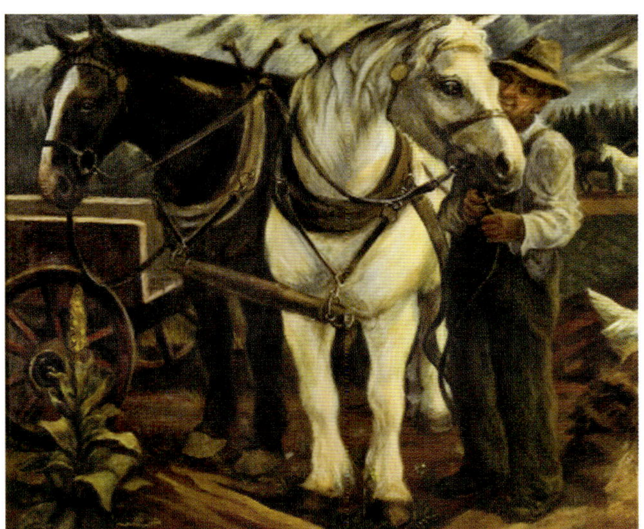

WISCONSIN

With tenuous threads and gossamer shreds of fantasy and illusions we weave the stuff of our personalities, all striving toward some self-esteem and self-appreciation against our "baser alloys," hoping for some good in us to justify and give reason to great thanks for our existence. CWT

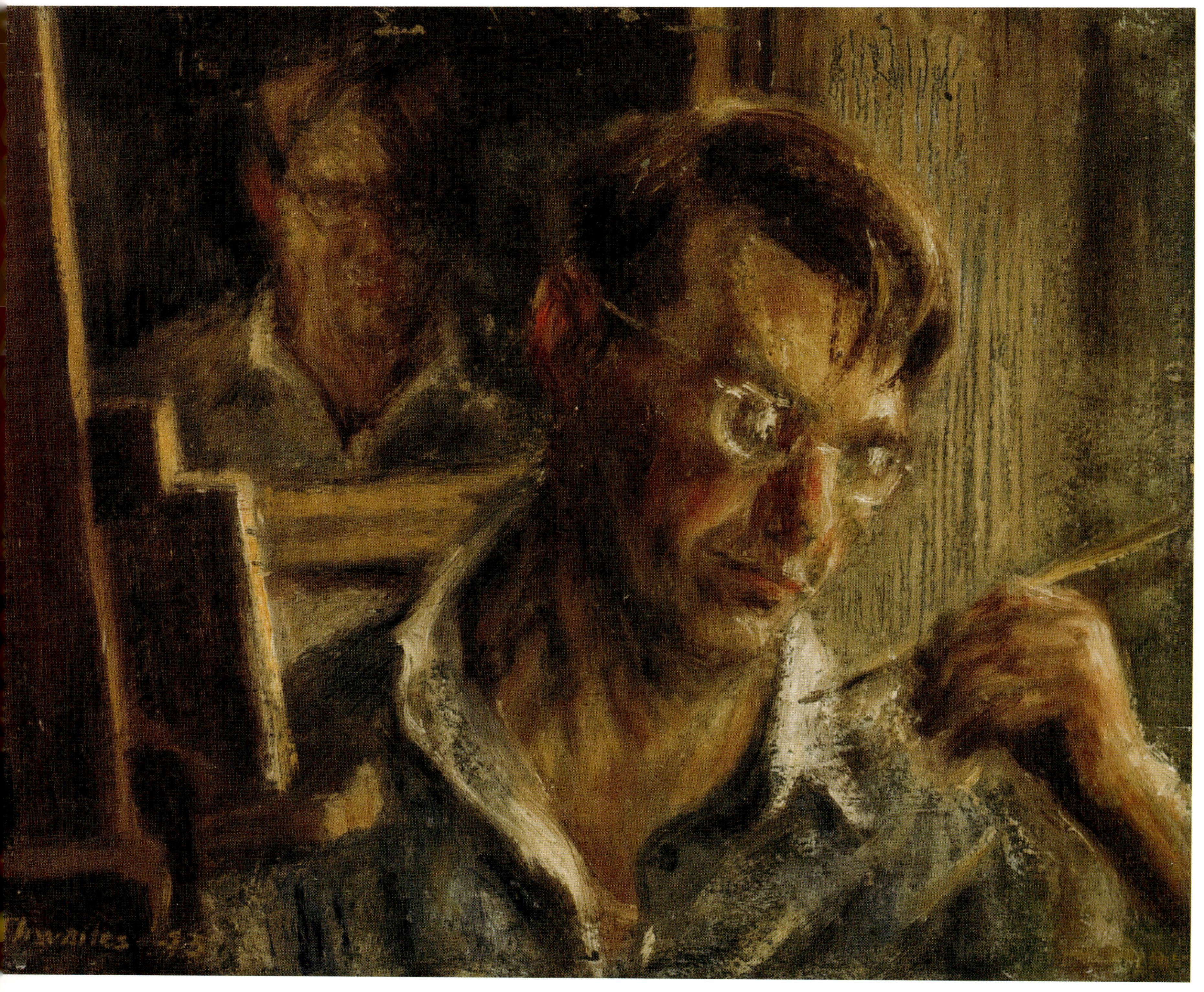

SELF-PORTRAIT (WITH SELF-PORTRAIT), 1943
oil maroger on masonite
8 x 10

ENVISIONING A CAREER

As is the tête-à-tête of young lovers, so too is the dialogue between a young artist and a work of art. It has to do with each other, with themselves, admiration, hope, dreams, fears, pain, inspiration, promise, and above all a desire to be good. If this be not true, then it be not love. CWT

Charles W. Thwaits was born on a cold March day in 1904 in Milwaukee, Wisconsin.[2] The youngest of five children, he was short in stature, standing five feet, six inches at maturity. Perhaps because of his size, he grew up a scrappy youngster, determined to build his physical prowess through exercise, swimming, acrobatics, and hard work. Throughout his school years, Charles worked with his father, who was a building contractor and manager of real-estate holdings, notably apartment buildings in Milwaukee. In his spare time, Charles reveled in family excursions into the countryside, particularly in the area around Cedar Lake, a natural paradise with rolling hills, forests, and grasslands that continued to lure him throughout his five decades in Wisconsin.

Too young to volunteer for World War I and too old to be drafted in World War II, Charles grew up in the era of prohibition, the rise of the labor movement, the Red Scare, women's suffrage, and the celebration of cultural identity among African Americans. The national art scene at the time was conflicted. The sensational 1913 Armory Show, which opened in New York, New York, and moved to Chicago, Illinois, introduced European modernism to a nation of relatively traditional painters. At roughly the same time, the New York Ashcan School followed by the American Scene painters championed a distinctly American art dedicated to realistic depictions of contemporary genre subjects, whether the ills of urban society or the idylls of rural life. Three Midwesterners, Grant Wood, John Steuart Curry (1897-1946), and Thomas Hart Benton (1889-1975), would become renowned for their dedication to the working man, and notably rural themes from their immediate surroundings in Iowa, Wisconsin, and Kansas. It is not known to what extent Charles was interested in art as a teenager attending Milwaukee's Riverside High School. His goals, however, included learning how to sail, getting a pilot's license, and studying civil engineering.

In the second year of his engineering curriculum at the University of Wisconsin, Madison, Thwaites observed students walking up to the second floor of the machine shop and decided to investigate. There he encountered Arthur Nicholson Colt (1890-1972) doing a portrait demonstration using what Thwaites described as an "interesting style and technique."[3] He stayed to watch, and that afternoon purchased paints, brushes, and canvas, and used himself as the subject of a self-portrait—a face and demeanor he interpreted throughout his life.

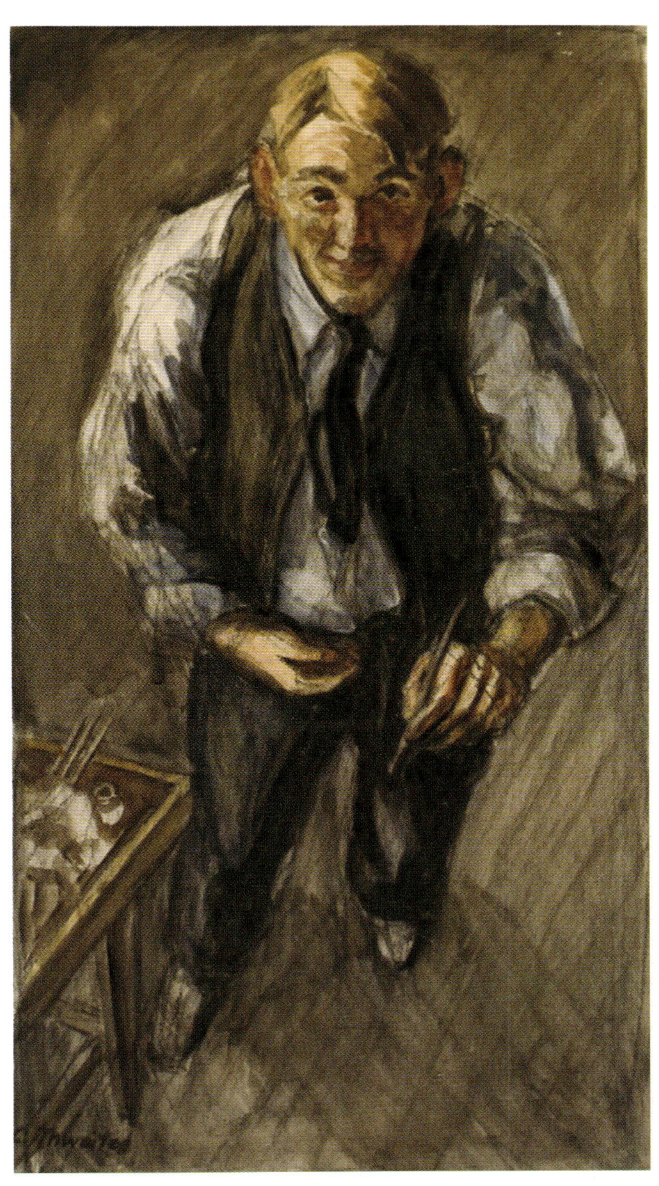

SELF-PORTRAIT (LOOKING UP), 1930
mixed media on paper
20½ x 11

Thwaites began skipping classes to paint. He soon came under the scrutiny of George Sellery, dean of the College of Letters and Sciences, who gave him permission to study as he wished for the remainder of the 1925 school year. The following year, Thwaites enrolled in a fine art program at the respected Layton School of Art, Milwaukee, which had been founded in 1920 by Charlotte R. Partridge and Miriam Frink.

Among Thwaites' notes in the estate archive is reference to Gerrit V. Sinclair (1890-1955), an instructor at Layton who influenced Thwaites' recognition of quality in art and perhaps his choice of medium. Thwaites described below what Sinclair called "the look" or a pattern that synthesizes the artist's personal response with universal emotions (also see The Look and The Look Again, Appendix B).

> It is to be seen in painting from all times and in nature and, looking long at nature, we see it change and vary and reappear in endless succession of emotion-satisfying relationships.... It exists in many, many forms and not the least important of which is the one imprinted in parallel pattern on your subconscious in the conduct of your own life.... Thus, as we were saying, this "look" ... this best spot on the canvas ... is just as valid on the canvas of your life. It is what really sets some canvases and certain lives apart and above the many.

Sinclair worked in a form of egg tempera that was described by Janet Treacy, curator of a Sinclair exhibition. "For painting, [Sinclair] favored tempera, a mixture of oil, varnish, egg, water and color. It is said that he kept this special amalgam in the family refrigerator. The mix was used to develop color and build texture."[4] Thwaites also worked in tempera incorporating egg, a mixture he may have learned from Sinclair or extrapolated from recipes provided by Max Doerner's book *The Materials of the Artist and Their Use in Painting, with Notes on the Techniques of the Old Masters*.[5] Olof Dahlstrand, an architect and former teacher at the Layton School who knew Thwaites beginning in the late 1930s, describes his mixture thusly:

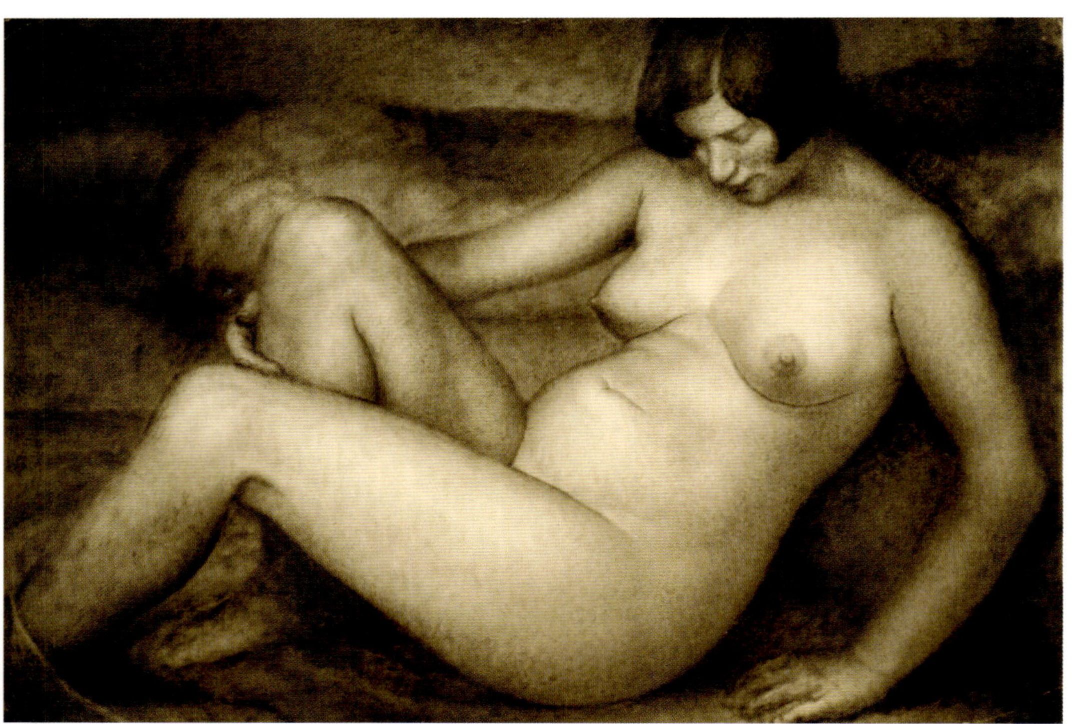

> He would prepare the egg medium, usually using the whole egg instead of just the yolk. Using dry pigments, he would wet the brush in the medium, dip the brush in the dry pigment, which would adhere to the wet brush, after which he would mix the paint on the palette and proceed as though it were oil. He would add medium or pigment as needed (or even thin with water as necessary). The process was really more akin to gouache than the traditional egg tempera methods, allowing greater freedom and faster response.[6]

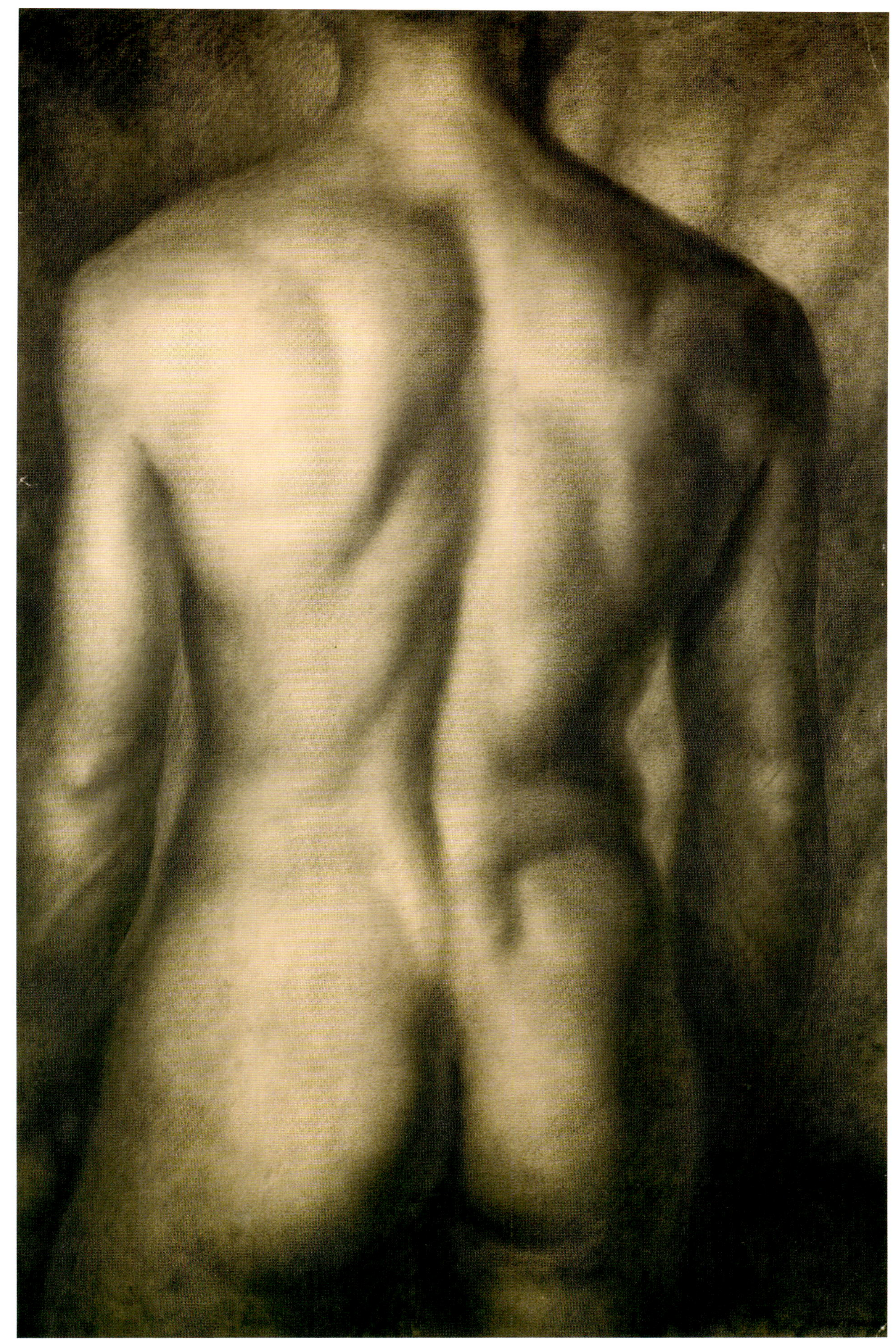

TORSO, 1935
dry oil on paper
35 x 23

Opposite:
RECLINING NUDE, 1935
dry oil on paper
23 x 35

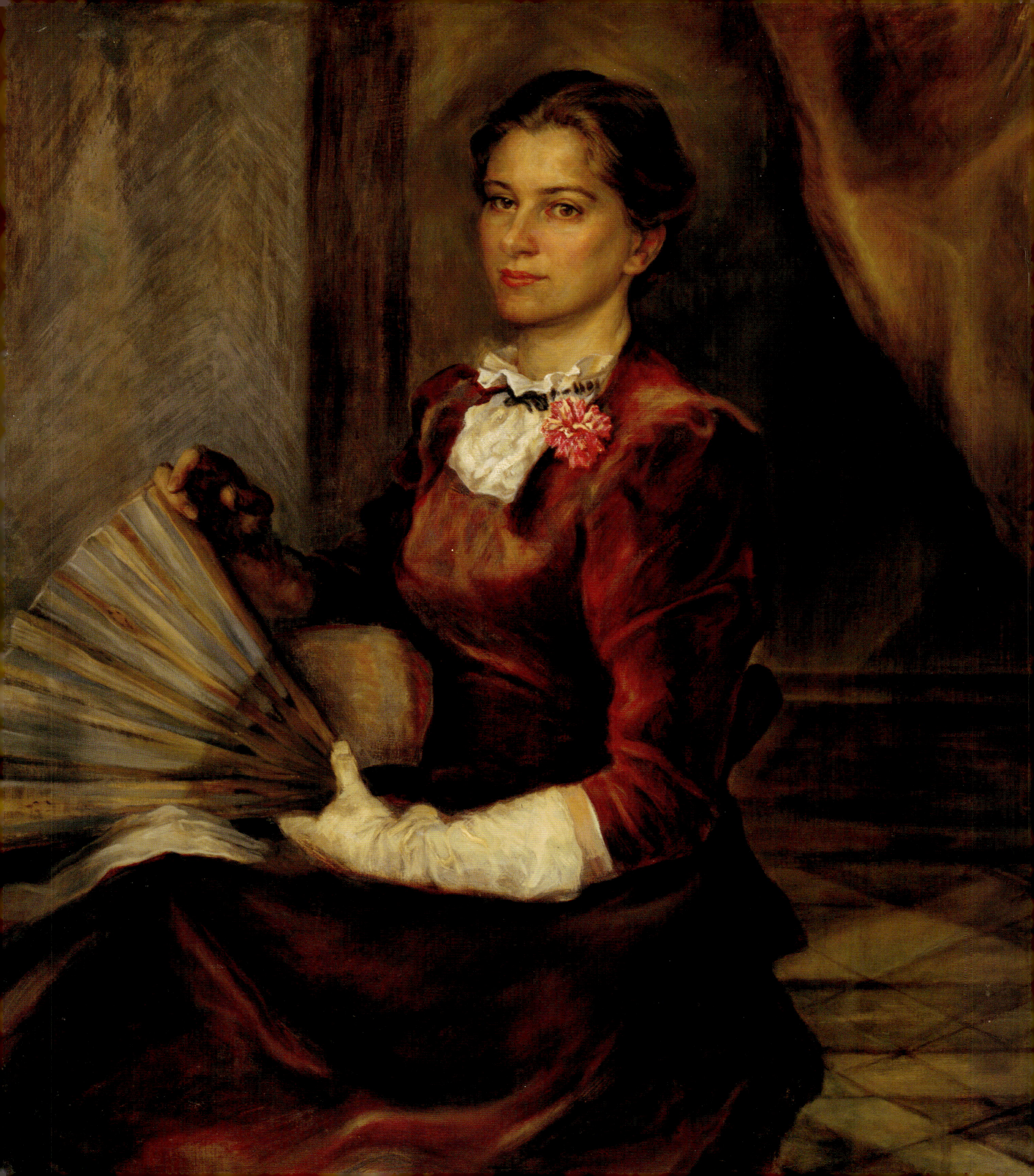

Dahlstrand also comments that Thwaites loved materials and experimented with a wide variety of media throughout his lifetime. Indeed, in addition to the tempera mixture, which was used to create *Waltz*, he also worked in oils, including oils maroger, an Old Master medium that in the 1930s was named after French expatriate Jacques Maroger, who resurrected its formula and published it in the handbook *The Secret Formulas and Techniques of the Old Masters*. Thwaites identified several of his portraits and still lifes as using the maroger medium, including *Spring Portrait, Self-Portrait (with Self-Portrait), Summer Nude*, and *Pomegranate*.

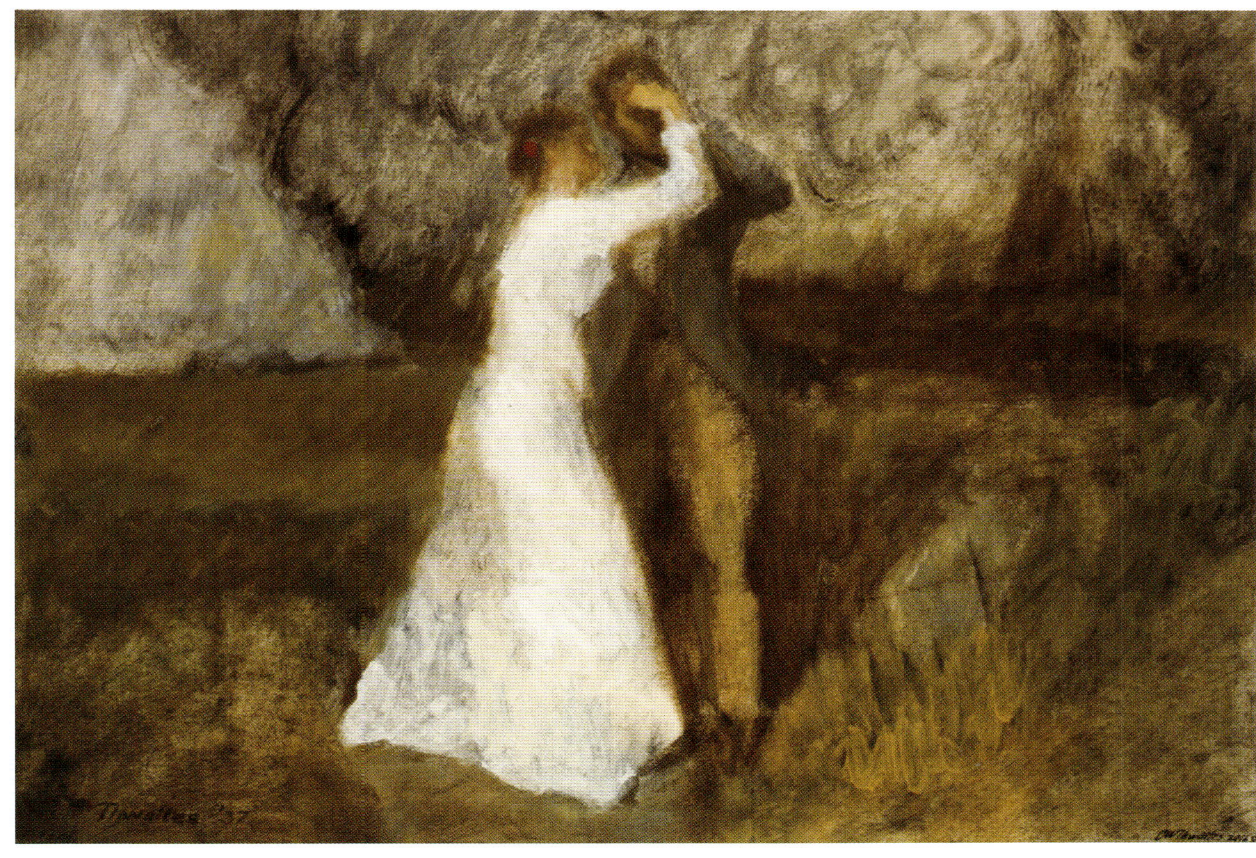

WALTZ, 1937
egg tempera on paper
17½ x 23

In an article published in the January 1946 *The Studio*, author Samuel N. Manierre noted that "the true artist has been a profound student of his medium. Charles Thwaites is such a painter. His close analysis of pigment, his study of color and glazing, his penetrating scrutiny of the human face, have made him the leading portrait painter in Wisconsin today." Manierre also referenced Thwaites' self-portraits, including a painting of his own eye (see page 95), describing them as having the "beautiful fluidity and rich color harmony of a Renoir, a master who Thwaites particularly admires."[7]

Opposite:
PORTRAIT WITH FAN, 1940
oil on masonite
42½ x 37½
private collection
John Cisco, Photographer
Printmakers Chicago

Thwaites also worked in dry oils, a stick form of oil pigments that dries to a hard surface like oil paint. He used dry oils as both a preparatory and finished medium, as in a series of large-scale nudes commissioned in the late-1930s and exemplified by *Reclining Nude* and *Male Torso*.[8] In the late 1940s, as his paintings became increasingly expressionistic and abstract, Thwaites added encaustic, which incorporates wax with pigments, to his list of media. When commercial acrylics were introduced in the mid-1950s, he embraced them as well, creating increasingly larger works. Throughout his career, he also experimented with print media such as lithography during the 1930s and serigraphs in the 1970s. In all of his paintings, Thwaites worked quite thinly, glazing colors over one another but rarely building up physical textures, preferring instead to create the illusion of texture.

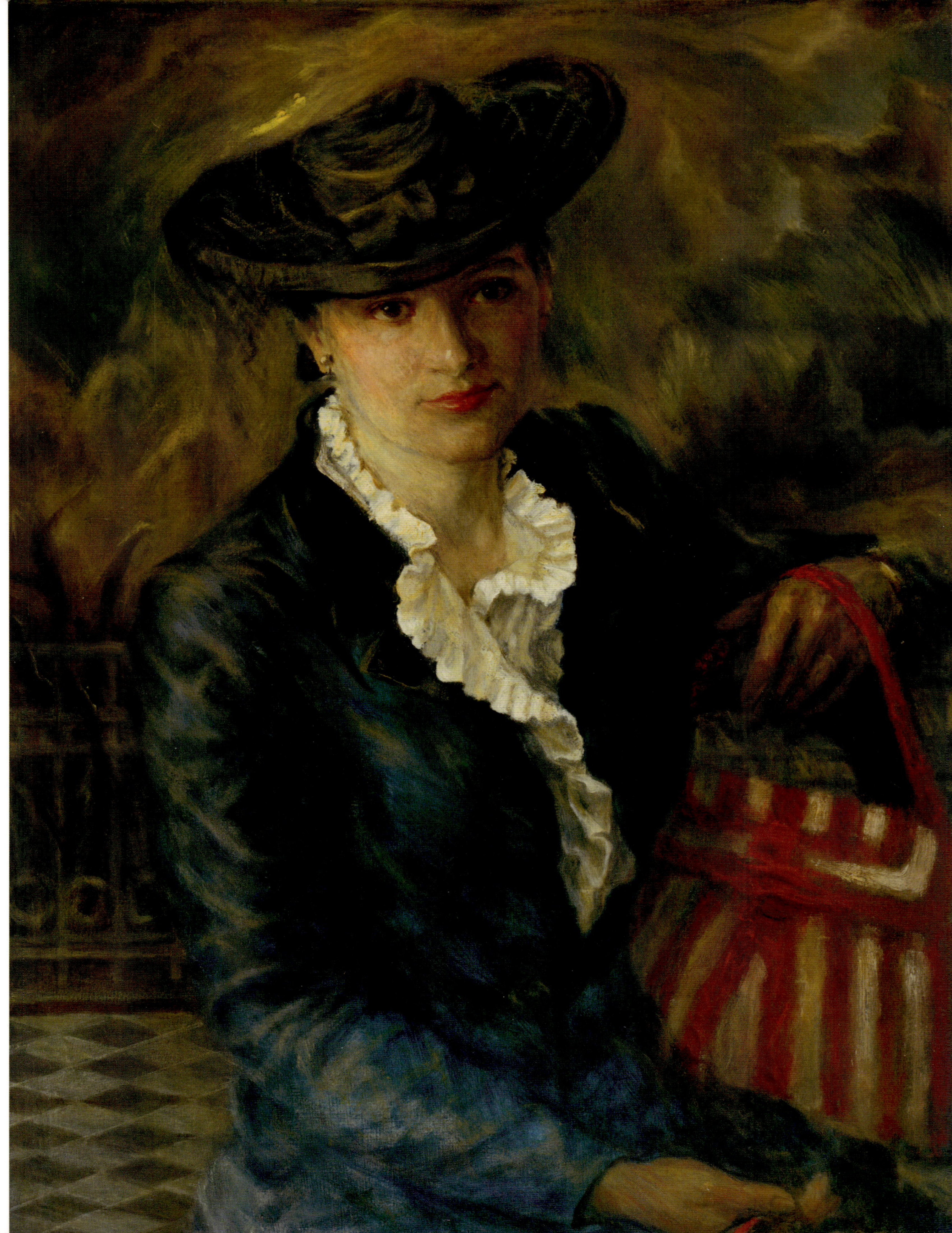

APPLYING THE LESSONS

It should be clear that three things are unavoidable: repetition, variation, and self-expression. All art has these three elements. The difference in the great bulk and the masterpieces is in the quality of that third element, self-expression. Self-expression must be transformed into expression through organization. It is not the illusion of realism, nor the so-called literary content, but the nerve-jangling ideal of organization of contrast that realism aims at and which we call art. CWT

Still single and attending Layton, Thwaites briefly served, in 1928, as director of the Dubuque Little Institute and taught at the Dubuque Art Association in Iowa. He graduated in 1929 determined to pursue a career in fine art just as the Great Depression brought the nation, including Thwaites' father, to an economic nadir. Undaunted, Thwaites embarked on a strategy of building his name by competing in major juried exhibitions at the Art Institute of Chicago, including International Watercolors and Drawings (nine years), Artists of Chicago and Vicinity (twelve years), and American Paintings and Sculpture Exhibition (five years). He also joined the Wisconsin Painters and Sculptors, exhibiting with the group from 1933 through 1948 and taking numerous awards. (See Exhibitions & Awards.)

During the early 1930s, Thwaites focused on figure painting, often submitting paintings in which he used models or himself as the subject. Reviews in Milwaukee newspapers applauded his knowledge of human anatomy, noting that his reputation was synonymous with the figure as a subject. He was also described as "a quiet sort of person ... consistently hard working ... [with] a real mastery of form,"[9] and "his own severest critic."[10]

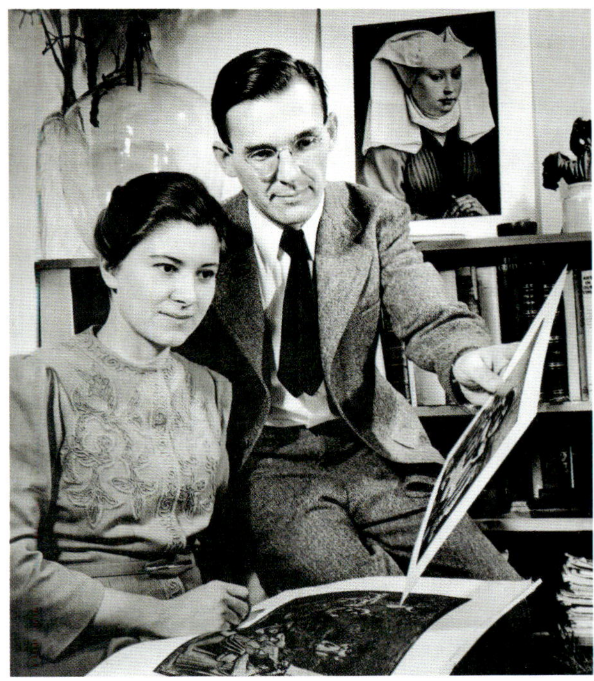

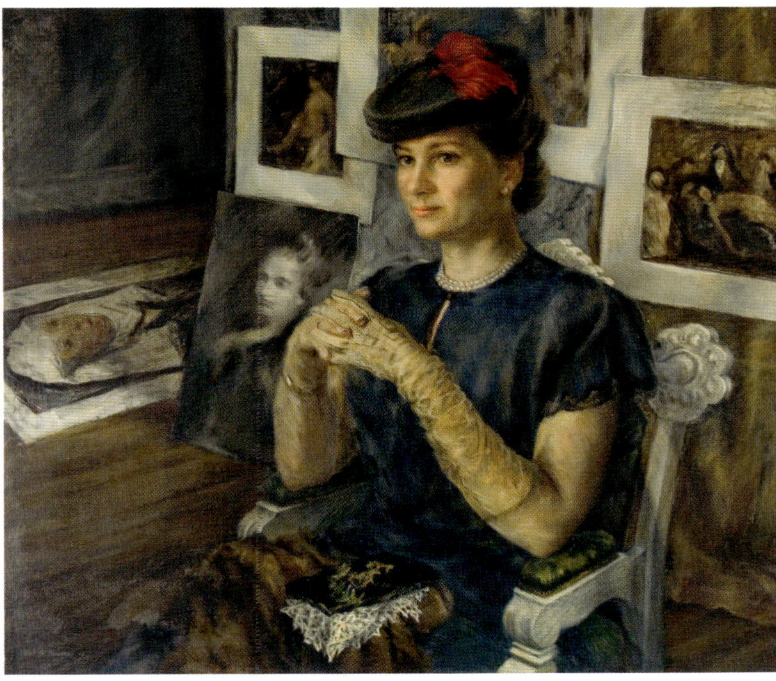

Left: Antoinette and Charles looking over Antoinette's collection of prints in their Wisconsin living room, circa 1940s.

Right:
ANTOINETTE IN THE STUDIO, 1945
oil on masonite
42½ x 37½
private collection
Alison Dunlap Photography

Opposite:
SPRING PORTRAIT (WHANNE THAT APRILLE), 1942
oil maroger on masonite
28 x 22
private collection
John Cisco, Photographer
Printmakers Chicago

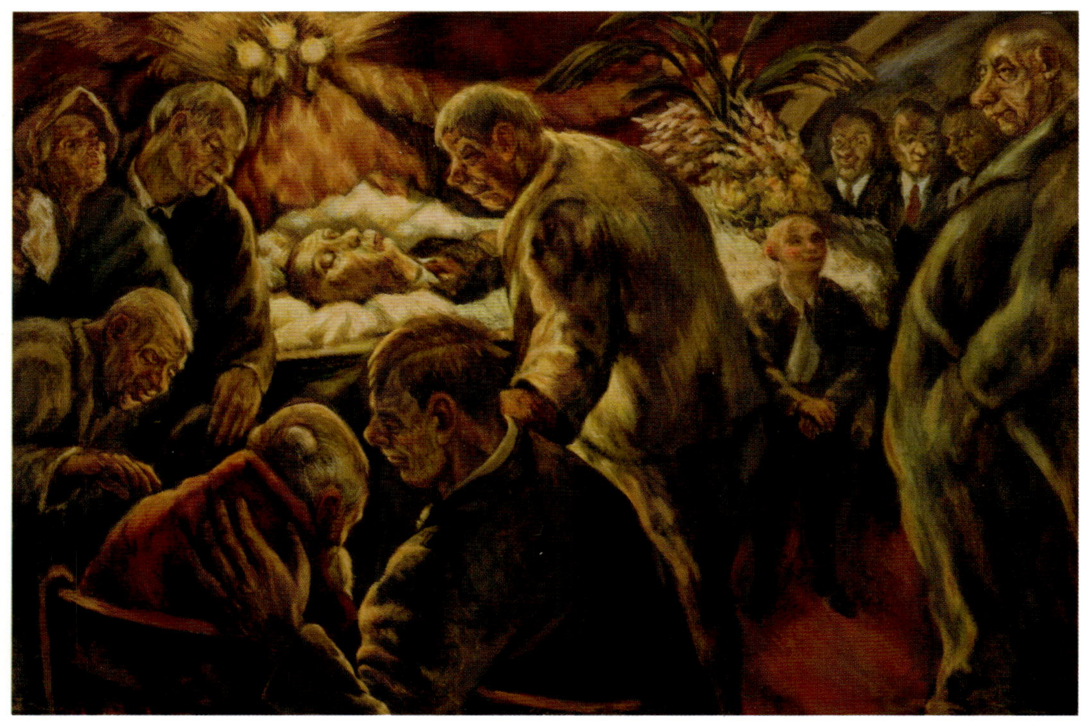

ALIKE IN TREMBLING HOPE REPOSE, 1940
oil on masonite
24 x 36

By 1931, Thwaites had changed the spelling of his birth name, Thwaits, adding an "e" to become Thwaites.[11] A few years later, he met Antoinette Gruppe, a fetching art student attending Layton School of Art, and in 1935 they eloped against the wishes of her family. Antoinette soon became Thwaites' model. Typically shown seated, she was portrayed in a variety of indoor settings and, in three of the estate paintings, her hands are distinguished by wearing one glove. Several of them were submitted to exhibitions, including *Portrait with a Fan*, which appeared in at least three exhibitions, and *Rosie*, which garnered awards in the 1943 Wisconsin Painters and Sculptors exhibition at the Milwaukee Art Institute. Both of the paintings are in the estate, and they were probably intended to be Thwaites' "calling cards" for pursuing portraiture in that he often priced them not to sell.[12]

Antoinette was a very competent painter in her own right. She showed in numerous exhibitions, and the estate includes several of her still-life compositions, a market scene, and studies created in a foundry from around 1934 and 1935. In a 1935 letter from Antoinette to Charles, who was in New York learning how to frame paintings at the time, she references a "factory project" that they were working on together and describes her experiences overlooking the furnaces and workers at the local Falk Foundry.[13] The professional training Thwaites received in framing during this time was the source and inspiration for him to make the majority of his frames.

Childless throughout their marriage, Charles and Antoinette's romantic love and devotion, as well as respect for one another was profound and expressed in correspondence during their rare separations. One series of exchanges took place during Antoinette's August 1938 hospitalization at the Mayo Clinic for an operation to remove a fistula. Her recuperation in Rochester, Minnesota, lasted about three weeks, during which time Charles wrote to her about their partnership in life and art.

> We should ... lay down a course that we can follow with little definite ends along the way to bigger ones.... It's never too late to begin and the thought of planning and shaping our lives together around painting, giving real purpose to living.... I can think of no more exciting nor exhilarating adventure than to strike out with you on the road of improvement that leads to lands of as yet unknown possibilities and achievement. If we could do this, we would add immeasurably to our self-respect, which has had reason to suffer much in the past.[14]

In addition to painting, Antoinette joined Charles in all his passions, including boating, camping, and getting her pilot's license. She also fostered his love of art history, lecturing on the subject, following the art scene, and collecting reproductions of famous paintings, past and present. Thwaites depicted her surrounded by these prints in *Antoinette in the Studio*. In his comments on "the look" referenced earlier, he also wrote, "Antoinette knew the look from the experience of examining the many, many prints which she collected and many paintings in galleries and at exhibitions and her own paintings, comparing, appraising them over and over for years."

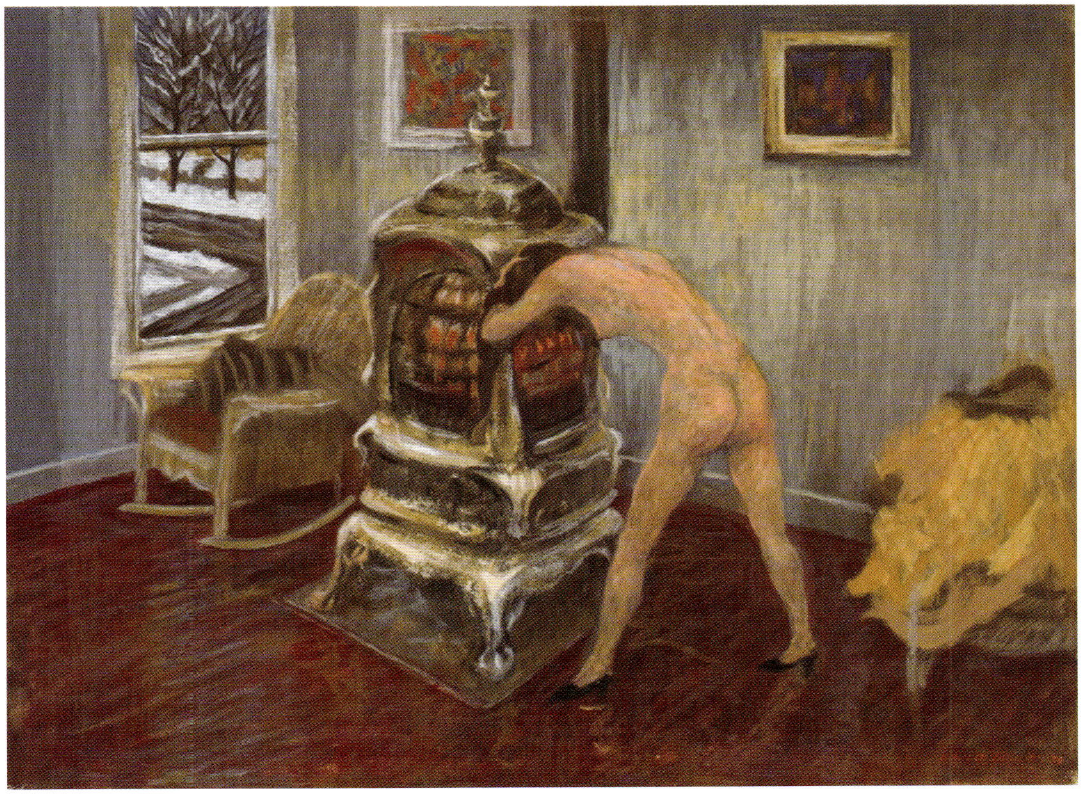

Antoinette's exposure to the American Southwest during a trip with her mother in 1935 was the catalyst for the couple's decision to winter in Tucson, Arizona, in 1941, and to travel throughout the Southwest, subsequently settling in Taos. In a letter to Charles on Santa Fe's Hotel La Fonda letterhead, Antoinette wrote, "In New Mexico and Arizona there are great spaces between towns and the largest town in New Mex. has a population of 25,000, while Taos is a little over 1,000. Gee, Charles, it would be grand to spend next summer there—I know you'd love New Mex. We just have to find some extra money somewhere."[15] Although Antoinette taught art at a private school and continued to exhibit paintings at least through the 1940s, she let her own career wane as she dedicated herself to helping Charles build his.

DRYING HER HAIR, 1936
egg tempera on paper
17½ x 23

During the worst years of the Depression, the couple struggled to stay alive, assisted in part by Thwaites' job creating easel paintings for the Public Works of Art Project, which was overseen by Charlotte Partridge of the Layton School. He went on to work for the Creative Painting and Sculpture Unit for the Works Project Administration, through 1937, for which he also supervised painting projects. Realistic depictions of local subjects dominated most WPA projects, but the artistic styles were as diverse as the artists themselves. Thwaites counted many of the artists in these projects as both colleagues and friends, including the witty and colorful Schomer Lichtner (1905-2006) and his artist-wife Ruth Grotenrath (1912-1988), precisionist Edmund Lewandowski (1914-1998), and artist-art historian James Watrous (1908-1999). Thwaites' genre scenes from the period include tragic images such as a drowned man being pulled from a river in the Milwaukee Art Museum collection, and the somber *Alike in Trembling Hope Repose*. Others are more exuberant, as in *Circus Acrobats*, and the charming *Drying Her Hair*, which shows the couple's apartment, with paintings on the walls, a snow scene out the window, and Antoinette next to the pot-bellied stove before the era of hairdryers.

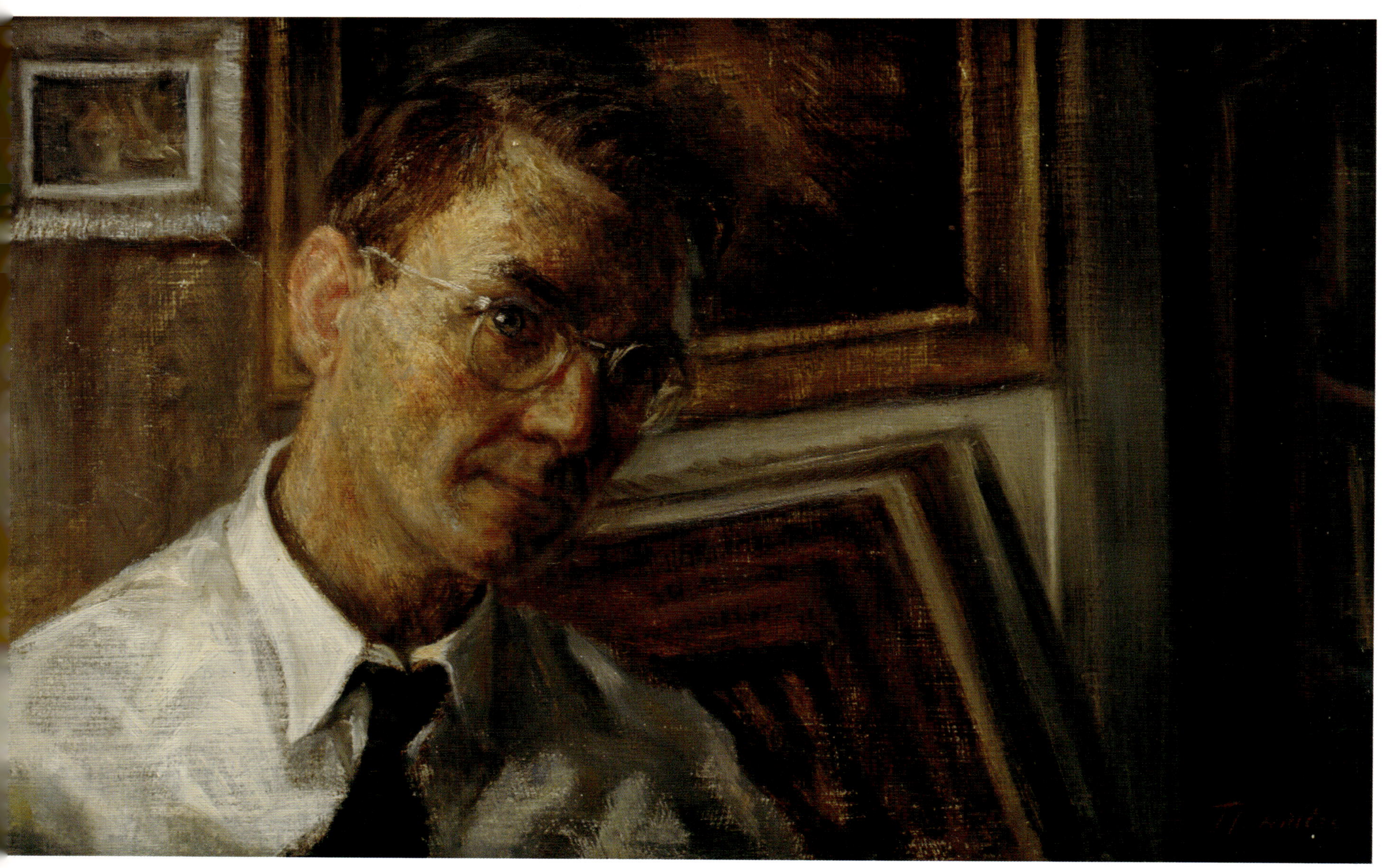

SELF-PORTRAIT (WITH PAINTINGS), 1945
oil on masonite
11 x 17
private collection
Cameron Wittig Photography
Awarded the Bronze Medal at the 1946 First Spring Annual,
California Palace of the Legion of Honor, San Francisco.

NATIONAL RECOGNITION

To have an interest in art, however humble, could be evidence that you are mysteriously compelled or destined to seek within yourself for answers to aesthetic questions not yet formulated in the conscious mind. To promote and cultivate a climate to help us all on this intimate journey of the spirit should always be our steadfast purpose and mutual goal. CWT

From the 1930s into the mid-1940s, Thwaites exhibited in no less than ninety exhibitions, many of which were major national forums. His accomplishments were routinely noted in the *The Milwaukee Journal*, whose reporters spoke of him as a favorite son. In New York, he showed in the National Exhibition of American Art (1936 to 1938), at the 1939 New York World's Fair, the 1942 Artists for Victory at the Metropolitan Museum, and the 1946 Paintings of the Year at the National Academy of Design.

Other national exhibits included the Biennial Exhibition of American Oil Paintings at the Corcoran Gallery of Art in Washington, DC (1939, 1941, 1947); the 1941 New Directions in American Painting at the Carnegie Institute in Pittsburgh, Pennsylvania, and the American Paintings and Sculpture juried competitions and invitationals at the Art Institute of Chicago (1937, 1940 to 1942, and 1945). In 1946, he exhibited in Contemporary American Paintings at the Virginia Museum of Fine Arts, and his *Self-Portrait (with Paintings)* received a bronze medal at the American art exhibition at the California Palace of the Legion of Honor in San Francisco. From 1937 to 1939, he was also included in Artists of the Great Lakes Region, a major annual exhibition that traveled widely.

In 1937, as a member of the Wisconsin Painters and Sculptors, Thwaites joined the jury of the annual exhibition, along with Minnesotan Dewey Albinson (1898-1971) and John Steuart Curry, who had just assumed the post of artist-in-residence at the University of Wisconsin, Madison, and with whom Thwaites struck up a friendship. Thwaites could not compete in the exhibit, however, his painting titled *Girl Ironing* was on the cover of the show bulletin of the Milwaukee Art Institute. The painting undoubtedly depicts Antoinette, wearing a slip, her head bowed, ironing a garment, with one of her prized prints hanging on the wall behind.[16] Inside the bulletin Thwaites' decorative, stylized image of seductive

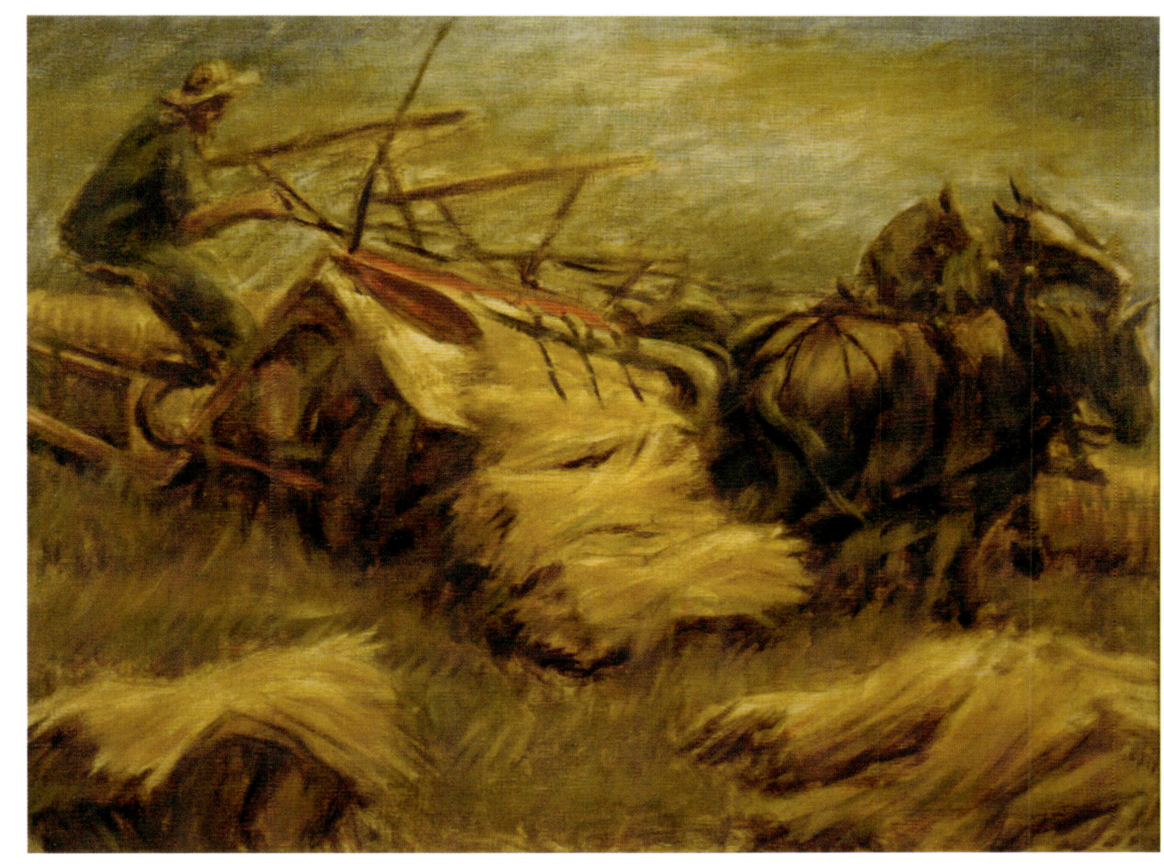

THE BINARY, circa 1938
oil on masonite
16 x 22
Museum of Wisconsin Art Collection, West Bend

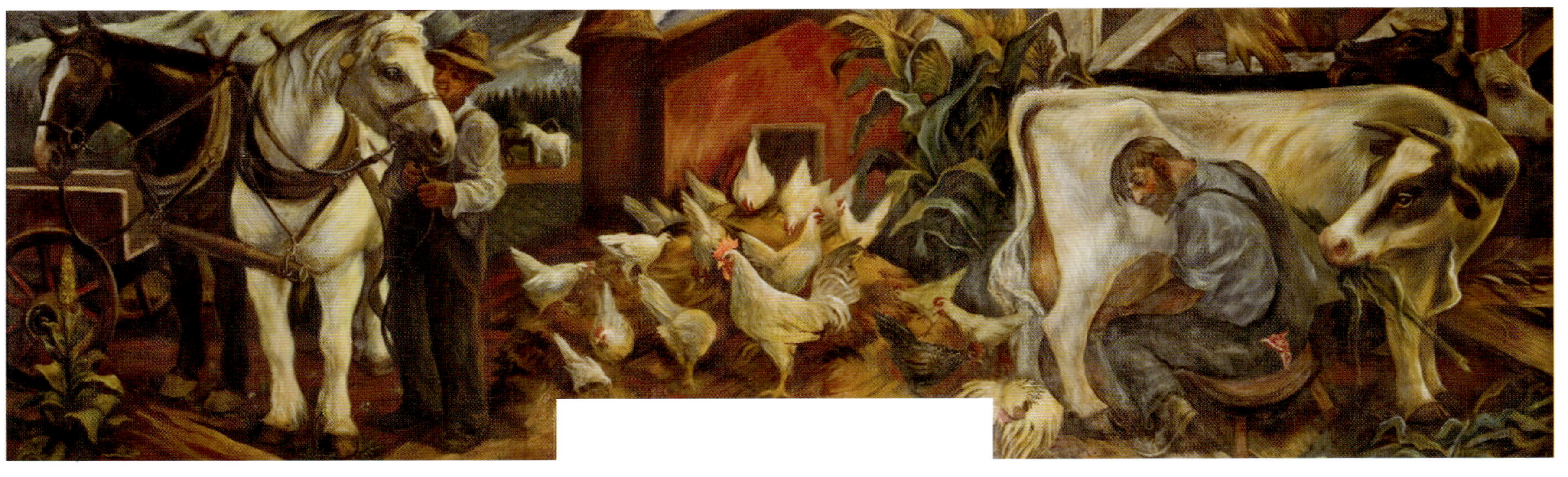

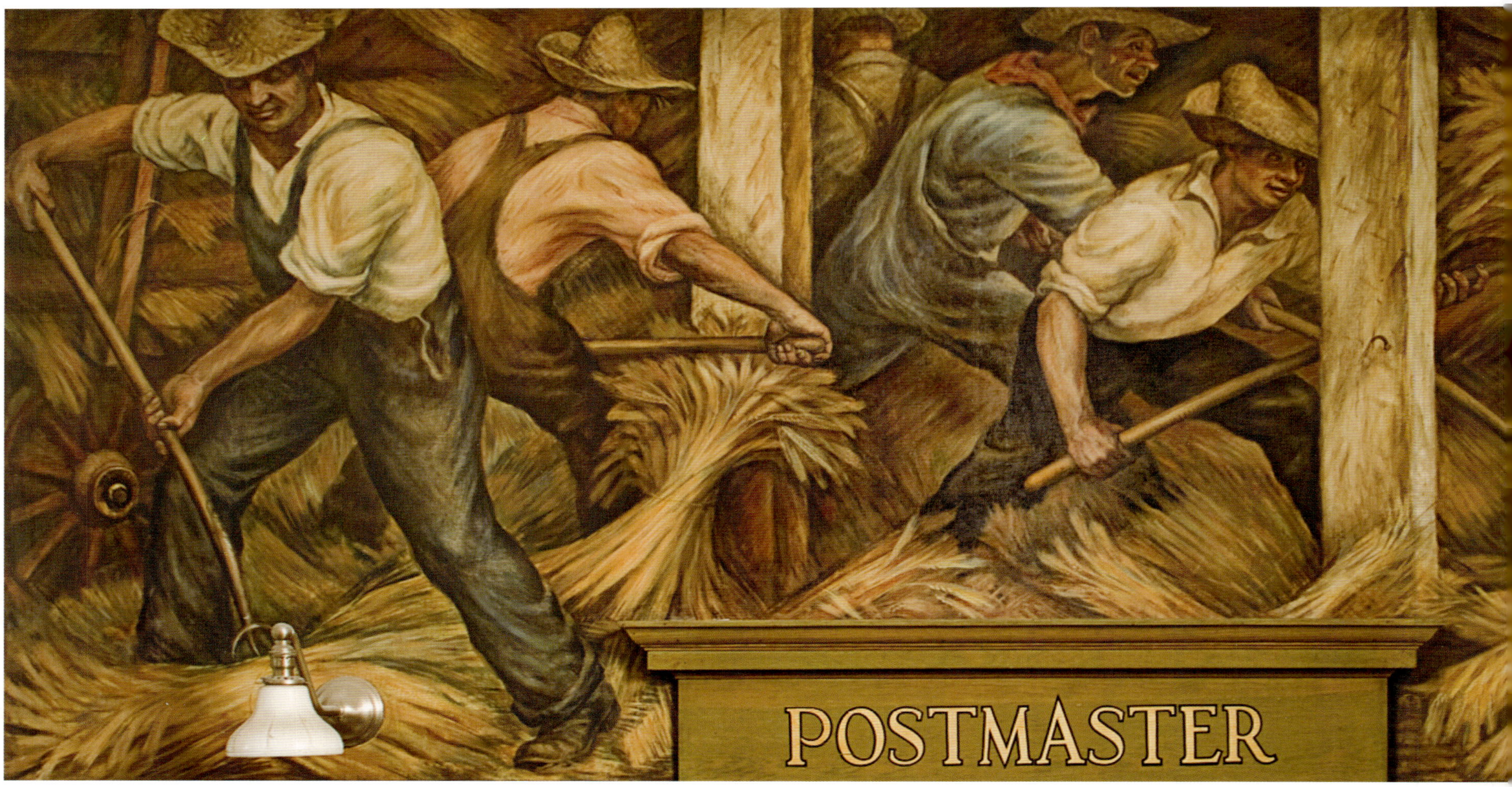

Pitcher Plants was reproduced, and he was described as "masterful in his unobtrusive but beautiful modeling in paint ... [and] intuitively a frequent follower of the older painting traditions. [He is] self-effacing and meditative ... [His paintings] receive profound consideration for a certain painterly quality rarely apparent in most contemporary painting."

Thwaites' reputation expanded further when he entered the Forty-Eight States Competition to create murals for the Section of Fine Arts of the U.S. Treasury Department. His winning design for the post office in Chilton, Wisconsin, was exhibited at the Corcoran Gallery in 1939,[17] and received considerable critical acclaim, including being pictured in *Life* magazine and the *New York Times*.[18] It was also acknowledged in the *New York Herald Tribune* where Royal Cortissoz applauded its "thoughtfully assembled" design qualities with balance, order, and a "beginning, middle and an end."[19]

For research, Thwaites visited Calumet County to observe threshers at work. He created the 5-by-12 foot canvas in warm golden tones of tempera using a rhythmic composition that begins on the left, showing men with hayforks lifting shocks of barley onto a conveyor on the right. Divided by vertical motifs that center on either side of the post-master's doorway, it appears as a triptych and is reminiscent of regionalist viewpoints. However, the compressed space in which the farmers work and the decorative treatment of the barley give the image a contemporary feel. Thwaites' use of dividing motifs and his following comments in a local paper suggest that he was familiar with Thomas Hart Benton's murals and theories of dynamic sequences and opposing lines and curves. "I wished to make a rich pattern of human beings and grain, giving voice to their relation both by their portrayal and especially by the related movements that figures, bundles of grain and implements perform."[20]

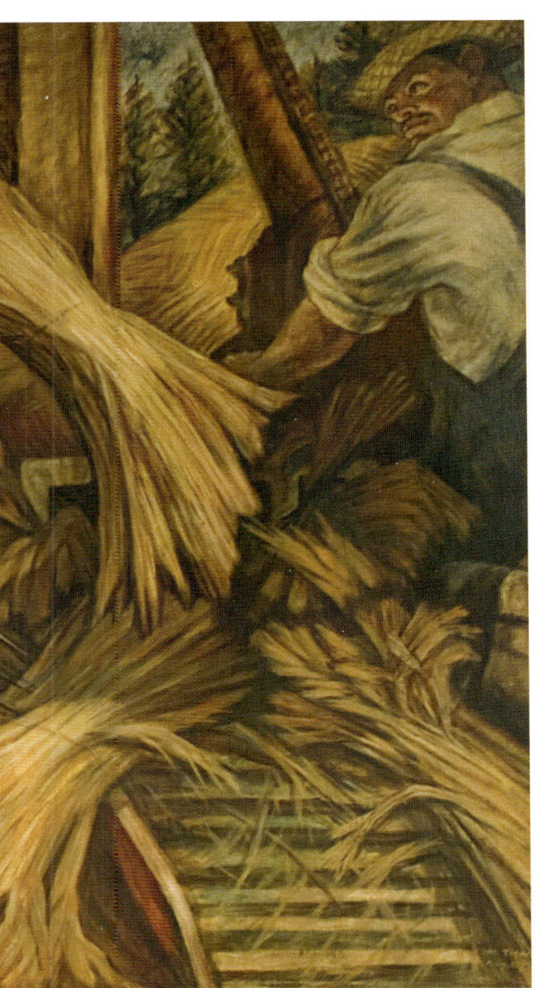

Based on the success of the Chilton mural, Thwaites was commissioned to paint three additional post-office murals in which he compressed the figures and landscapes into decorative shapes and lines that conveyed movement. Local industries were his themes: an old-time rural cheese-making factory for Plymouth, Wisconsin; a farmer with a team of horses separated by a flock of chickens from another farmer milking a cow for Windom, Minnesota,[21] and lumberjacks in Greenville, Michigan.

For the Greenville mural, Thwaites created a rich tapestry comprising a team of horses and eight men, some with axes removing stylized branches from a downed tree that two lumberjacks are sawing. In correspondence with the postmaster, Thwaites was informed that the foreground lumberman, dressed in red, bore a striking resemblance

Above:
FARMING MURAL, 1943
egg tempera on canvas
Collection Cottonwood County Historical Society
Windom, Minnesota
Cameron Wittig Photography

HARVEST (THRESHING BARLEY) MURAL, 1940
oil on canvas
60 x 144
Post Office™, Chilton, Wisconsin
Don Stolley Photography Studio

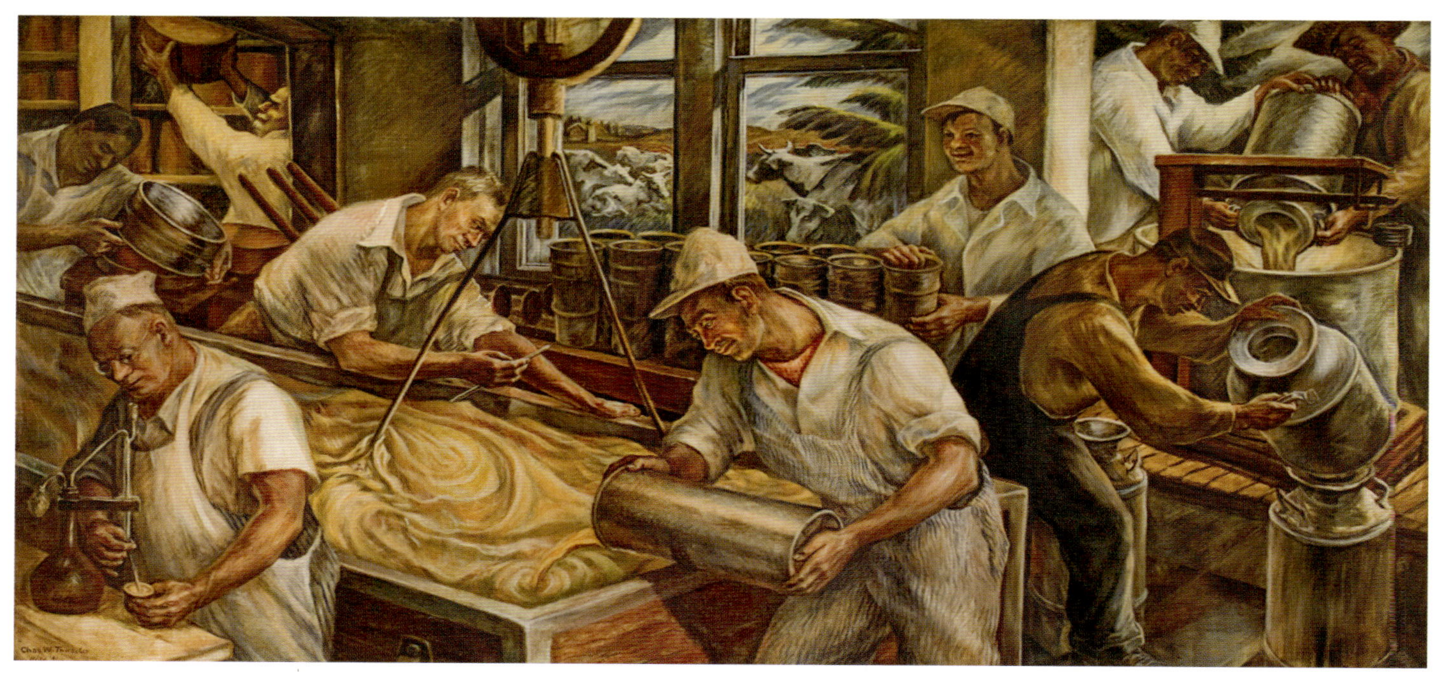

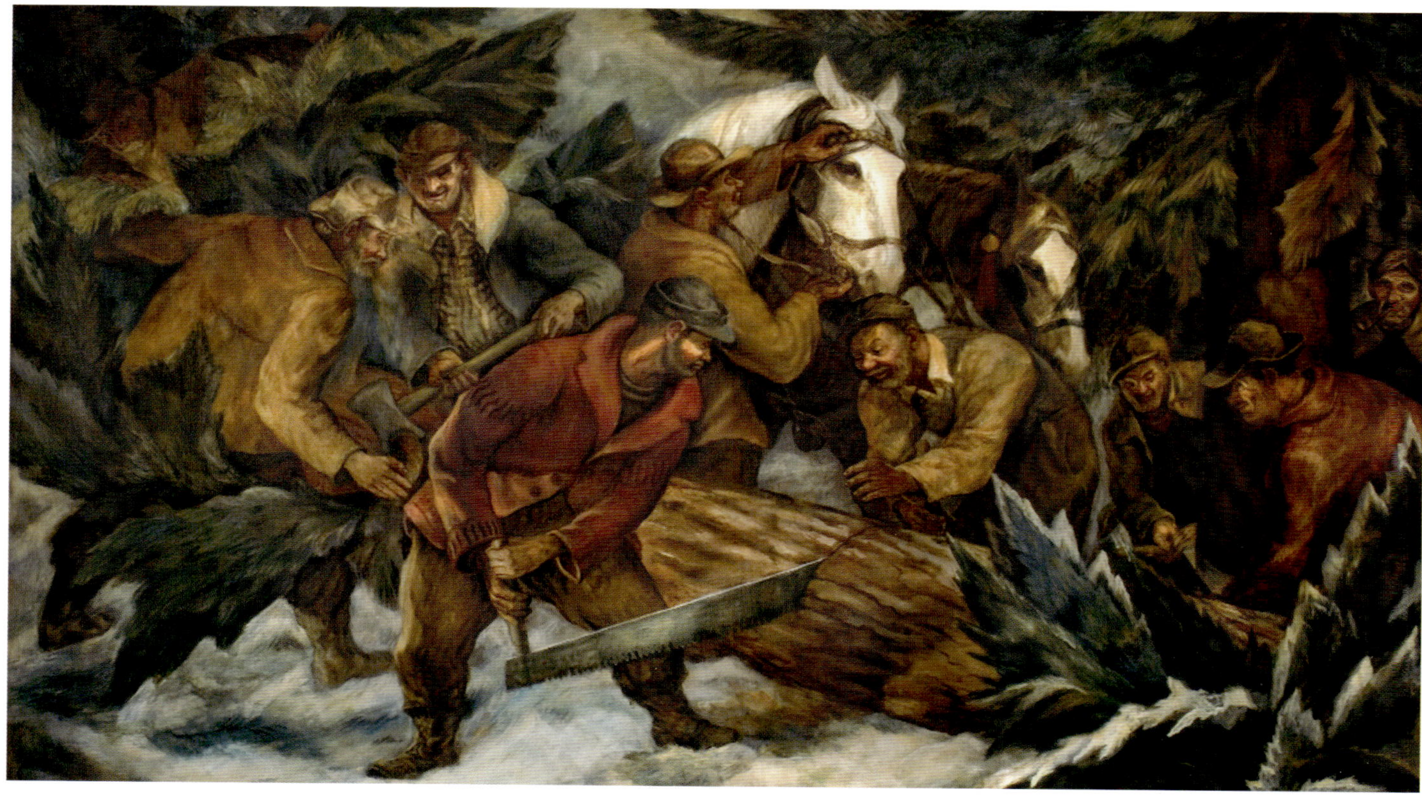

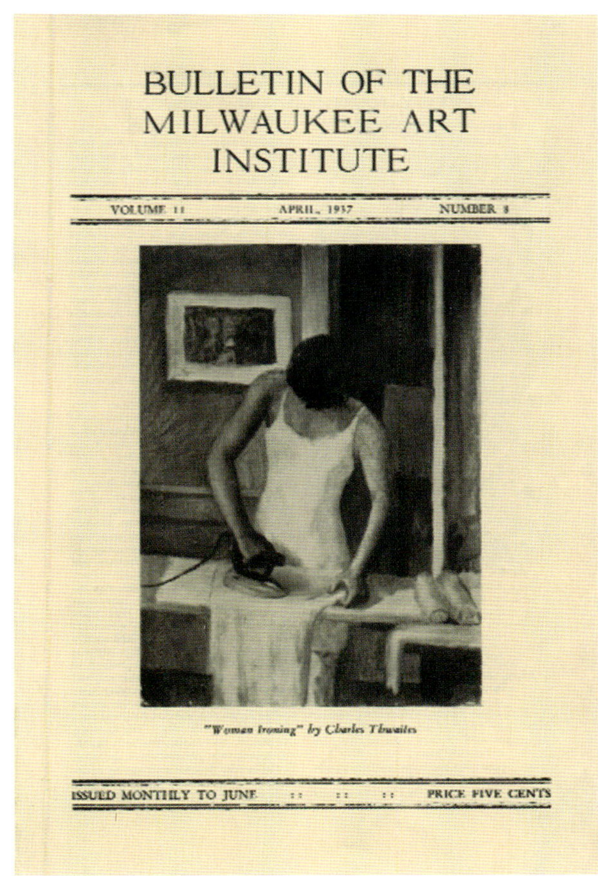

BULLETIN OF THE MILWAUKEE ART INSTITUTE

VOLUME 11 APRIL, 1937 NUMBER 8

"Woman Ironing" by Charles Thwaites

ISSUED MONTHLY TO JUNE :: :: :: PRICE FIVE CENTS

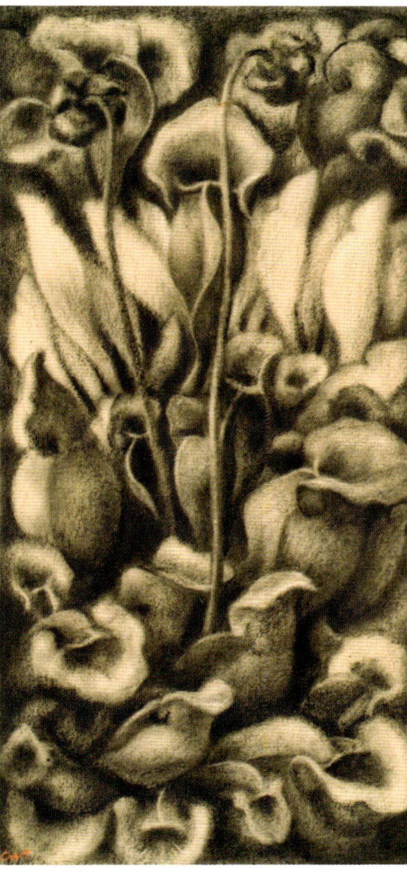

Left:
WOMAN IRONING on the cover of the Bulletin of the Milwaukee Art Institute, April 1937.

Right:
PITCHER PLANTS, 1936
dry oil
17 x 8½

Opposite:
MAKING CHEESE MURAL, 1941
oil on canvas
Post Office™, Plymouth, Wisconsin
Don Stolley Photography Studio

Opposite:
LUMBERING MURAL, 1940
egg tempera on canvas
Post Office™, Greenville, Michigan
Chuck Heiney Photography

to a renowned local lumberman—a man Thwaites never met. He later recounted in Notes to Myself a paranormal experience in which a woman he did not know and never saw again happened into his studio while he was painting the mural. She informed him she knew something about lumbermen and recommended that he redo the foreground figure, which Thwaites did (see the full description in Greenville Mural, Appendix B).

In writing about his goals on this work, Thwaites stated, "I have tried to take advantage of the rich decorative possibilities found in naturalistic forms. The movements of these forms have been directed toward a relationship wherein logic, rhythm, and variety are the controlling expressive forces, changing them from otherwise dead illustrative material into a vital design."[22]

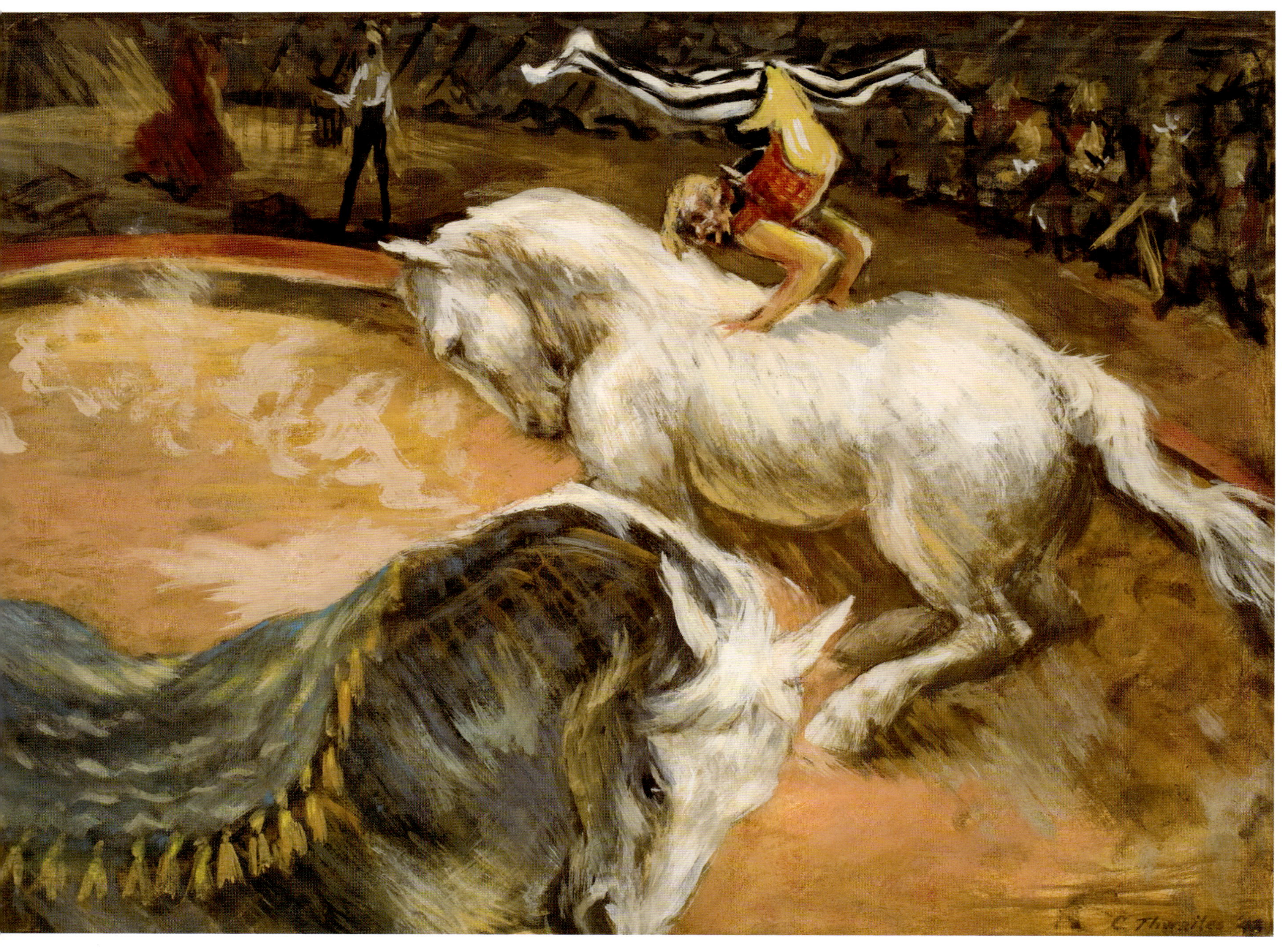

LIFE'S VITAL DESIGNS

Because there is a basic pattern for all things and particularly a basic human need, the pattern which forms the base of our psychological responses results in our emotions, and thus the arts are possible. CWT

The conflicted politics of World War II were reflected in the art world by clashes over modernism versus traditional art. In the 1941 Wisconsin Painters and Sculptors exhibition, Thwaites became a part of the debate when he received an award for "the best conservative painting." His winning *Self-Portrait with Pieta* was pictured in Milwaukee newspapers and in *The Studio* magazine. In it, the businesslike artist wears his customary shirt and tie and looks directly at the viewer, minus his glasses, with a relaxed yet pointed stare. Behind him on the wall is a print of the *Pieta of Avignon* by Enguerrand Quarton (French, active 1444-1466) with the dead Christ's head appearing to touch Thwaites' ear.[23] In one newspaper account, Thwaites was quoted as questioning the award, stating, "'distinctions between modern and conservative only add to the general confusion,' pointing out further that he knows only two types of painting, good and bad."[24] In another article, he is identified as "one of the state's best known artists, who has sometimes been labeled a 'modernist' by the controversialists."[25]

Opposite:
CIRCUS ACROBAT, 1943
egg tempera on paper
16 x 23

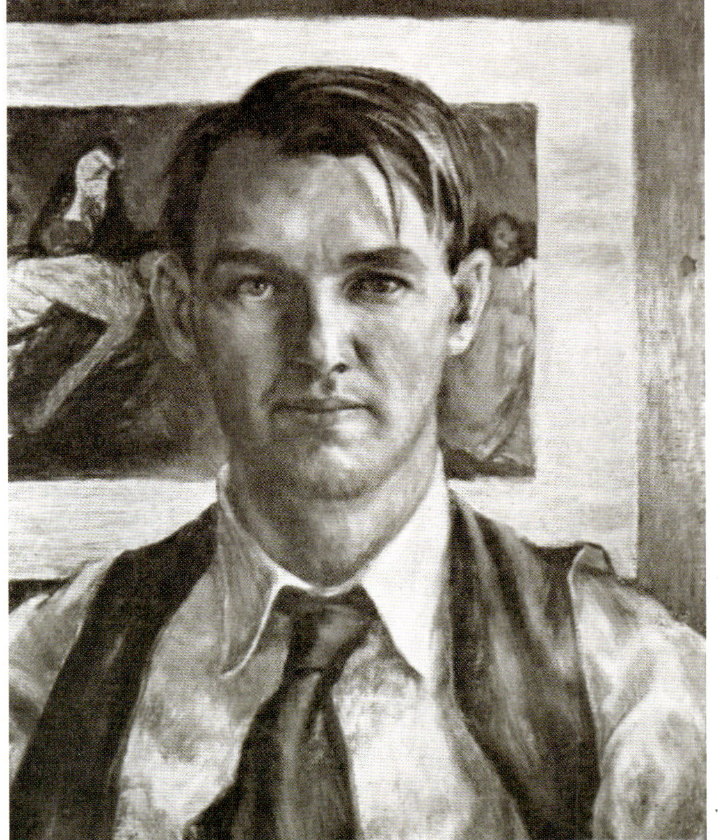

SELF-PORTRAIT WITH PIETA, 1940
oil maroger on masonite; size and location unknown. Reproduced in *The Studio* magazine, January 1946. Winner of two awards at the 1941 Wisconsin Painters and Sculptors annual exhibition.

Perhaps the *Self-Portrait with Pieta* was Thwaites' nod to old traditions and new trends "butting heads." Although he was primarily a representational painter, Thwaites adhered to modernist concepts about the primacy of formalism inherent in depicting a three-dimensional world on a two-dimensional canvas. As he observed numerous times, "the abstract qualities determine the value of a work of art, whether realistic or nonobjective, since art is a reaction to the world in abstract terms."[26]

That philosophy was also the foundation of *Verve*, an avant-garde quarterly magazine, the first 1938 volume of which was included in Thwaites' library. Published in France with an English language version, *Verve* was lavishly illustrated with covers and artworks by the era's leading contemporary artists, including Matisse, Braque, Rouault, and Picasso, alongside some of the first color reproductions of art from antiquity onward.[27] The publisher's mission was to show the continuity of art across centuries and cultures—a unique mixture to which Thwaites ascribed and which was complemented by commentary by leading philosophers and critics. In the fall 1938 issue, artworks by Rouault and Miro were juxtaposed against reproductions of the month's labors from the fifteenth-century illustrated manuscript Les Heures de Rohan. The late summer and fall months show men gathering shocks of wheat that fill the majority of the image—an idea that may have contributed to Thwaites' design for the Chilton mural.

Thwaites' attraction to contemporary visions, as well as imagery created prior to the discovery of mathematical perspective and vanishing points, undoubtedly was fueled by the decorative potential of art, a goal he ascribed to as follows:

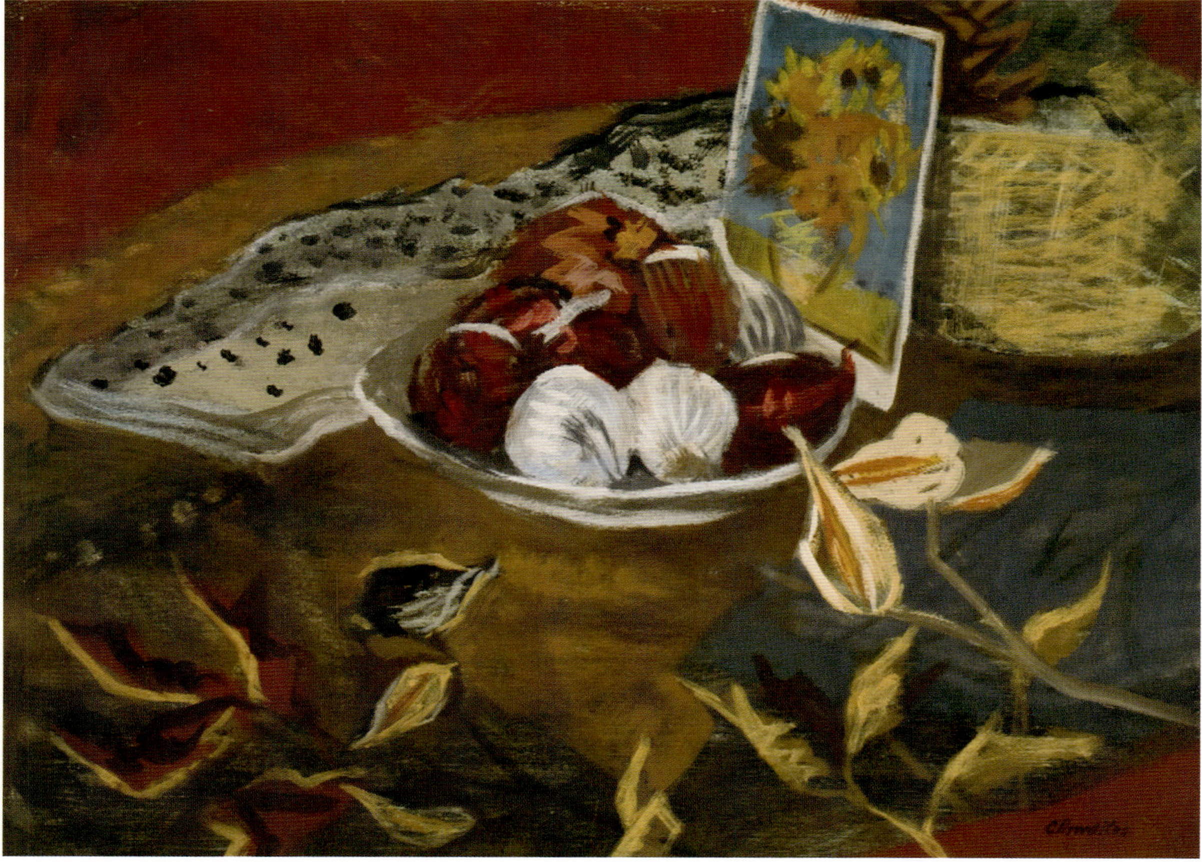

> The elements of decorative design are those units which contain two contrasting forces held together by a third—as hot, medium and cold in color, or black, gray and white, or large, medium and small in area, or circular, square and triangular in shape, or long, medium and short—and many more. These visual elements are also those used for strictly [rendering] purposes or strictly for design, or a combination of both when illusion is the initiating inspiration.
>
> The aim and essence of art is decoration. The language is the decorative-visual. The law is only achieved in the decorative. The means of art is the decorative or the decorative is the means necessary, as well as the end in its highest sense. Decoration parallels life in the relativity of its parts and total unity of its organization. The Law is absolute and also infinitely flexible.[28]

STILL LIFE WITH VAN GOGH PRINT, 1945
egg tempera on paper
17½ x 23

Opposite:
FADING BOUQUET, 1941
egg tempera on paper
23 x 17½

Just as important to decorative contrast was the element of color. Thwaites quoted Cezanne on the subject, "Color is the place where the mind and the universe meet. That is why it appears so dramatic to real painters," and "Color is everything." In his own words, Thwaites wrote:

> Color is the universal in painting. Any spot of color is at one and the same time (1) hue, (2) intensity, (3) tone or value, (4) texture, (5) shape, (6) area, (7) gesture, (8) has relation to its immediate [surroundings] and to the whole, (9) is subject to the laws of optics, (10) has varying qualities of edge, and (11) has magnetic psychological or gravitational force, creating tension, plus carrying power (or the distance at which it can be seen). Color is, because of all this, the building unit—all components individually represent forces of contrast and are the same employed to make larger groups of contrasts that relate to the entire canvas.[29]

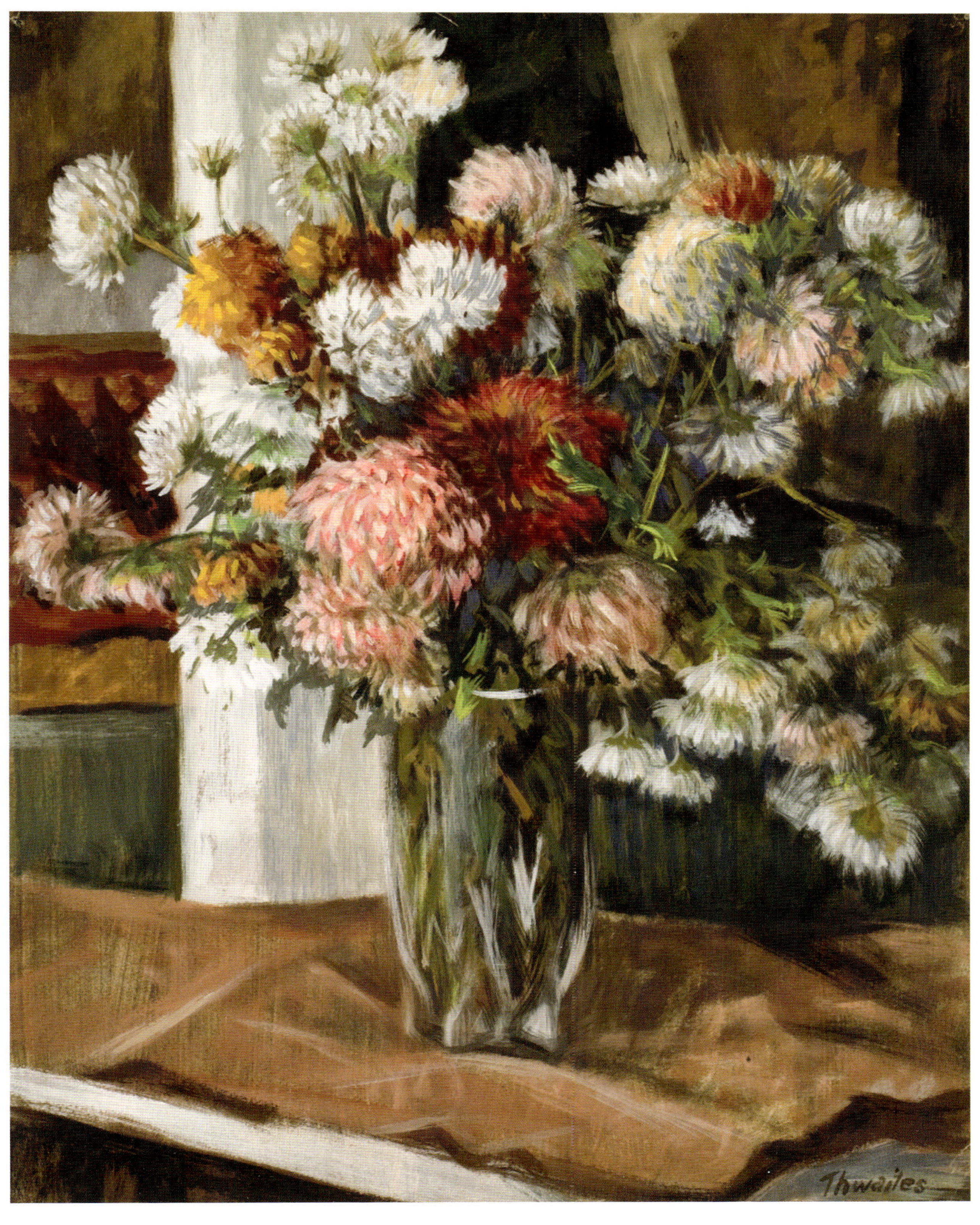
Thwaites

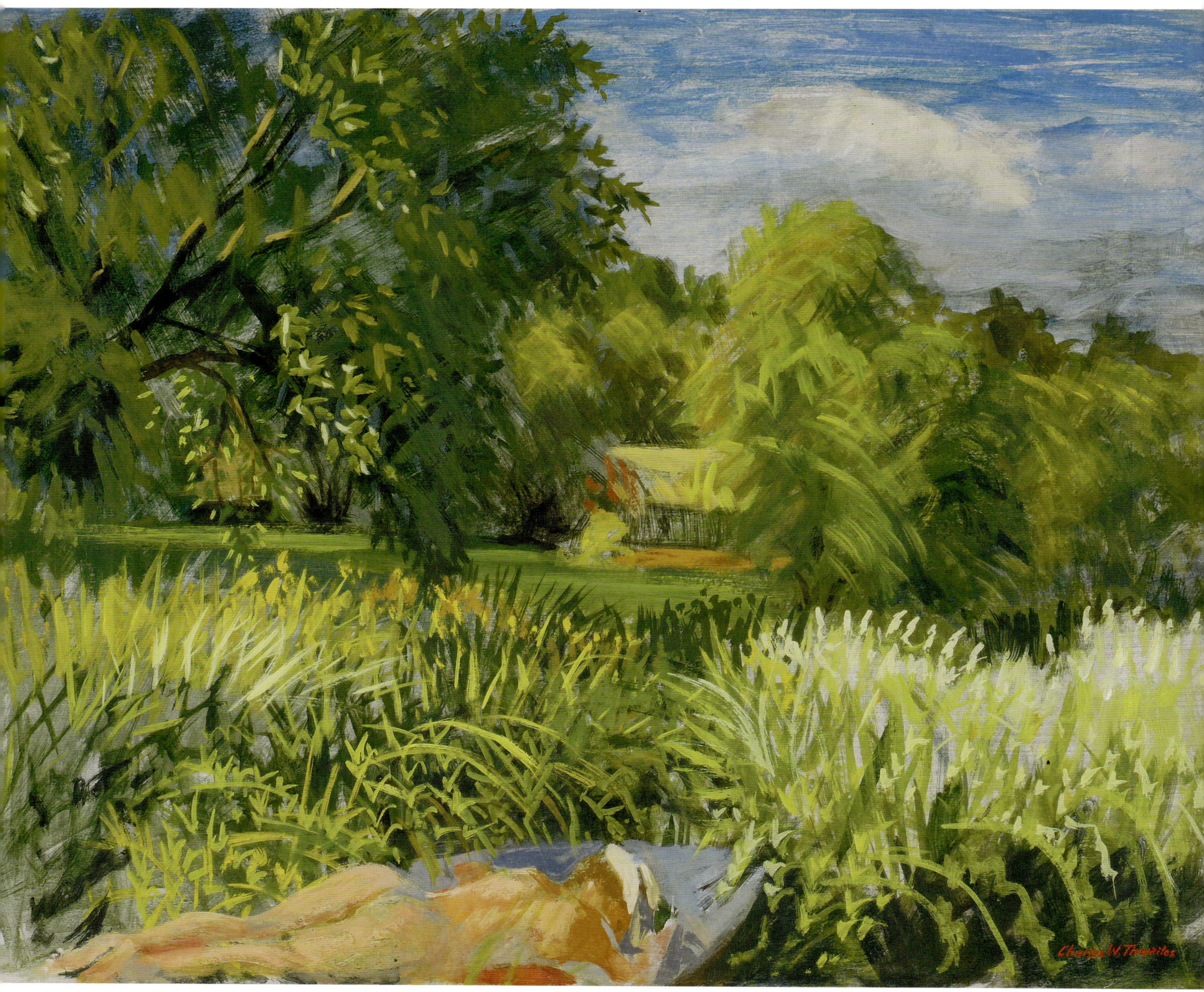

LANDSCAPE WITH NUDE, 1942
egg tempera on paper
17½ x 23; private collection
Dennis Wyszynski Photography

ALLURE OF NATURE

There is no greater blindness than lack of interest. The masters always saw the means for a universal statement in the visual aspects of nature. They could pick out those visual aspects which coincided with their inner picture of the universe. Their personal choices represented their built-in attractions and repulsions directed by a highly original philosophy of existence, resulting in a most significant statement of unity. CWT

Throughout their years in Wisconsin and later in New Mexico, the Thwaiteses were avid outdoors people. They drove across country using Conoco Travel Bureau maps, setting up their tent and cooking equipment at campsites along the way. They spent countless hours on the water, whether lakes or streams, using an ingenious "fold boat" that Charles designed and built in the early 1940s.[30] The remarkable plywood, two-seater had a vee-shaped hull and flat sides held together by water-tight hinges. It measured 11½-feet in length and could be propelled with paddles or rigged with a sail (see illustration on page 103). Once folded, it was easily strapped to the side of the car or transported up the narrow stairway to their small apartment. The couple routinely set out for the country-side, spending the day on the water, sketching and picnicking. Thwaites often depicted himself and Antoinette in the boat, as in *Figures in Fold Boat*, or he used it as a prop as in *Summer Nude*.

The estate includes a small number of Wisconsin landscapes, some of which depict barns and cows, while others show urban scenes, most likely views from Thwaites' downtown Milwaukee studio on Plankinton, including an interior scene with the Chilton mural in-process. Nonetheless, Thwaites loved to paint nature, typically isolating its elements and showcasing them to fill the image space as if a naturally designed still-life composition. The award-winning *Canadian Thistle* and *Milkweed Pods* are examples.

In that same vein, the still-life paintings from this period typically incorporate fruits, vegetables and plant forms, often dried as in *Dried Plant Forms* and *Still Life with van Gogh Print*. In a 1947 newspaper account of the Thwaiteses' apartment, the writer delighted in "rooms alive with handsome paintings, with milkweed pods and other feathery autumn weeds and strange graceful stalks in Chinese vases.... Not only milkweed but Queen Anne's lace and all of the dying summer in the plant world allure Thwaites. He arranges the lacy blossoms adding whatever they need in the line of color, through still life."[31]

Green Bananas includes pomegranates, which appear in numerous still lifes, including *Pomegranate*, which pays homage to El Greco and was exhibited at the 1949 Artists of Chicago and Vicinity. Thwaites discovered the fruit while he and Antoinette spent the winter of 1941 in Tucson, Arizona, living in a small casita with a garden of agaves, surrounded by cholla and saguaro cactus, and a view of the Santa Catalina Mountains. While there, Charles painted a pomegranate still life including olives and a Navajo blanket.

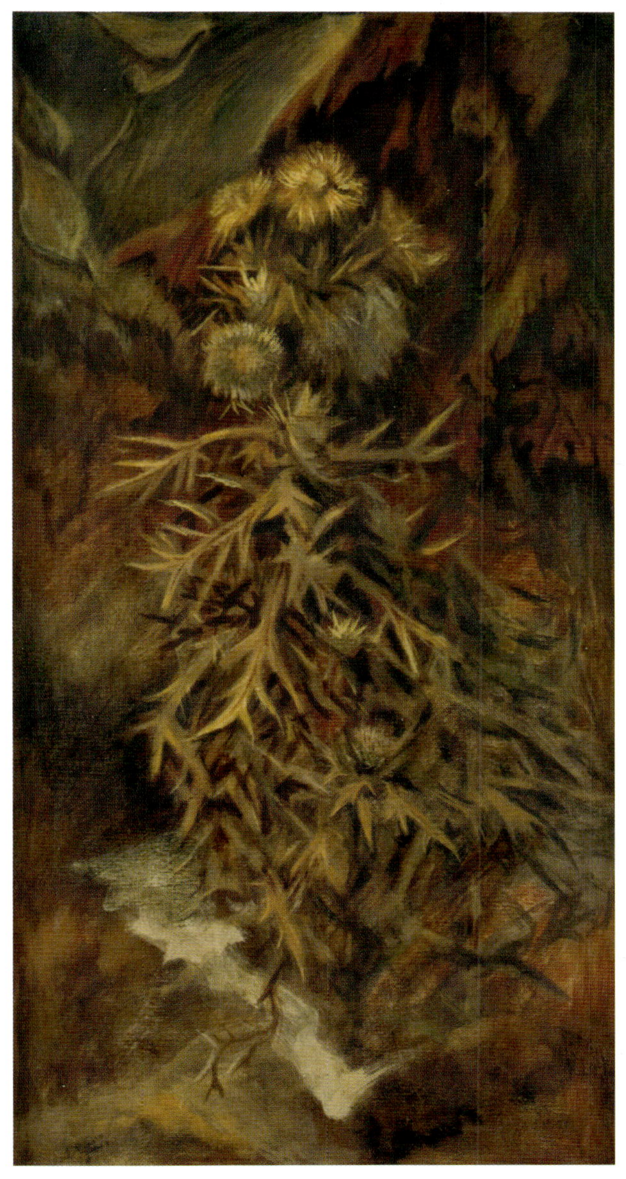

CANADIAN THISTLE, 1940
oil on masonite
30½ x 20½

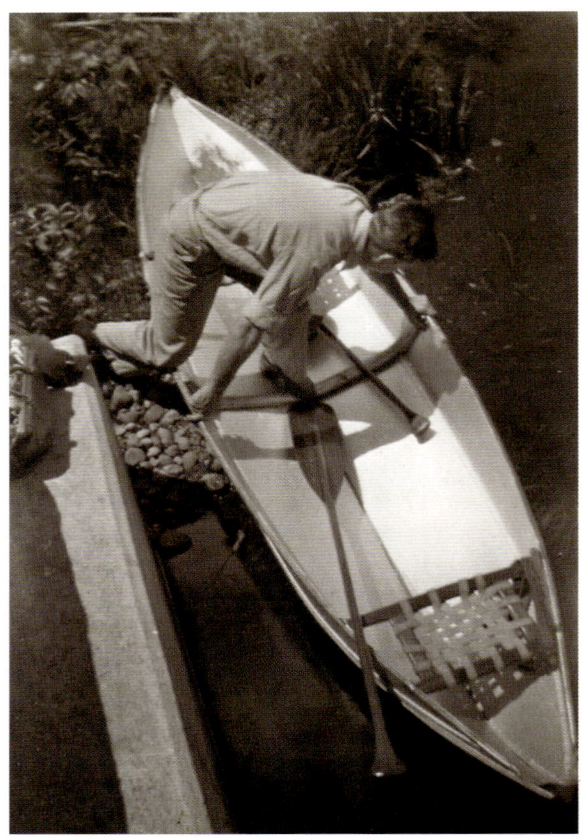

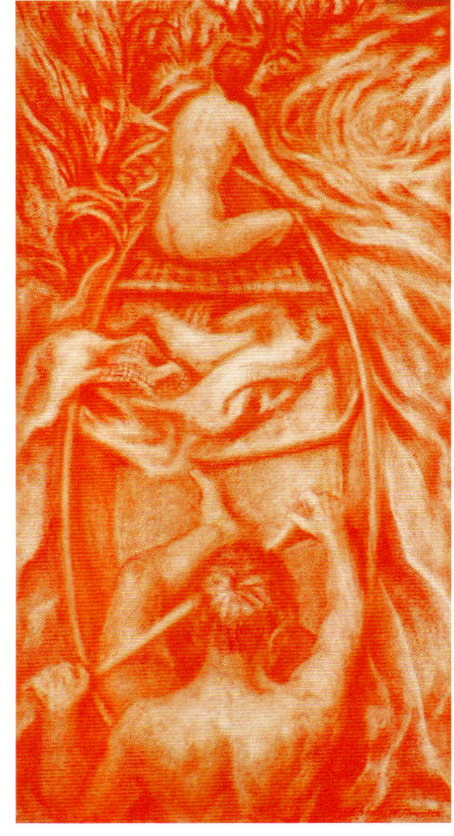

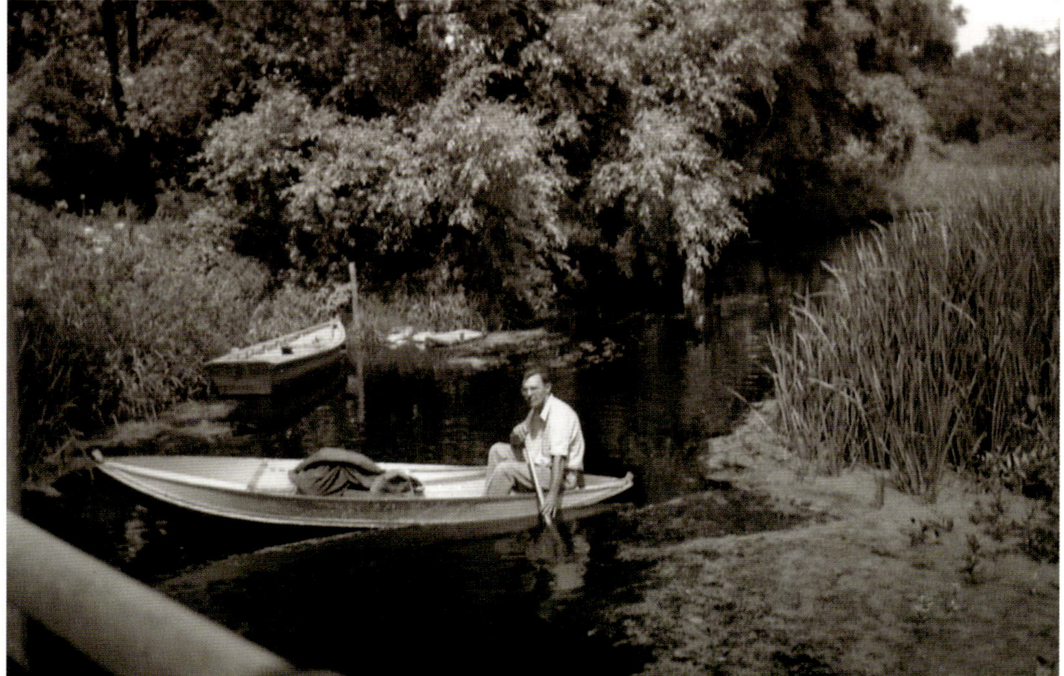

FIGURES IN FOLD BOAT, 1942
dry oil on paper
$17\frac{1}{2}$ x $9\frac{1}{2}$

Thwaites stepping into the fold boat and paddling on a Wisconsin waterway.

Opposite:
SUMMER NUDE, 1942
oil maroger on masonite
$9\frac{1}{2}$ x 14
private collection
John Cisco Photographer
Printmakers Chicago

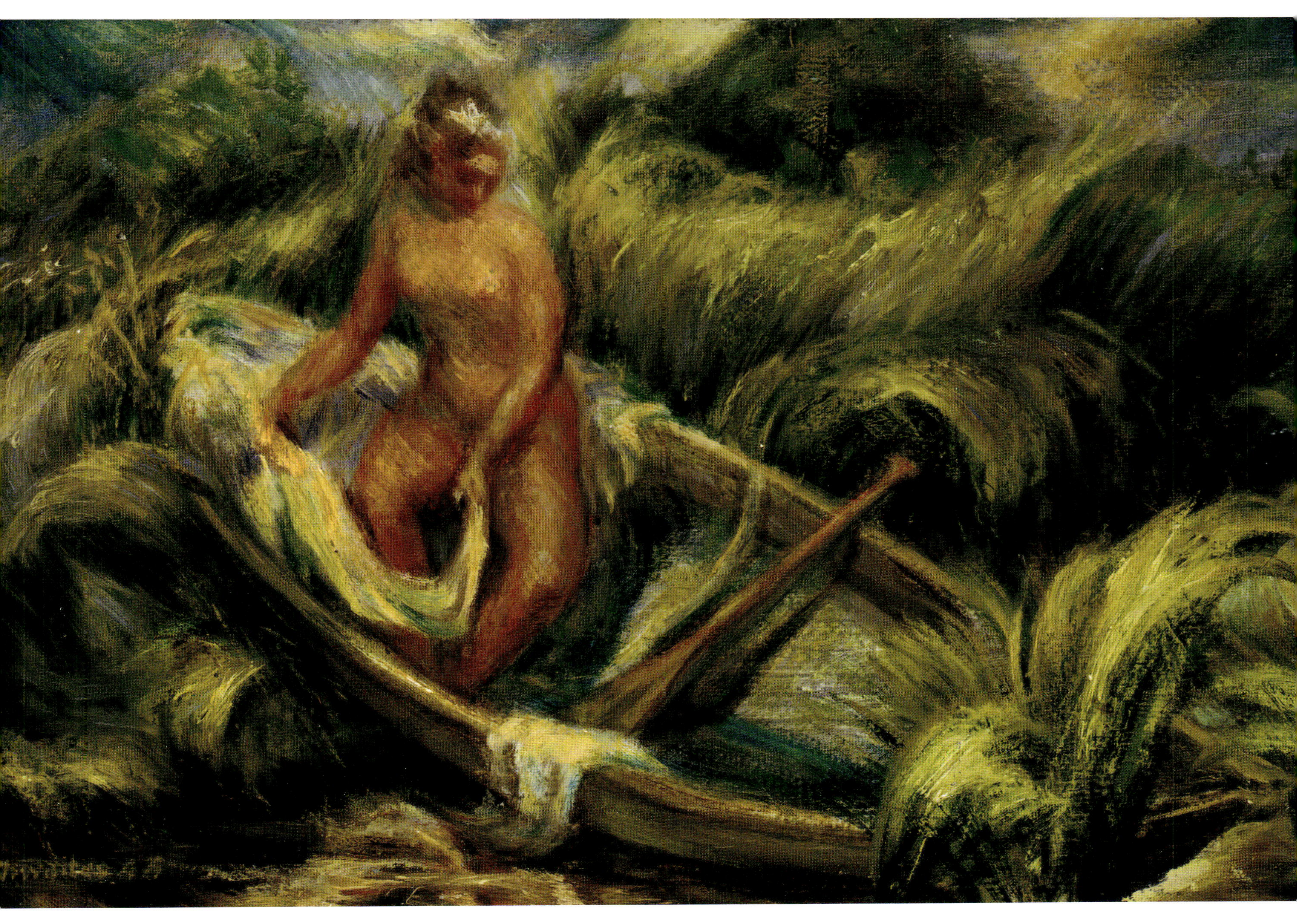

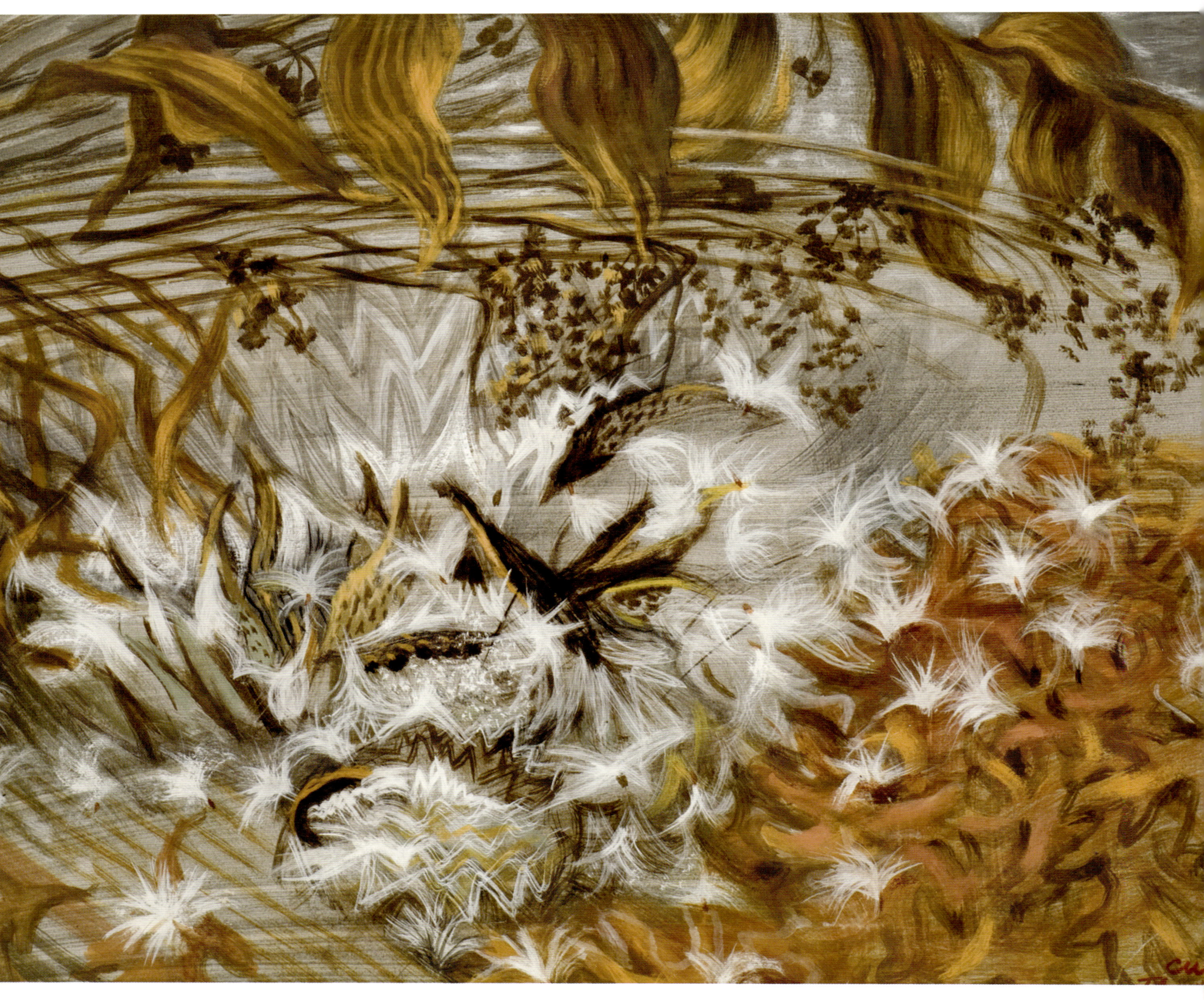

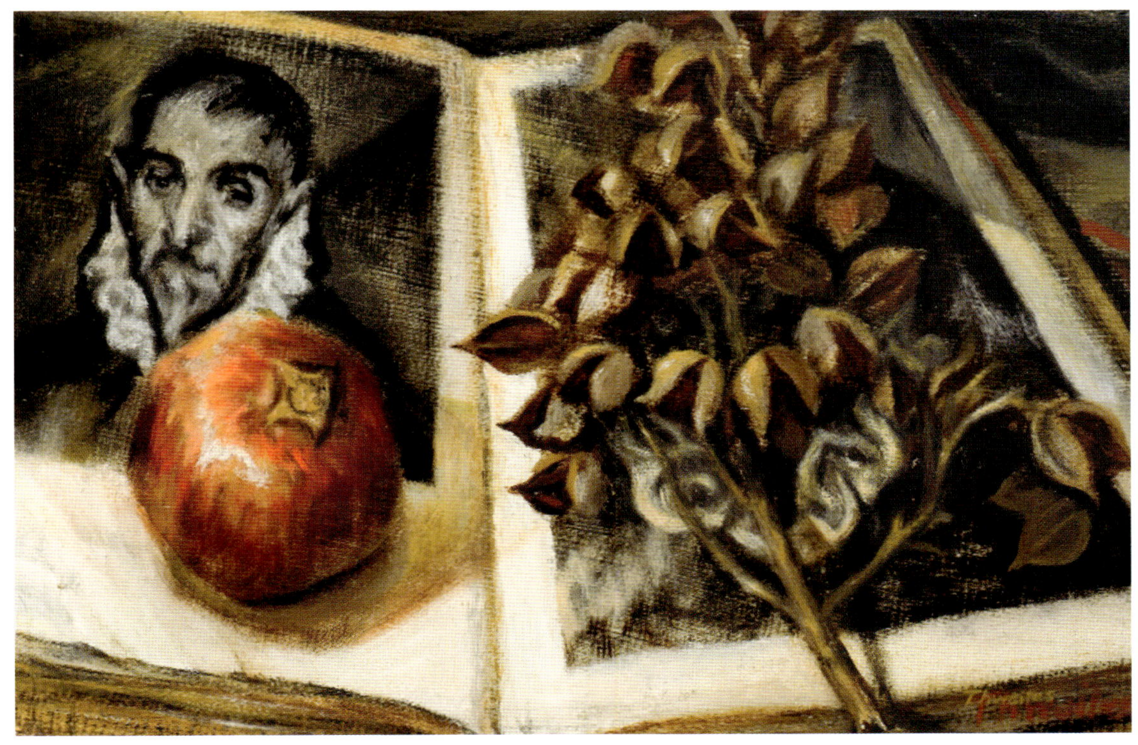

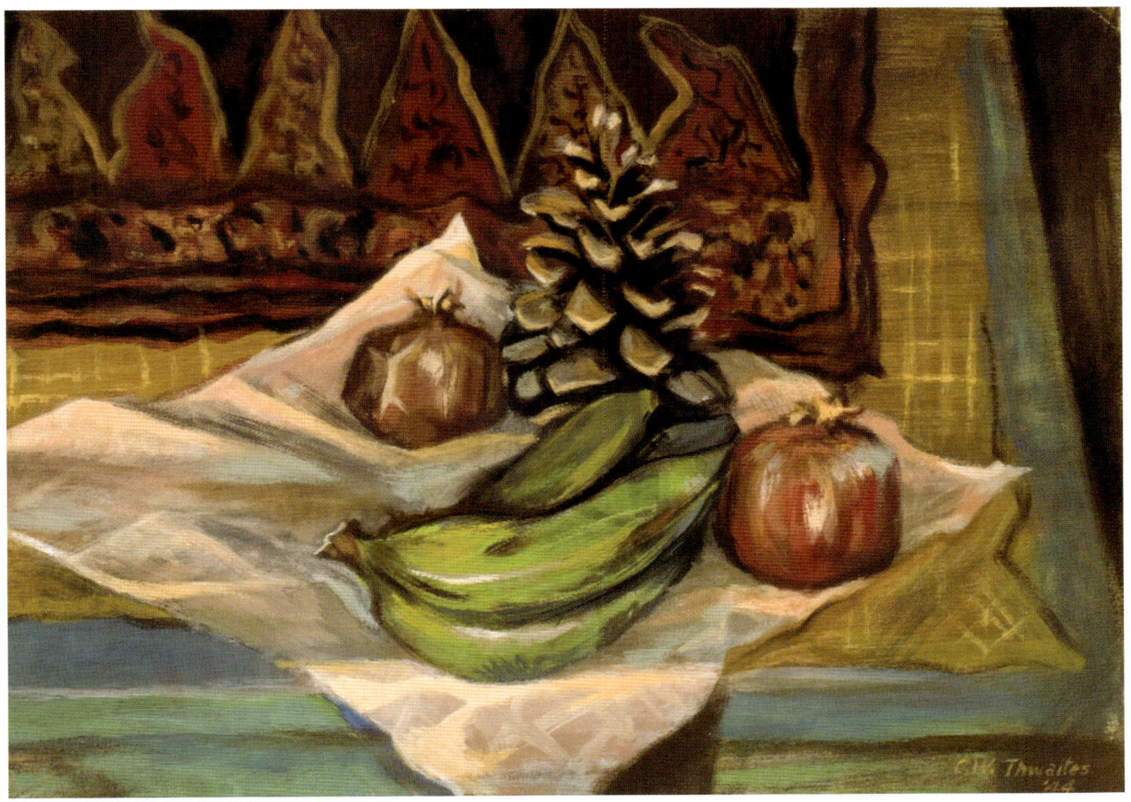

Above:
POMEGRANATE, 1949
oil maroger on masonite
$9\frac{1}{2}$ x 14

GREEN BANANAS, 1944
egg tempera on paper
16 x 22

Opposite:
MILKWEED PODS, 1949
egg tempera on paper
$24\frac{1}{2}$ x $29\frac{1}{2}$

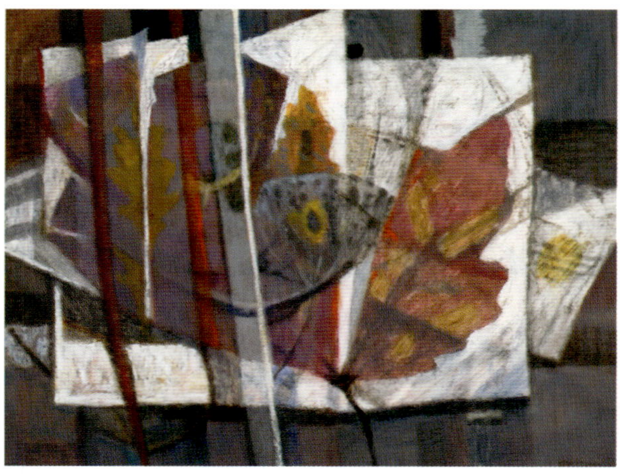

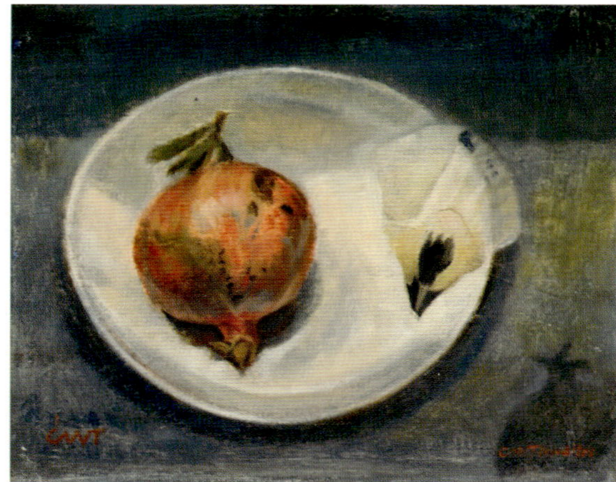

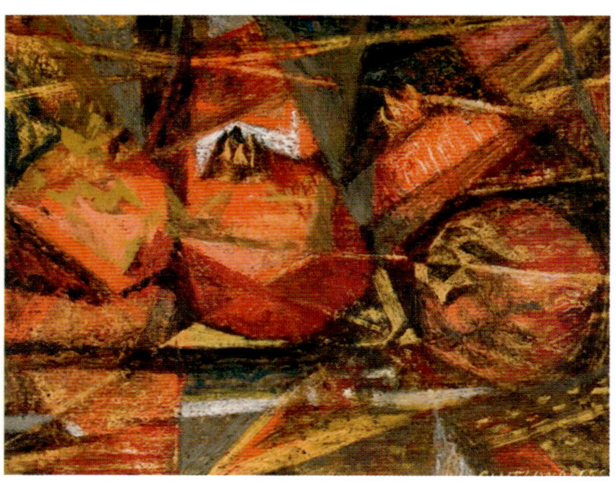

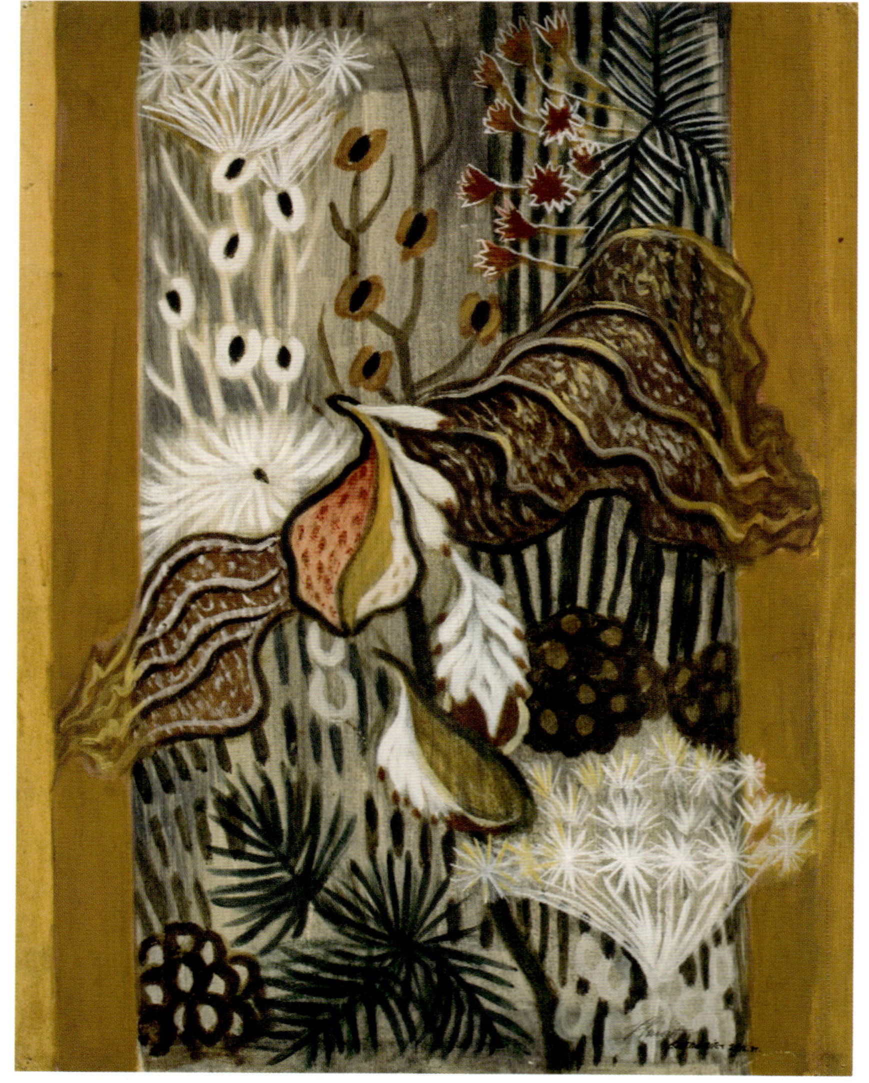

Clockwise from top left:
RED LEAF MOTIF, 1965
acrylic on paper
24 x 29½

POMEGRANATE AND PETAL, 1950
oil on masonite
8½ x 10½

POMEGRANATES (FRACTURED), 1952
oil on masonite
14½ x 16
private collection
Alison Dunlap Photography

DRIED PLANT FORMS, 1949
egg tempera on paper
23 x 17½

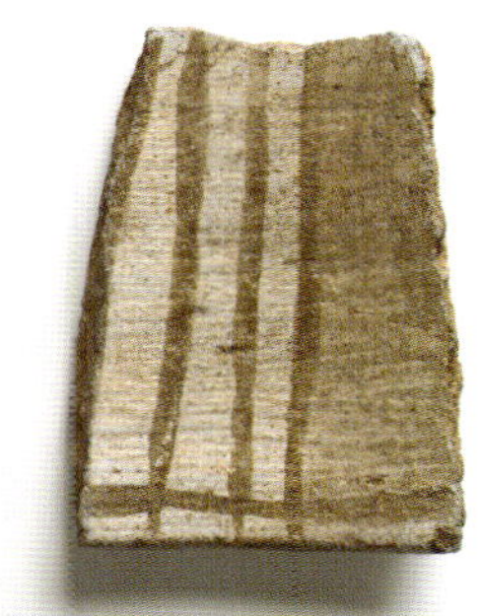

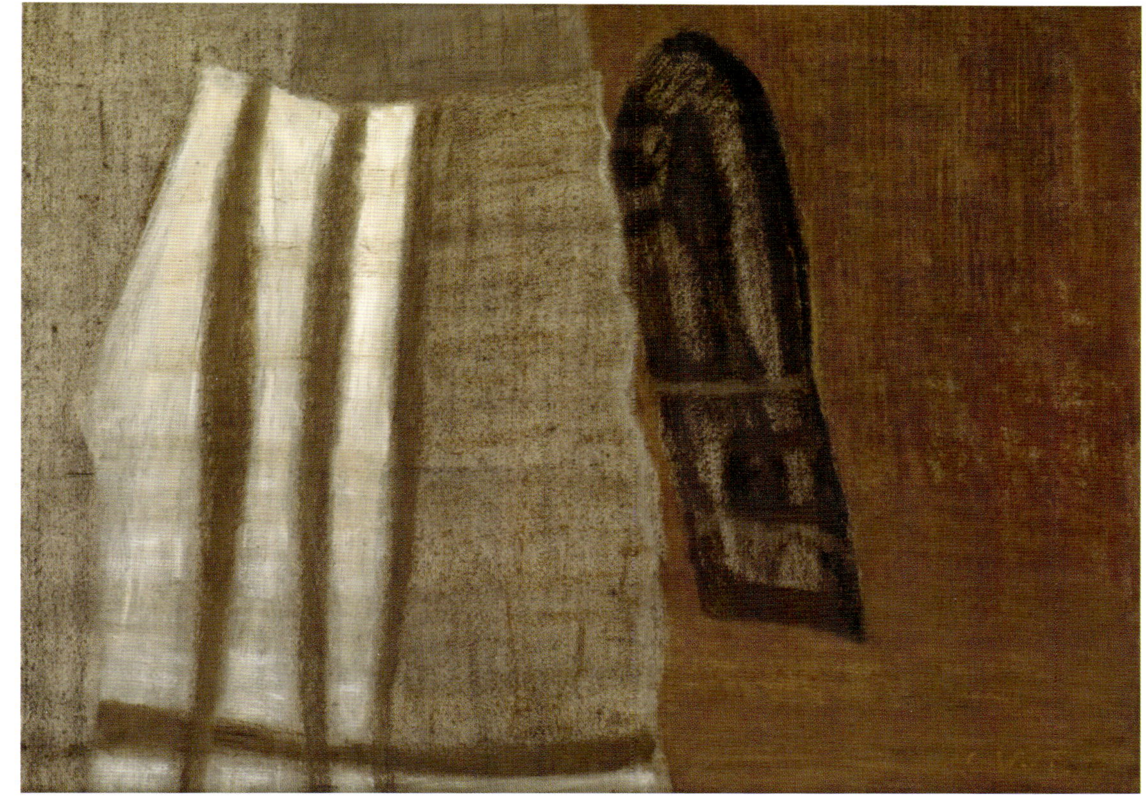

It was submitted to the 1945 Painting in the United States, Carnegie Institute, where it was purchased by the Edgar Kaufmann family and hung in their Frank Lloyd Wright designed Fallingwater residence.[32]

As the still-life paintings suggest, Thwaites was well aware of modernist tendencies, notably those of Braque, in which the tabletop is tilted forward, filling the painting surface with color that contrasts and complements the shapes of the objects on it. He also routinely added decorative elements and patterns from plant forms or fabrics. Still lifes also were a place for Thwaites to experiment with almost Zen-like simplification, as in *Pomegranate and Petal* and *Shard and Stone*, with decorative shapes as in *Red Leaf Motif*, and with abstraction, as in *Pomegranates (Fractured)*.

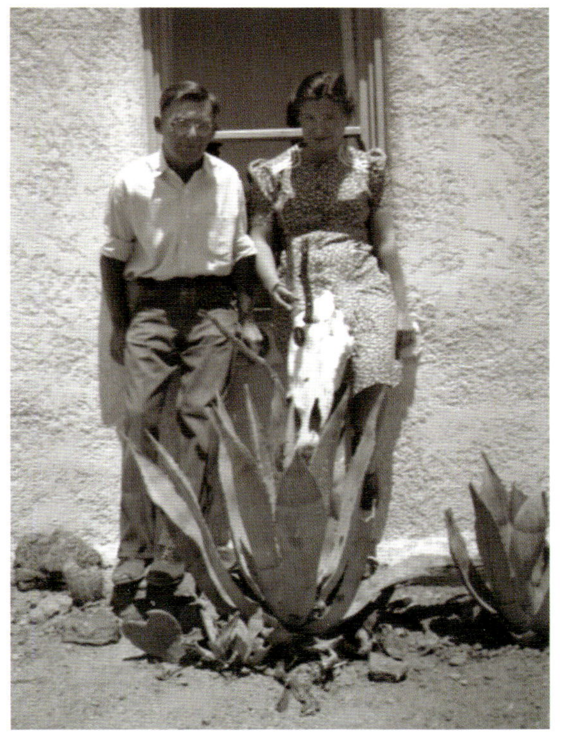

Above:
SHARD AND STONE, 1958
dry oil on paper
17½ x 23
private collection
Also shown is the actual shard which Thwaites placed in an envelope on the verso of the painting.

Charles and Antoinette in front of their casita in Tucson, Arizona, 1941.

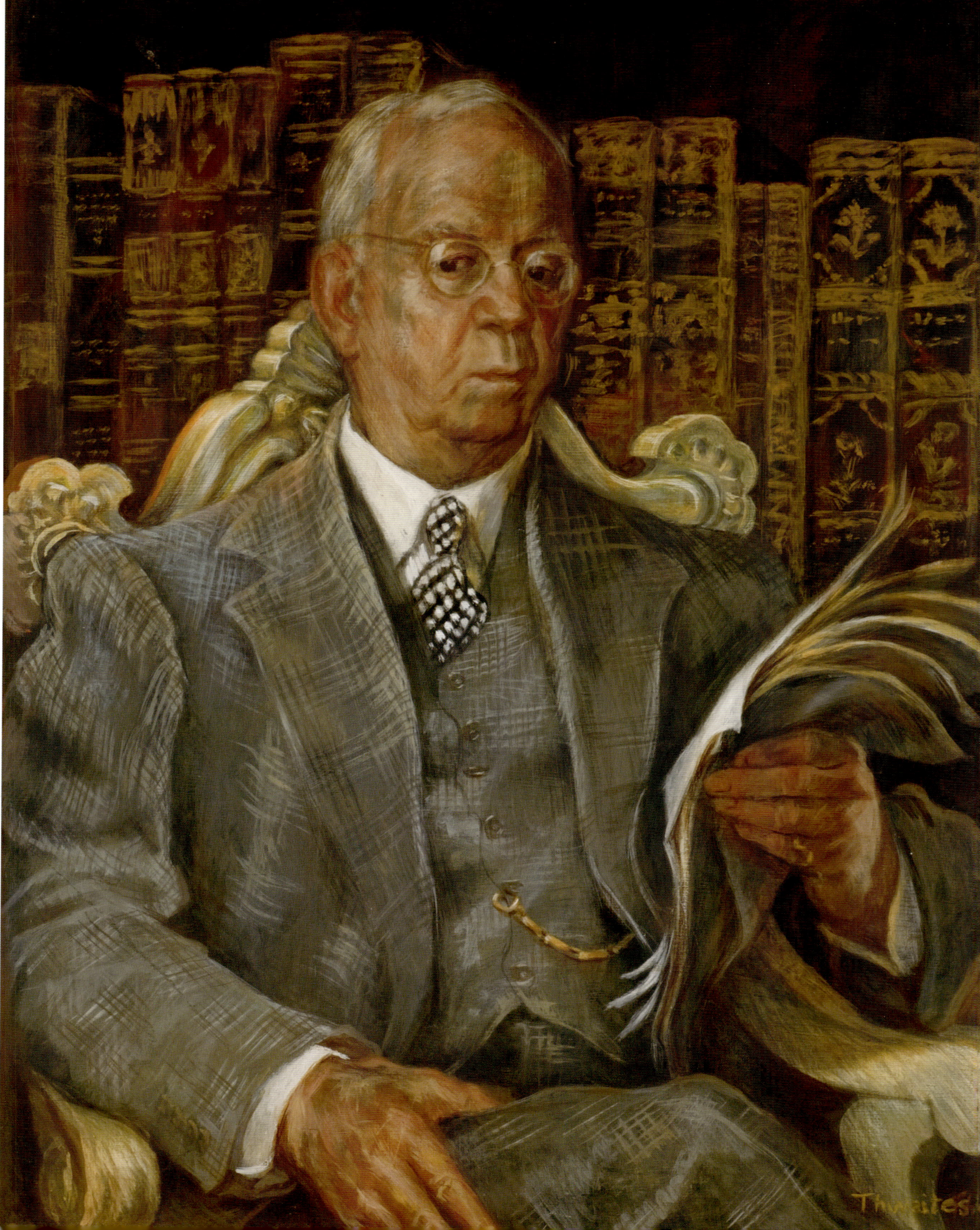
Thwaites

WISCONSIN PORTRAITS

The portrait artist who reads the information coming to his vision as a score of a great symphony, a score that can be read in infinite variations, but always with the unity of organization parallel to the entire universe, achieves his portrait as a byproduct of the most wonderful sensory material and his canvas as a direct result of this same means. It is only these portraits conceived and executed with this type of vision that we call great. CWT

In 1943, as he was installing the last of his post-office murals in Minnesota, Thwaites received one of the first of more than thirty portrait commissions. Fittingly, he was asked to paint Dean Sellery, who was retiring from the University of Wisconsin. Thwaites painted Sellery's portrait from life, and according to Olof Dahlstrand, it was common for him to do two portraits, allowing the sitter to select the likeness he preferred. Accordingly, there are several "unofficial" portraits in the estate, including one titled *The Professor*, which depicts Dean Sellery. Thwaites did at least ten portraits of prominent professors and deans at the University of Wisconsin, and for the next fifteen years, portraiture would be a lucrative source of income for the couple (see Portrait Subjects).

While the majority of the portraits were done from life, Thwaites also did several that were posthumous. One of the more renowned was a 1949 portrait of Frederick Jackson Turner (1861-1932), a professor of history at the University of Wisconsin from 1892 to 1910 and proponent of the frontier thesis identifying westward expansion with the spirit and success of the United States. Commissioned by the University of Wisconsin and American Historical Association, the portrait was gifted by the State Department to the Panamerican Institute of History and Geography at the University of Mexico. Working from photographs, Thwaites also visited with Mrs. Turner, who was age eighty-eight at the time, and interviewed friends of Turner in Madison. According to newspaper accounts, people who knew the historian considered Thwaites' portrait "more like the man than any or all of the photographs. Thwaites has succeeded in grasping what Turner's friends call his 'perpetual boyishness.' This is an openness to impression which not only characterized his writing of history but his reactions to all of life."[33]

Opposite:
THE PROFESSOR—GEORGE SELLERY, 1943
oil on masonite
36 x 27½

DAISY, 1945
oil on masonite
16 x 22

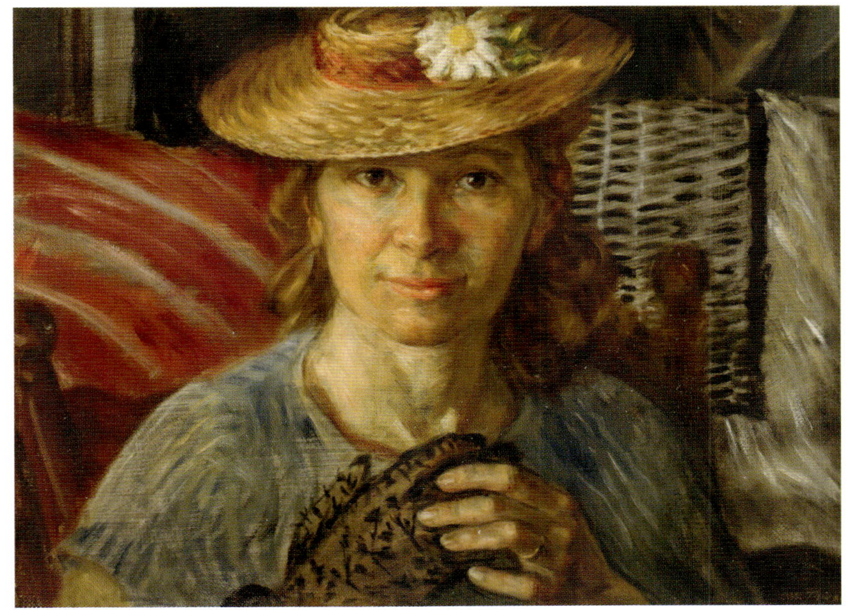

In addition to painting men of higher education, Thwaites also painted portraits of local industrialists and civic leaders, including Henry Bills Sr., Harry Bragarnick, Alfred James, Joseph Johnson, Frederick Pabst, Joseph Schafer, Charles Whitnall, and Carl Zeidler. In the judicial system, he recorded the faces of F.A. Geiger, John Gregory, Charles B. Rogers, and E. Ray Stevens. There are only a few female sitters, including a 1946 posthumous portrait of Mrs. Alexander Mitchell, founder and first president of the Women's Club of Wisconsin.

Portraiture was a reputation builder for Thwaites. Milwaukee newspapers acknowledged each of the paintings, proclaiming Thwaites to be "Wisconsin's leading portraitist."[34]

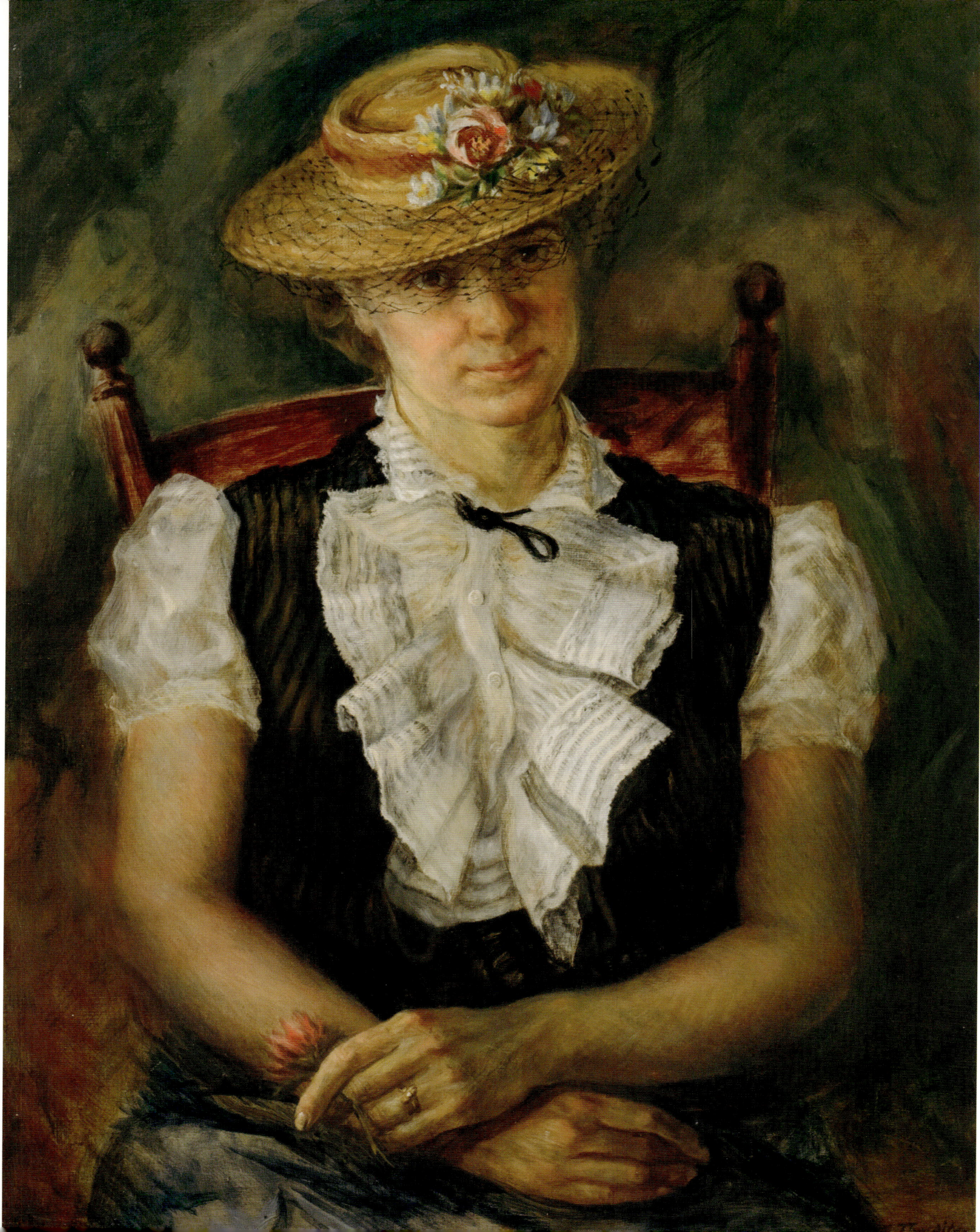

NO LABELS, PLEASE

Well, we have all been bored with: He who lives by the sword shall perish by the sword. However, because the sword of the critic is a very special doubled edged one, he cannot avoid hacking himself along with the object of his criticism, whether favorable or unfavorable. CWT

Opposite:
ROSIE, 1942
oil on masonite
32 x 24
Winner of an award at the 1943 Wisconsin Painters and Sculptors annual exhibition.

In November 1944, as the Allies turned the tide on the war's European front, Thwaites had his only one-man show in New York. It took place at Contemporary Arts Gallery, directed by Miss Emily Francis and located at 106 East 57th Street.[35] The seventeen paintings on display included a self-portrait, *Rosie*, *Summer Nude*, *Spring Portrait*, *Street Car*, and *Green Bananas*. Also included in the exhibition were depictions of cactus, a desert landscape, and a painting of the *Expulsion of Adam and Eve*, which includes a quail in the landscape.[36] The gallery flyer identified the paintings as "graphic evidence of his aesthetic quest for relativity—the outweighing of the complex by the simple, the seemingly important by the unimportant. Thru [sic] thoughtful organization of closely inter-related elements, he makes clear the quality of what he paints."[37]

In *The Art Digest*, the exhibition reviewer identified Thwaites as

> a substantial and satisfying painter [whose] pleasure in his media is evident ... and handled skillfully.... The portrait of *Rosie*, with its charm of characterization and fine rendering of fabric detail, should delight everyone. *Summer Nude* in lush verdure and sunlight is equally charming. The numerous still lifes are well painted, if not strikingly original, and Thwaites should be especially commended for not sacrificing substance for decoration in his cactus studies.[38]

The reviewer added that the painting *Street Car* bore a similarity in point of view with Reginald Marsh (1898-1954).

In the November 19, 1944, *New York Times*, Howard Devree reported that "this is earnest, arresting work." And Carlyle Burrow, in the November 26, 1944, *New York Herald Tribune*, wrote, "Attractive portraits are included in the show, but simple subjects, such as corn on the stalk, cactus and pomegranates, are more impressive in their low-keyed vibrant colors. This artist shows feeling, well supported by keen observation and drawing."

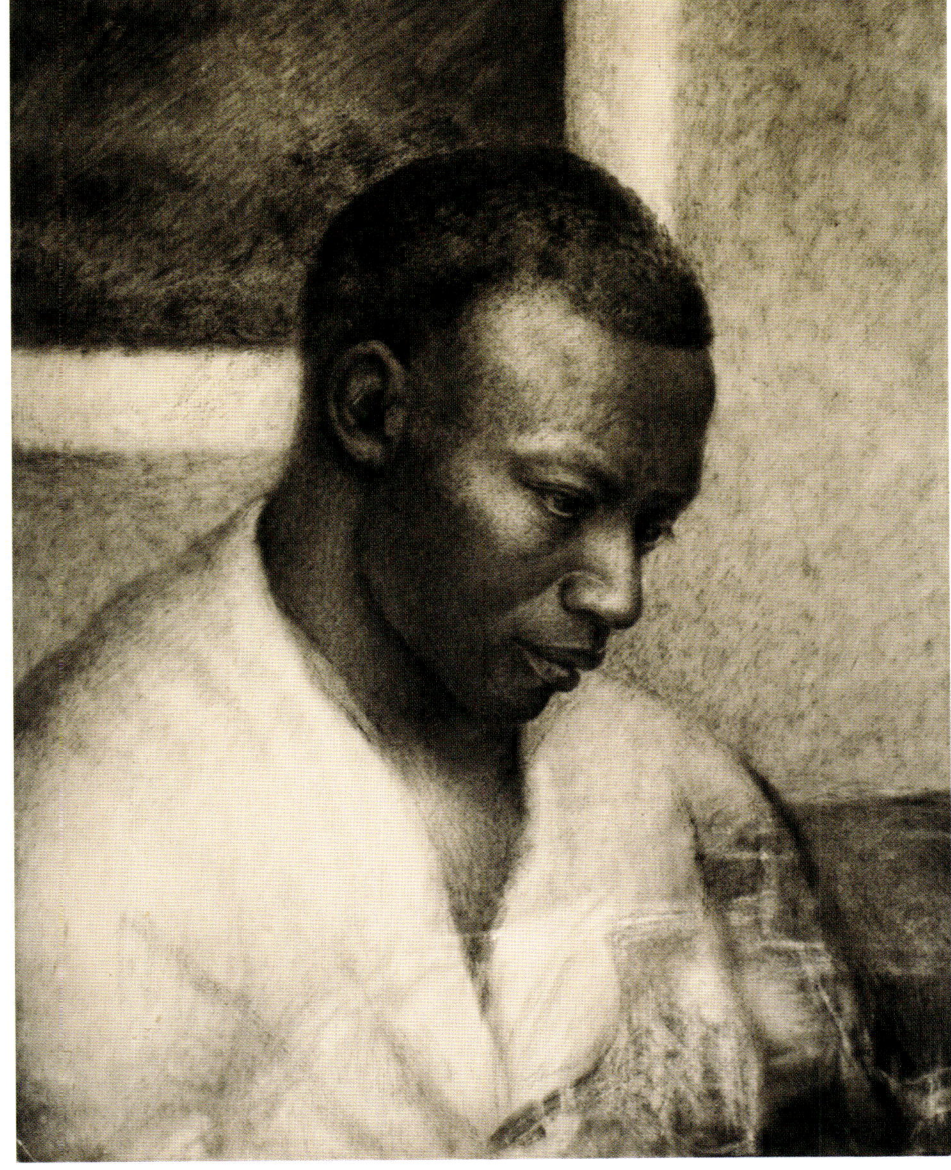

AFRICAN AMERICAN, 1940
dry oil on paper
23 x 17½

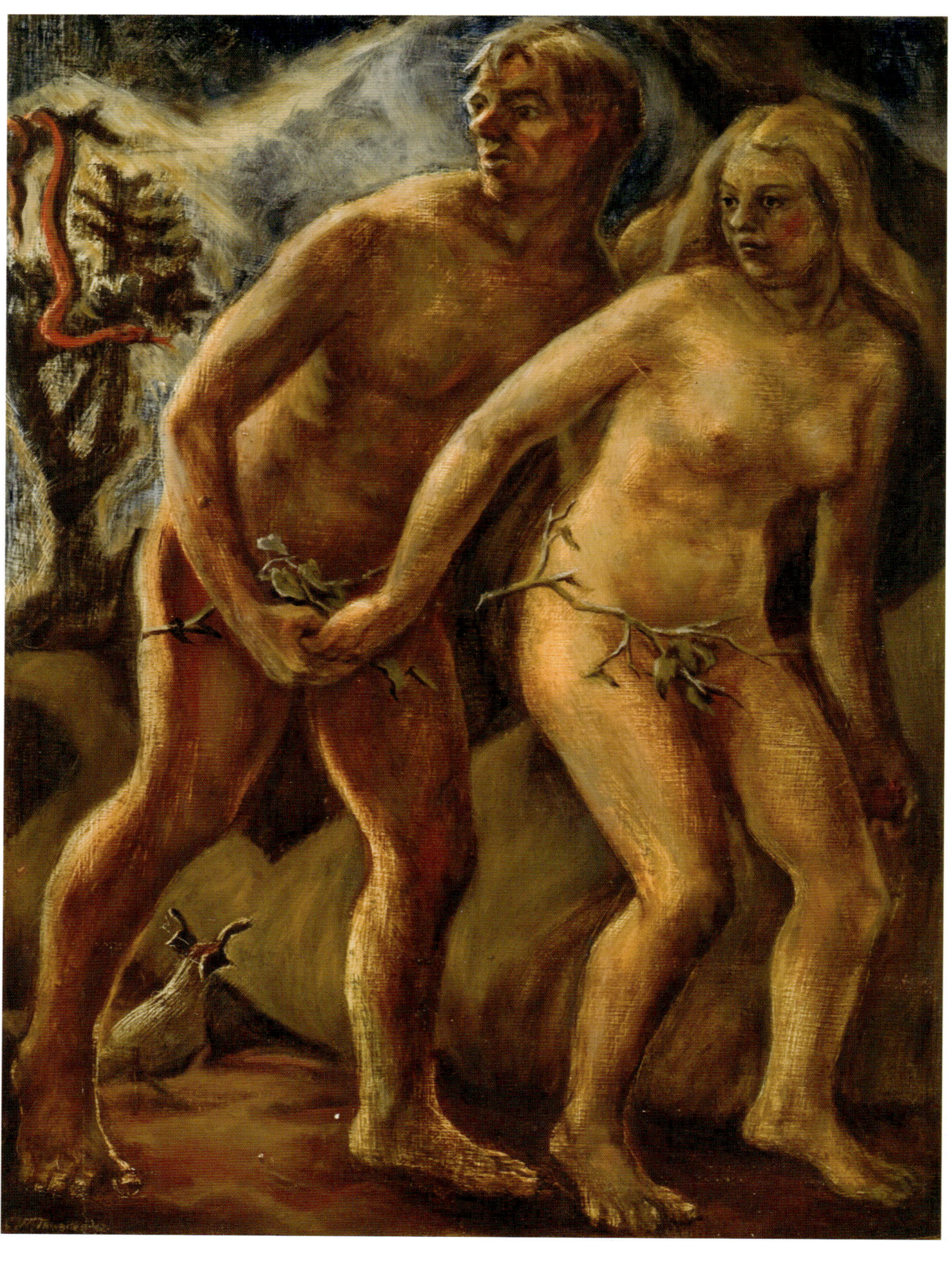

Despite the positive feedback and the chiding of his brother who lived in New York, Charles and Antoinette neither attended the opening nor the exhibition.

Three years later, in November 1947, Thwaites' work was the subject of a one-man show at the Milwaukee Art Institute. A newspaper reporter observed that Thwaites had a deep underlying philosophy controlling his work, making him sensitive to the works of others. He went on to quote Thwaites, who articulated his personal philosophy:

> There are 1,000 ways to paint, why limit yourself to one manner? It is of no importance whether a picture is "modern," "academic," or what have you. Is it good art, is it bad painting, or is it just indifferent? Some painters have illusions which carry them farther than others. Therefore, they have greater variety in their work. To my way of thinking, an artist practically relives all art history—he goes through all of the phases of art in his own experience.... The language of art is "decorative" and whether a painting is deeply significant or merely decorative is a question of the extent to which it parallels nature in its universal principles.[39]

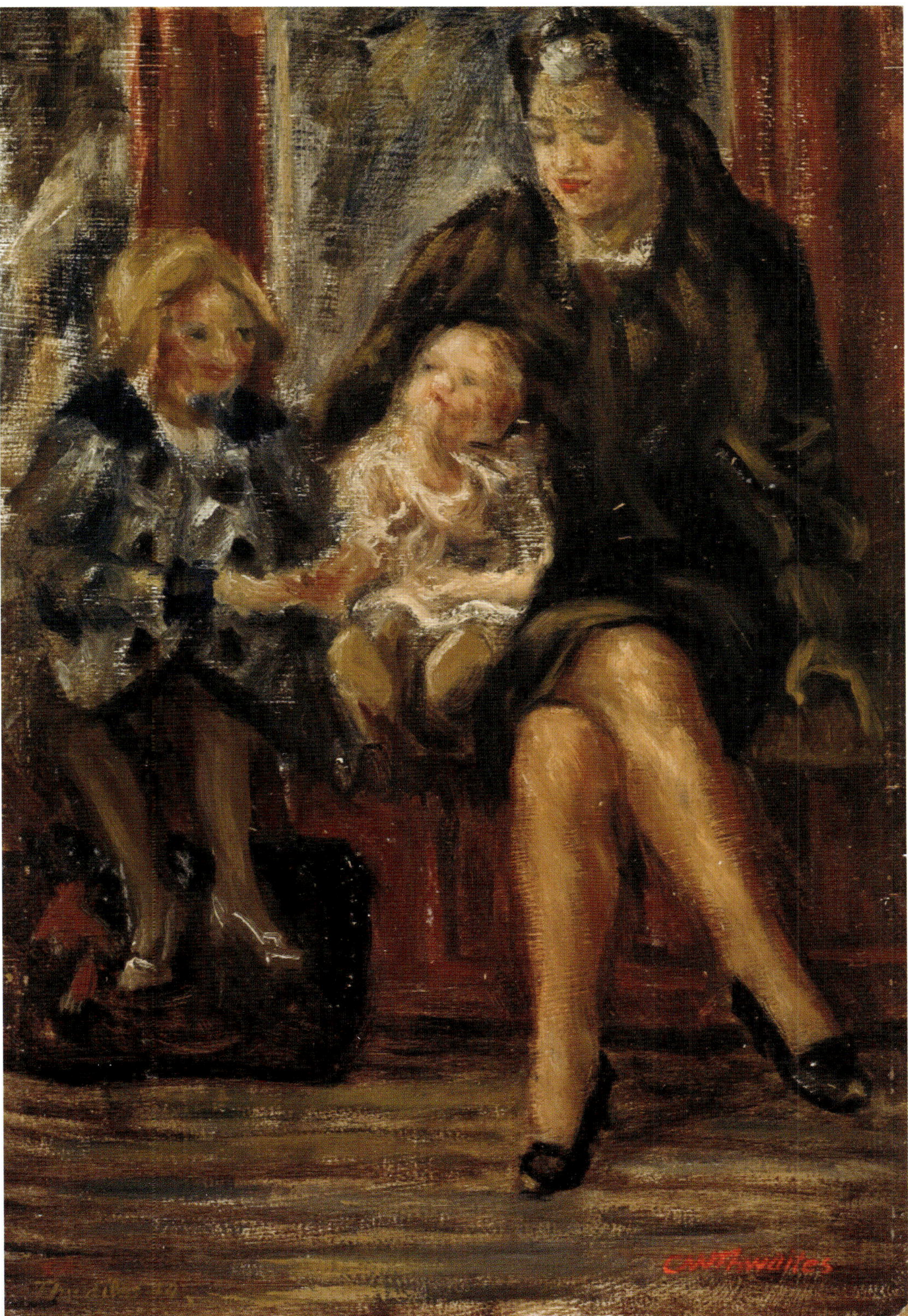

STREET CAR, 1940
oil on masonite
14 x 9½

Opposite:
EXPULSION OF ADAM AND EVE, 1942
oil on masonite
17 x 14

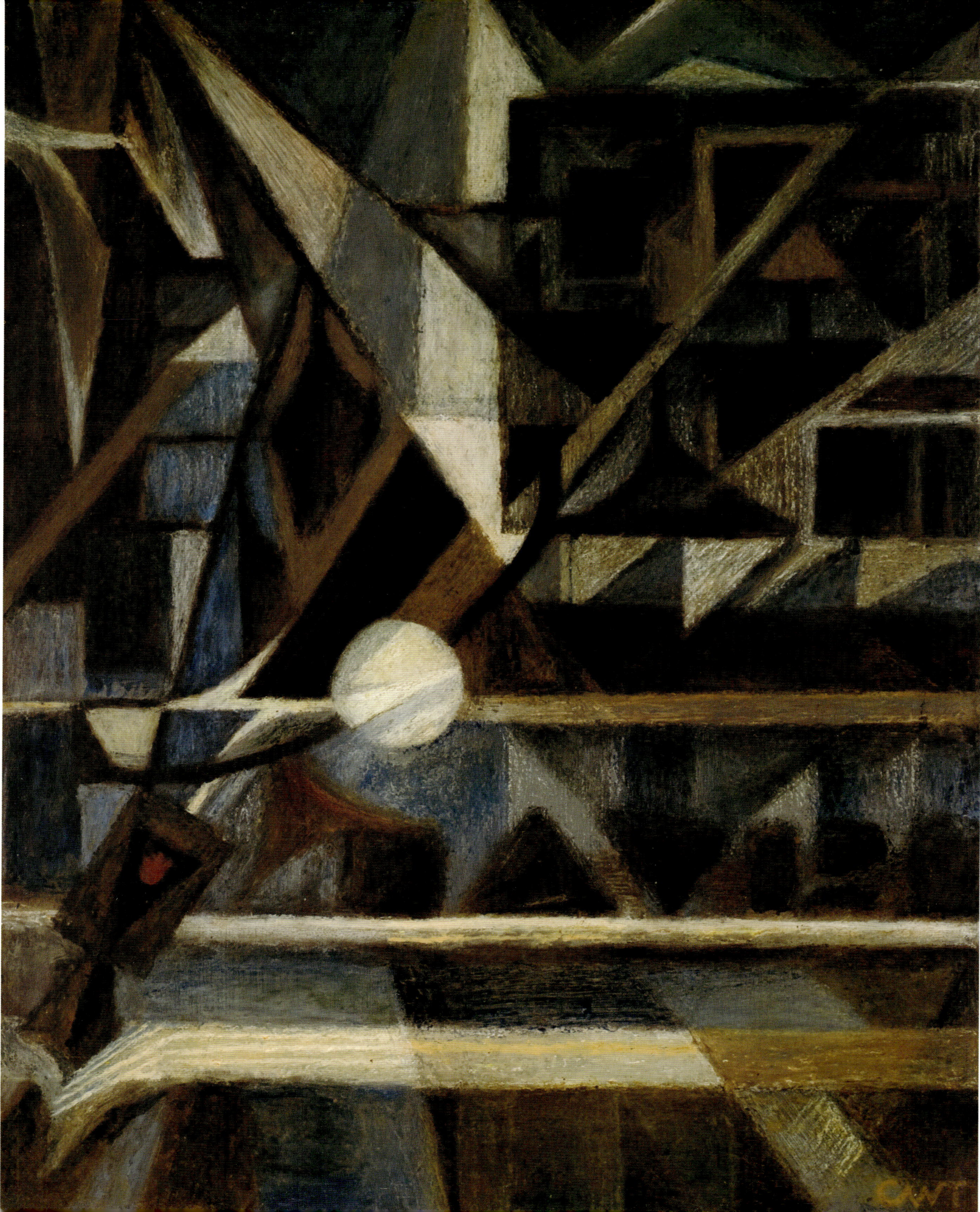

NEW DIMENSIONS

Modern art is not a search for modern idioms for old pictorial illustration, but a search for new patterns to illustrate and demonstrate the principles of art. CWT

Thwaites was very active throughout the late 1940s and early 1950s. He was teaching drawing and design in the extension division of the University of Wisconsin and portrait and figure painting at the Milwaukee Art Institute. He was also judging art shows, entering juried competitions, painting portraits, and caring for his elderly parents.

During the late 1940s, a major transition took place in Thwaites' work. He began looking at landscape subjects in a new way, breaking up their elements into decorative patterns, including angular geometric shapes as in *Night Patterns* and *Clouds of Lake Michigan*. He also began working in encaustic. The reasons for the change are unclear. However, even though he was not included in the 1948 AIC American Paintings Exhibition which focused on surrealism and abstraction, Thwaites undoubtedly saw the exhibition in which he was exposed to a range of modernist approaches, including those of prominent New Mexicans such as Georgia O'Keeffe, Cady Wells (1904-1954), Emil Bisttram (1895-1976), and Tom Benrimo (1887-1979).

Opposite:
NIGHT PATTERNS, 1952
encaustic on masonite
30½ x 23½

CLOUDS OF LAKE MICHIGAN, 1950
egg tempera on paper
17½ x 23

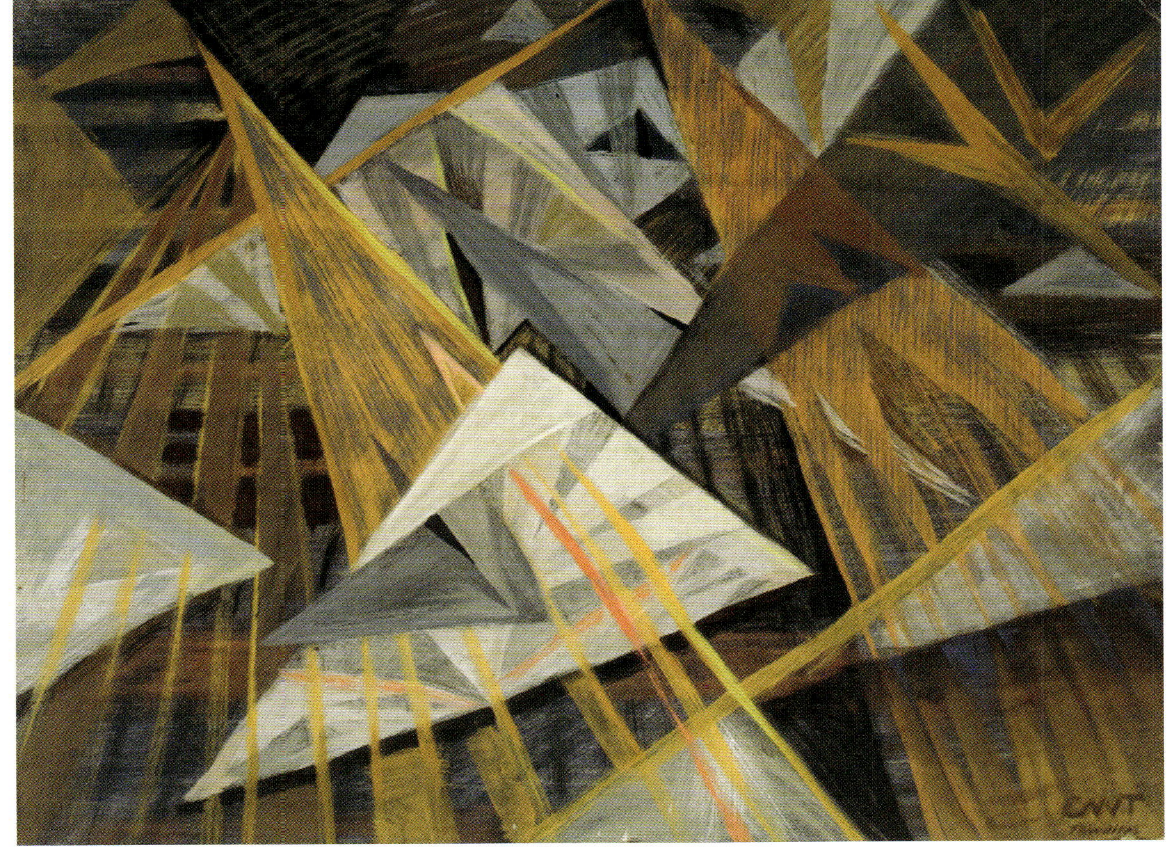

In 1950, the Thwaiteses took the summer off, tent camping as they drove westward, including a stay near Abiquiu, New Mexico, where they ran out of water. Noticing a road marked by a mailbox, they encountered a woman who instructed her maid to fill their container. Although names were not exchanged, Antoinette later identified the woman as O'Keeffe, who struck up a conversation acknowledging the couple's Wisconsin license plates. They talked about the beauty of the New Mexico landscape, and O'Keeffe informed them that her neighbor, who owned Ghost Ranch, was planning to sell it. The Thwaites archive includes correspondence from 1955 and 1956 in which Beatrice Van Bergh offers them the property for $15,000 (see Meeting Georgia O'Keeffe, Appendix A).

In 1951, Thwaites exhibited a nonobjective tempera painting titled *The Red Line*[40] at the Artists of Chicago

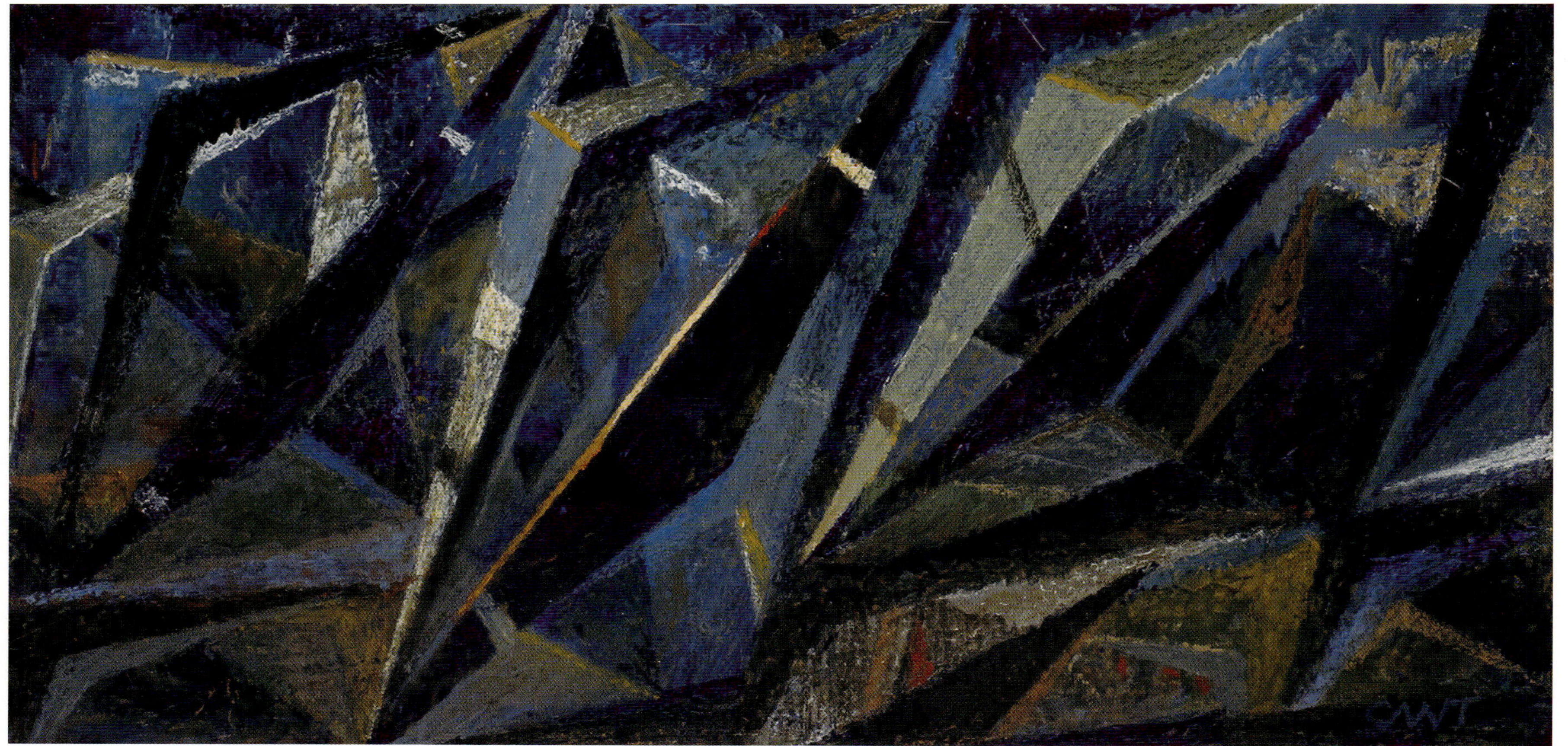

and Vicinity, followed in 1952 by an abstract encaustic titled *Desert*, and in 1954 an expressionistic encaustic titled *Sunflowers*. The catalyst for his experimentation with this new medium may have been the small handbook *Encaustic: Materials and Methods* by Frances Pratt and Becca Fizel published in 1949. Tracing the history of the wax and pigment medium from Pliny's references to contemporary painters, the book outlined recipes and working methods, including those of German expatriate Karl Zerbe (1903-1972),[41] an expressionist painter who headed the School of the Museum of Fine Arts, Boston, and revived the medium in the late 1930s. The fusion of an ancient technique with a new outlook would have appealed to Thwaites, and his encaustics became more expressionistic, as suggested by *Mukwonago*, which is most likely an interpretation of the Winnebago-Sac Indian legend about a phantom who pulled his bride into the depths of Phantom Lake near Mukwonago, southwest of Milwaukee. The large painting shows a distorted man and woman undulating across the top of a rhythmic composition with stylized water lilies in the foreground.

Late in 1951, a major chapter turned in Thwaites' life when his father and mother passed away in close succession. His ties to Wisconsin were severed. Having traveled extensively throughout the Southwest during the 1940s and living in Taos in 1952 and 1953, the couple was now free to look to brighter horizons in art and life. Late in 1954, they emptied the Milwaukee apartment they had lived in for nearly two decades and took up permanent residence in Taos.

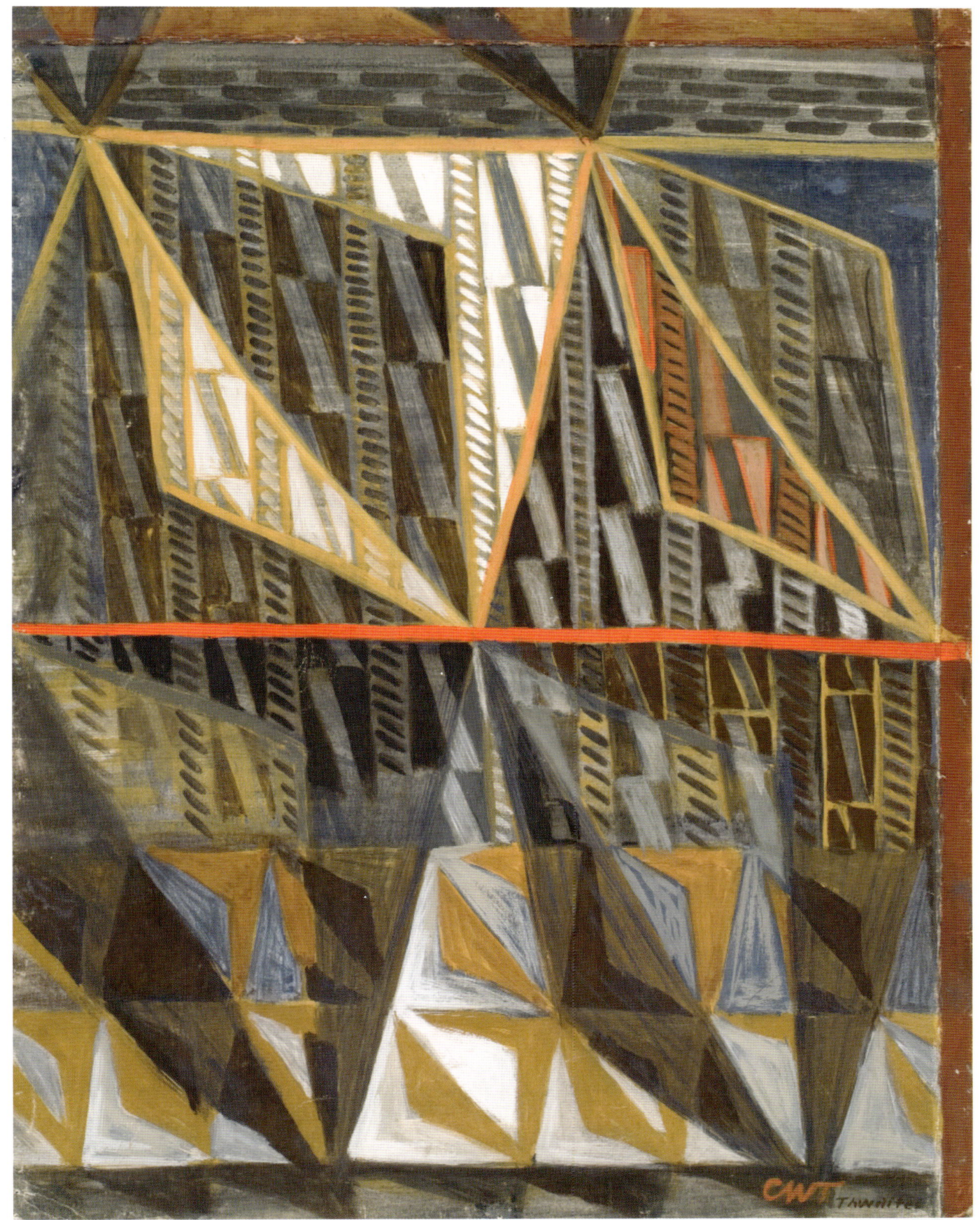

THE RED LINE, 1950
egg tempera on paper
23 x 17 1/2

Opposite:
WING PATTERNS, 1951
encaustic on masonite
18 x 36

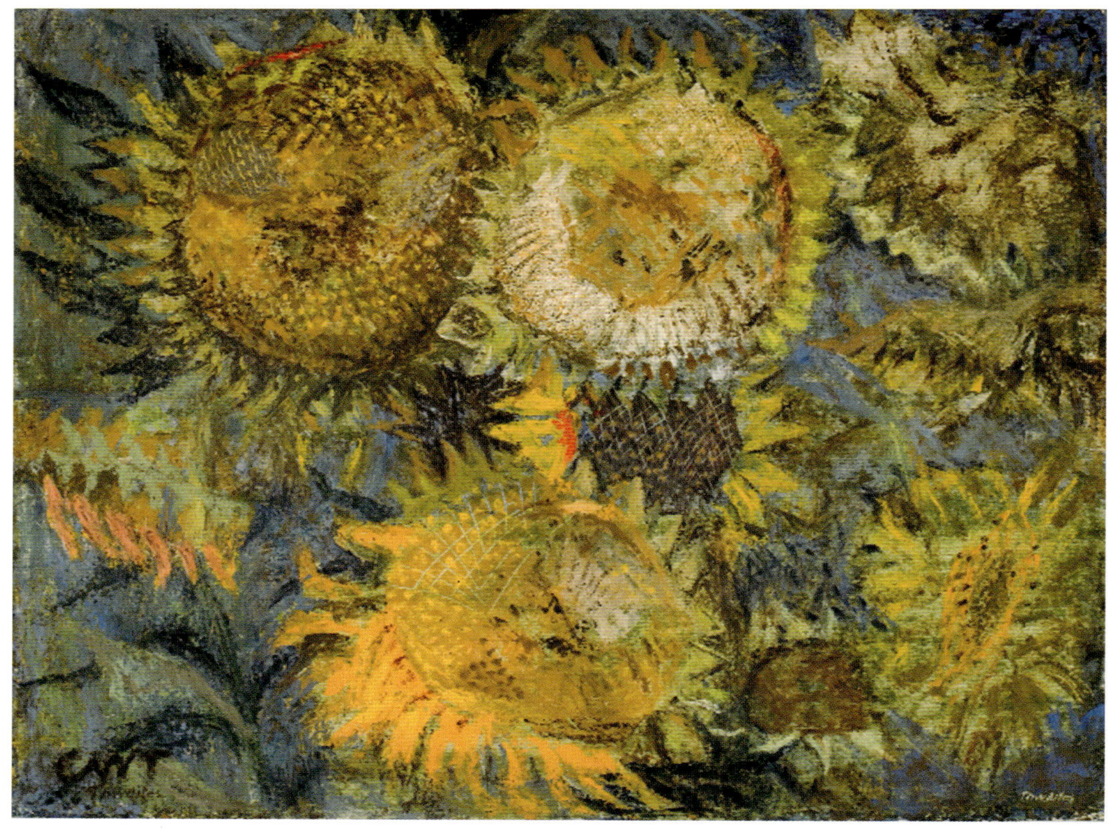

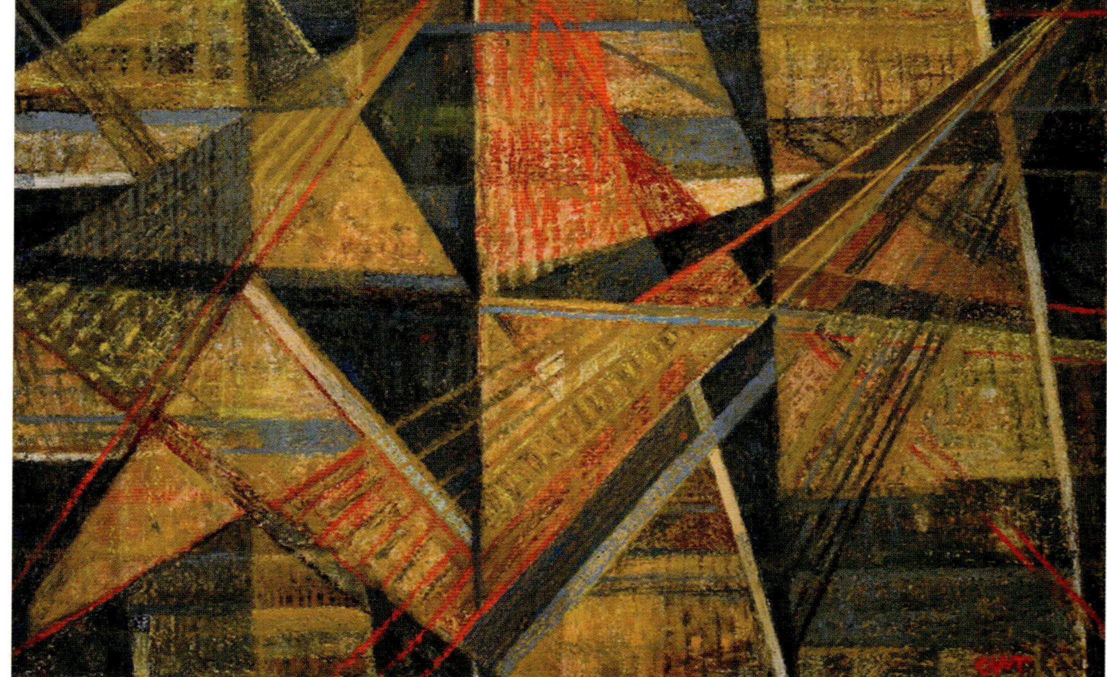

Above:
SUNFLOWERS, 1953
encaustic on paper
17½ x 23

PAINTED DESERT, 1953
encaustic on panel
26 x 39

Opposite:
MUKWONAGO, 1952
encaustic on masonite
36 x 48

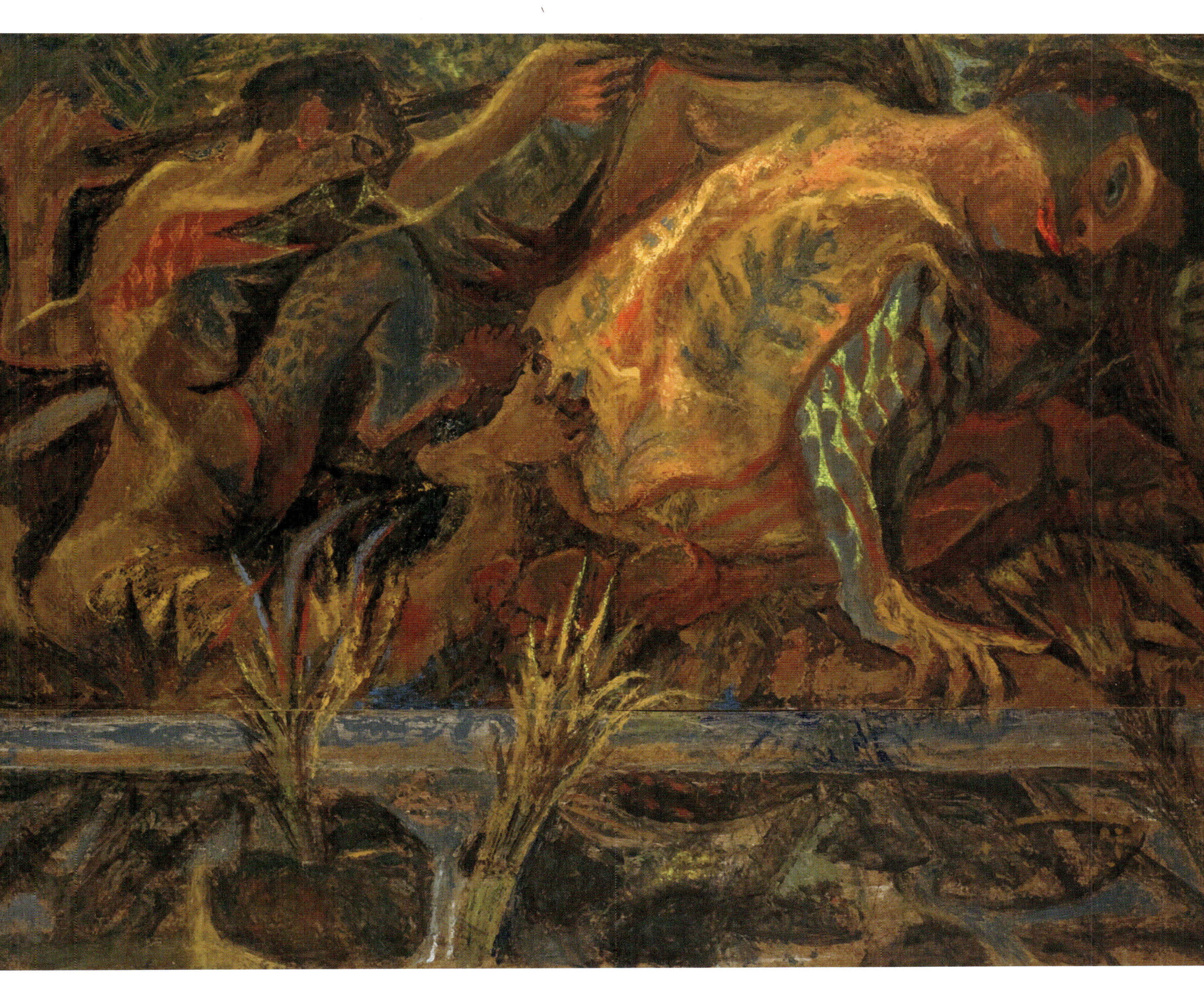

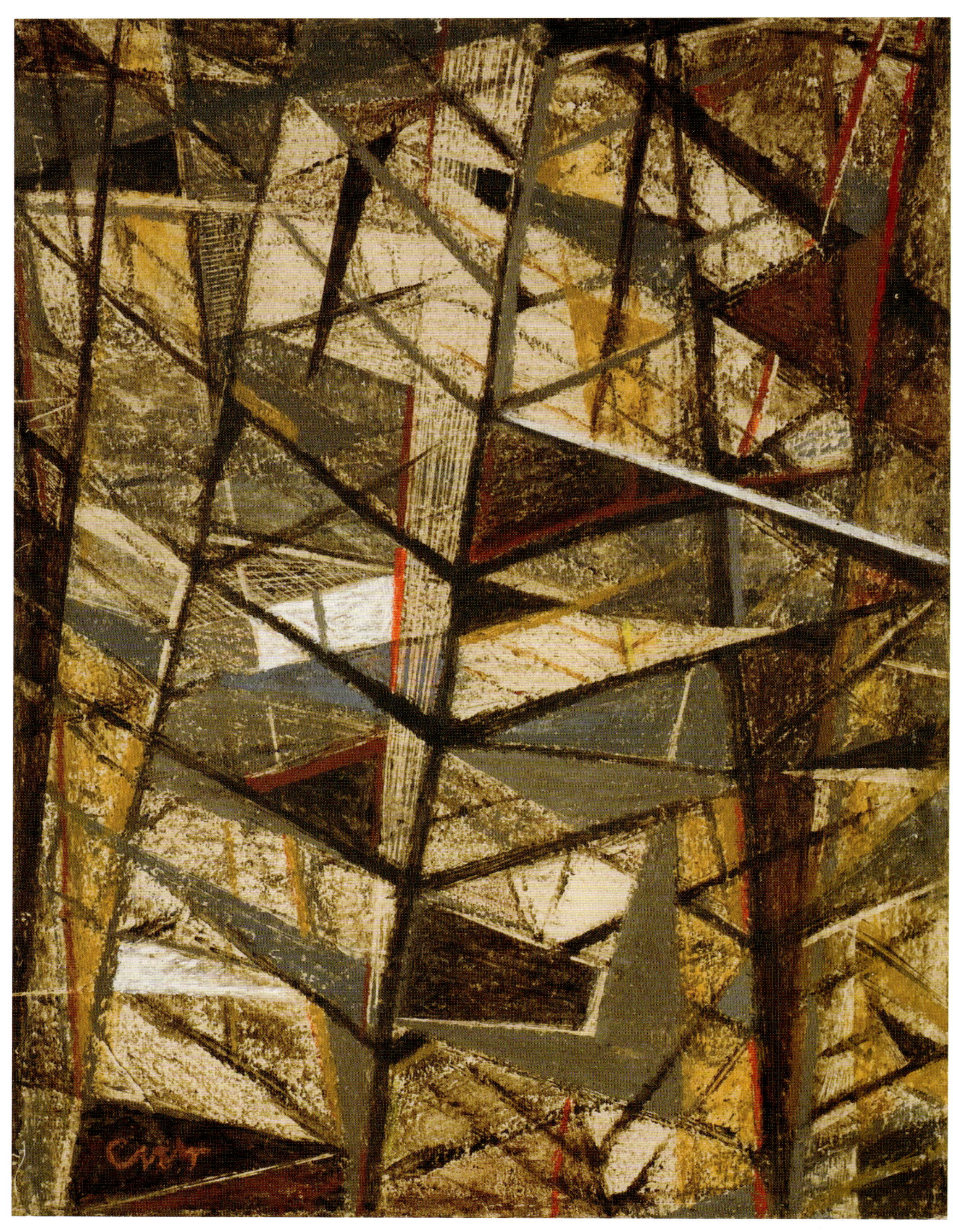

FOREST MOTIF, 1954
encaustic on masonite
23½ x 18

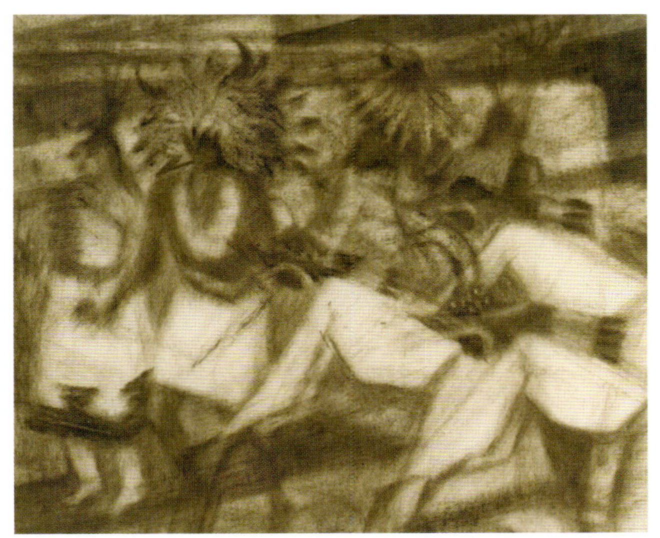

NEW MEXICO

We are out in lonely country now, far beyond our physical being … out there where the self begins, stripped of all associations, to be ourselves with ourselves, which, you might say, would be to cease to exist. But would it be? Do we not always exist in a state of isolation? That deeply personal isolation, whatever the associations and involvements, in pain or pleasure? Is there not always that theme of identity of the self consciously running through every minute? CWT

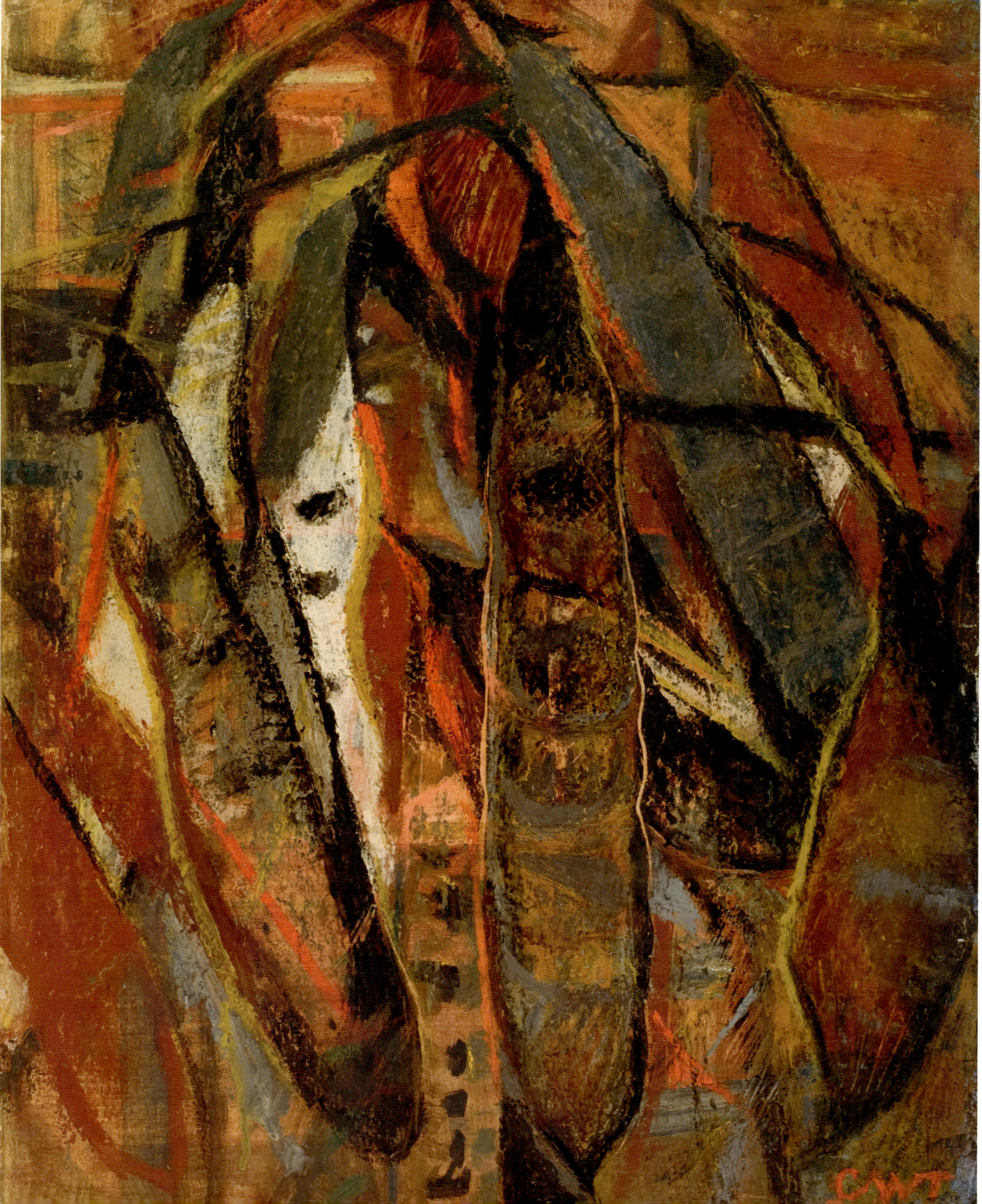

ONE WITH ALL

In art we are looking for an echo of our own being and all being at one and the same time. CWT

For decades, Thwaites had enjoyed the camaraderie of Wisconsin artists and the mix of traditional and progressive outlooks in the Chicago art community. He found that same energetic combination in the post World War II art community of northern New Mexico, which blended agrarian lifestyles with atomic-age science.

According to the Dahlstrands, the Thwaiteses were firm believers in synchronism, so the couple was not surprised that while wandering through town looking for a place to rent during the summer of 1952, they stumbled upon Taos artist Gisella Loeffler (1903-1977), whose daughter was leaving for two years abroad and looking to lease out the Pink House. Formerly a part of the Tony and Mabel Dodge Luhan compound, the small cottage was perfect for the couple and its proximity to Mabel (1879-1962) was a definite plus. Writer, activist, and doyenne of culture, Mabel had settled in Taos in the 1920s and married Taos Pueblo Indian Tony Luhan. While living a much quieter lifestyle in the 1950s, her home and compound still radiated the aura of a mecca that had attracted avant-garde artists, writers, poets, and celebrities for decades.

Opposite:
BLACK LOCUST PODS, 1956
encaustic on paper
23 x 17½

GISELLA, 1952
encaustic on paper
17½ x 23
private collection
Dennis Wyszynski Photography

Thwaites recorded his surroundings, including an expressionistic encaustic portrait of Loeffler titled *Gisella* and a light-filled tempera of the *Pink House Portal* (see page 108). In a 1952 letter from Taos that was printed in *The Milwaukee Journal* (see Pink House, Appendix A), Antoinette described in detail the interior of the house. The couple also evaluated the art scene of the time, with Antoinette commenting below on the remaining members of the Taos Society of Artists and the younger generation of modernists, many of whom exhibited at the Ruins Gallery, which Thwaites depicted in *Window Overlooking Ranchos de Taos Valley, Ruins Gallery*.

> There are one-man shows opening at the rate of one a week at the numerous galleries. Most of the work is representational, done with an eye to the tourist collector's taste. Some of it is very well done from an illustrative angle.

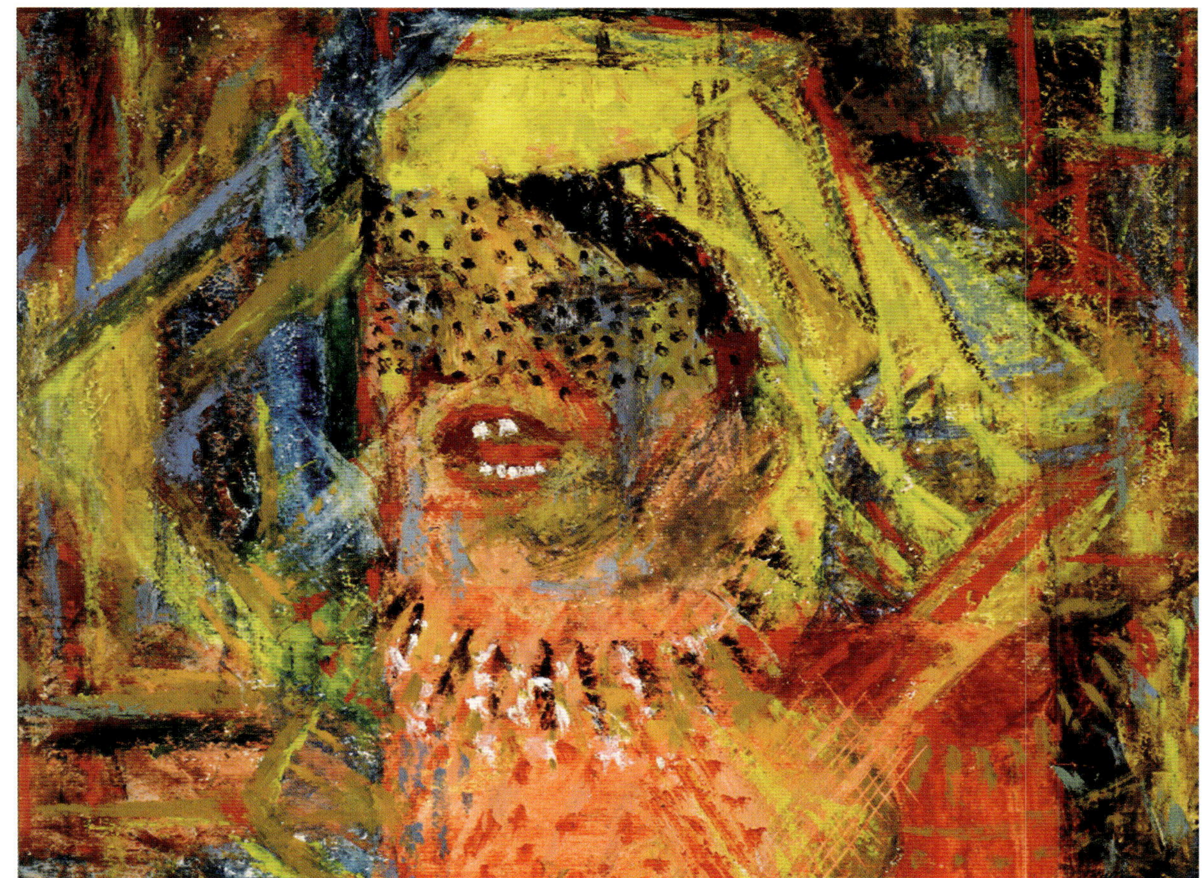

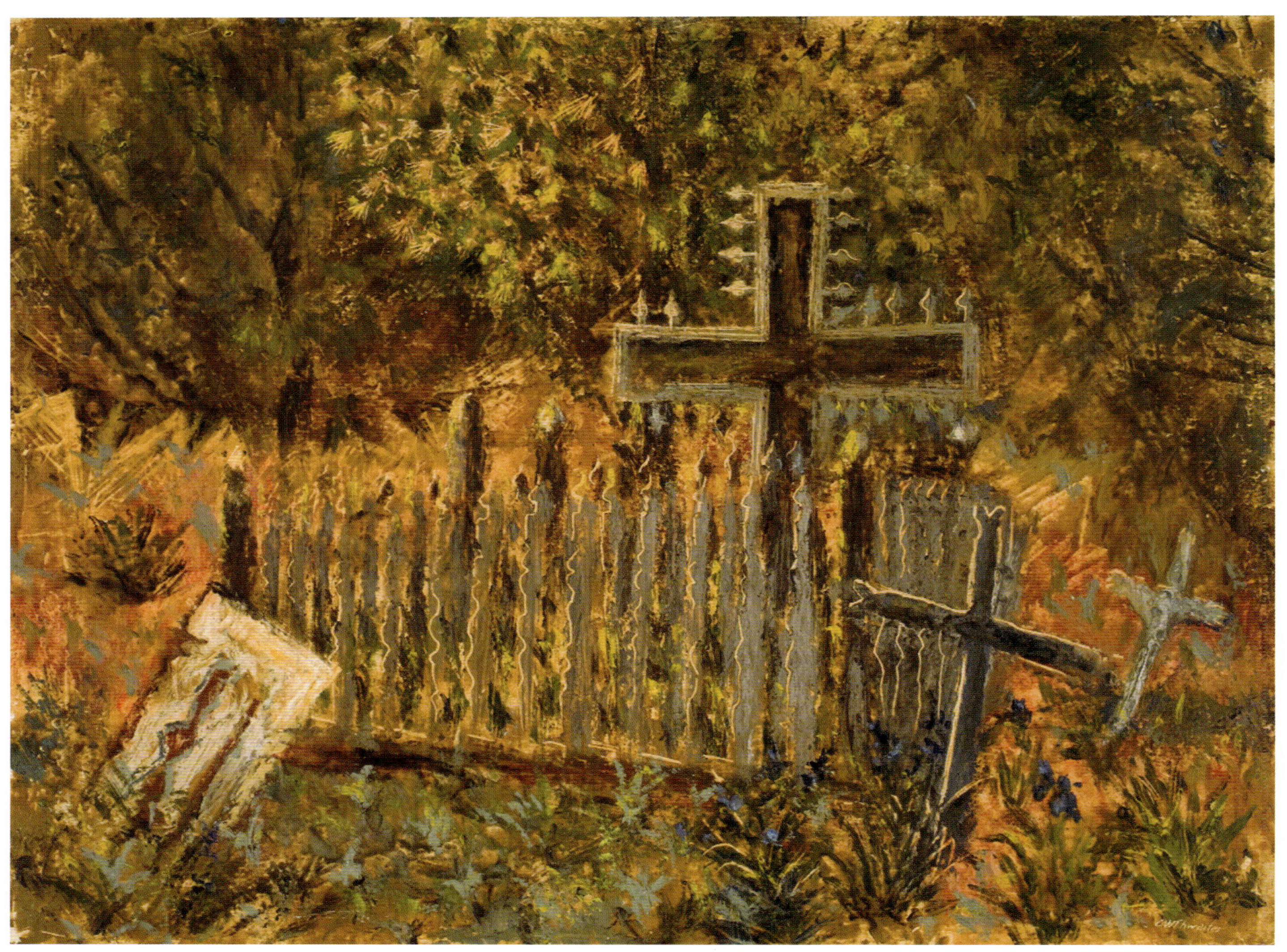

> Two galleries are devoted to expressionistic and nonrepresentational painting and sculpture, definitely not to the taste of the tourists. We visited with a number of artists in this particular group and have to admire their struggle to exist.

Their memorable summer of 1952 included dining with the Luhans at their second home in Embudo, New Mexico, during which they were entertained by Tony's stories. Antoinette further described her impressions of the physical environment, Mabel's lush irrigated gardens, and the dress and mannerisms of Taos Indians. The letter/article closes with this quote: "At the moment the sky is overcast and it looks as though the Indians' appeals through the recent corn dance are to be answered with rain for their crops."

The Thwaiteses spent the spring of 1953 in Arizona and summer and fall in New Mexico. Thwaites wintered in Rochester, Minnesota, where he painted a portrait of Byrl Raymond Kirklin, head of the radiology department at the Mayo Clinic, and in early

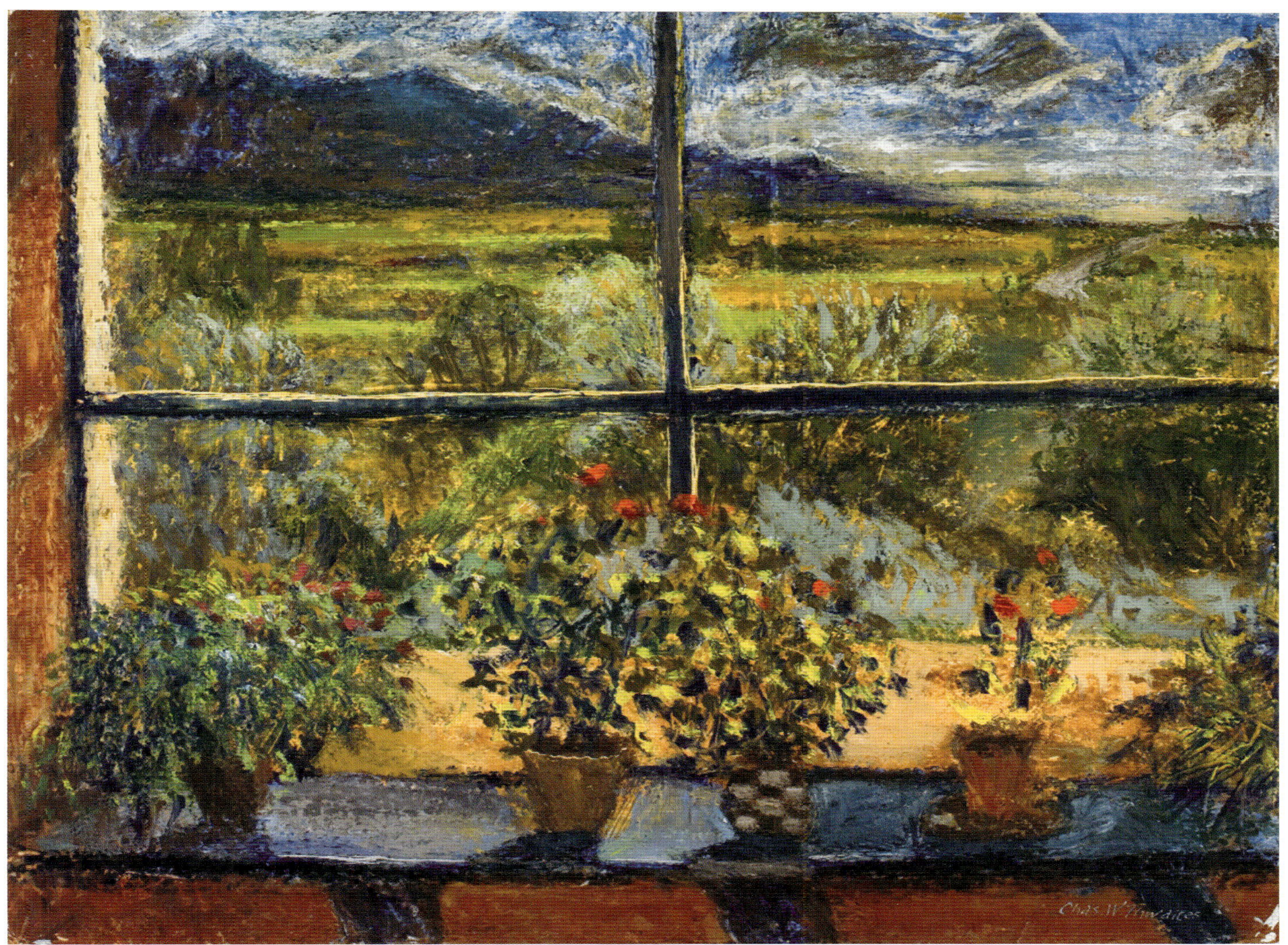

WINDOW OVERLOOKING RANCHOS DE TAOS VALLEY, RUINS GALLERY, 1952
encaustic on paper
17½ x 23

Opposite:
EL VALLE CAMPO SANTO, 1952
encaustic on paper
17½ x 23

1954, he opened a portrait studio in Dallas, Texas, working through Betty McLean Gallery. Founded in 1951, the gallery was directed by Milwaukee-born artist Donald S. Vogel (1917-2004).[42] Thwaites also began exhibiting at Dord Fitz Gallery, Amarillo, Texas, where he continued to show at least through 1961. Fitz (1914-1989) was an artist and teacher who attracted modernist painters such as Elaine de Kooning (1918-1989) and Louise Nevelson (1900-1988) to teach in the area.

Little is known of Thwaites' brief time in Dallas; however, it appears that the prospects for a portrait market were overstated. The couple contacted Mabel, who offered to not only rent them the Tony House on her property but to convert the garage into a studio. They would live in that rambling adobe bounded by Pueblo lands and looking east to sacred Taos Mountain for the next eight years.

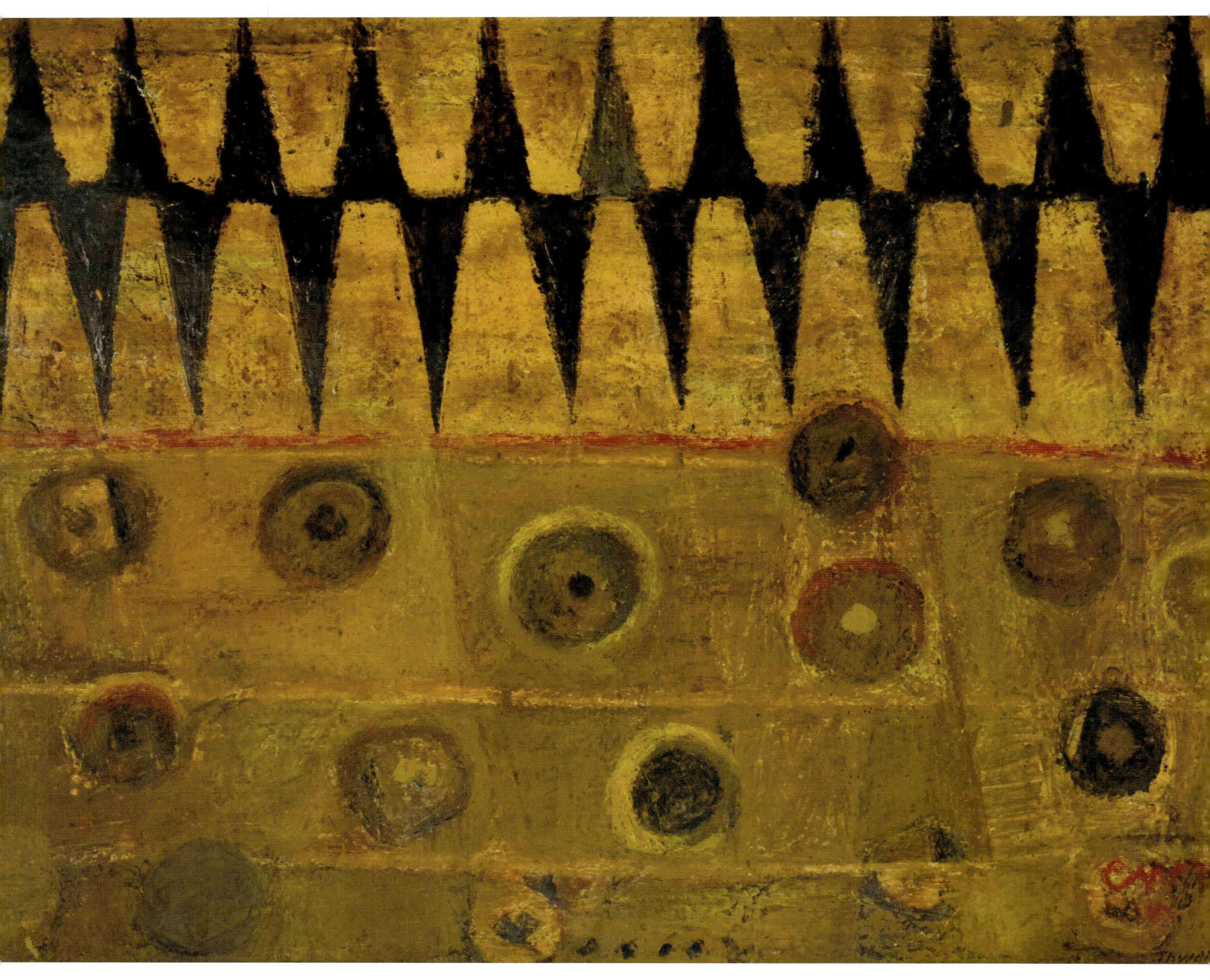

OLD AND NEW

Perhaps there is such a satisfaction in painting because not only can it be, it must be, all your own, through your own eyes, instead of others, your own selection, reflection, opinion, and judgments, and above all, your own synthesis, meaning, the formation of a unity of highly disparate parts. CWT

As the Thwaiteses decompressed into the mercurial mix of old and new in Taos, two encaustic paintings—the graveyard at *El Valle Campo Santo* and *Window Overlooking Ranchos de Taos Valley, Ruins Gallery*—were perhaps symbolic of the death of an old way of life and the couple's expanded views in a new land.

Art historian David L. Witt, who lives in Taos, has written extensively on that dynamic mix of old and new as it "rebirthed" countless artists who found themselves in Taos, and notably the Taos Moderns—the group of painters and sculptors that Thwaites was about to join.

> Most artists who [came to Taos and saw the Rio Grande gorge and Taos Valley] then remained for a summer or a lifetime have developed a personal, indelible creation myth of Taos. Their personal myths closely resemble American Indian mythology of emergence from a "lower world" to a "higher" one, referring both to spiritual development and to change in time and place.... Both the land and the indigenous cultures suggest nurturing: the ancient Pueblo culture is a permanent, "timeless" feature; until recently both Pueblo and Hispanic cultures have been largely agrarian; mysticism among all the cultures represented in Taos is more prominent than hard-edge urban thinking; even the mountains are rounded, feminine forms. These features suggest what traditionally has been thought of as feminine rather than masculine energy. Most Taos Moderns, who equated lack of change with artistic death, saw the same environment as symbolic of continual rebirth, with the result that artwork they completed in 1964 bore little relationship to works created in 1954 and 1944.[43]

The Thwaiteses undoubtedly experienced that synergistic rebirth. They were entranced by the landscape, committed to a new future, and mesmerized by the rituals and spirituality of Pueblo Indians, whose dances and feast celebrations they regularly attended. The estate contains several sketches and paintings that depict ceremonial dances, notably the Deer Dance, which takes place at Taos Pueblo on January 6, and a scene that Thwaites returned to repeatedly over the next two decades. He depicted it in a variety of media and styles, as indicated in the dry oil *Deer Dance (with Mountains)*, the acrylic *Deer Dancers (with Taos Mountain)*, the encaustic *Deer Dancers (with Blanket Motif)*, and the stark acrylic *Deer Dancers (in Black and White)*.

Opposite:
BLANKET MOTIF, 1959
encaustic on paper
17½ x 23
private collection

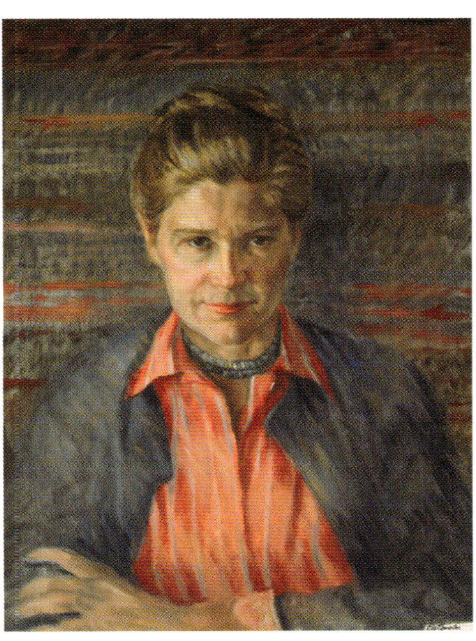

ANTOINETTE (IN RED SHIRT), 1958
egg tempera on paper
23 x 17½
private collection
Phillip Harsh Studio Photography

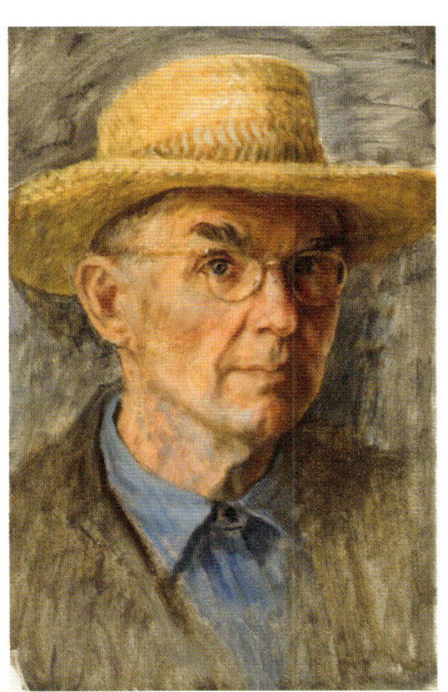

SELF-PORTRAIT (WITH STRAW HAT), 1958
mixed media on paper
19 x 11¼

DEER DANCERS (WITH TAOS MOUNTAIN), 1962
acrylic on masonite
20 x 28
private collection; Alison Dunlap Photography

DEER DANCE (WITH MOUNTAINS), 1961
dry oil on paper
17½ x 23
private collection

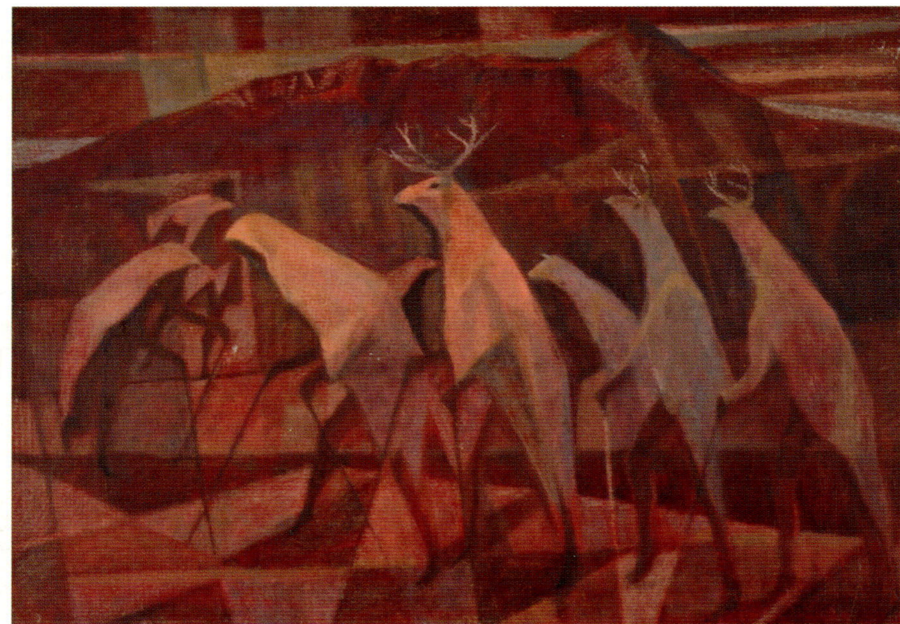

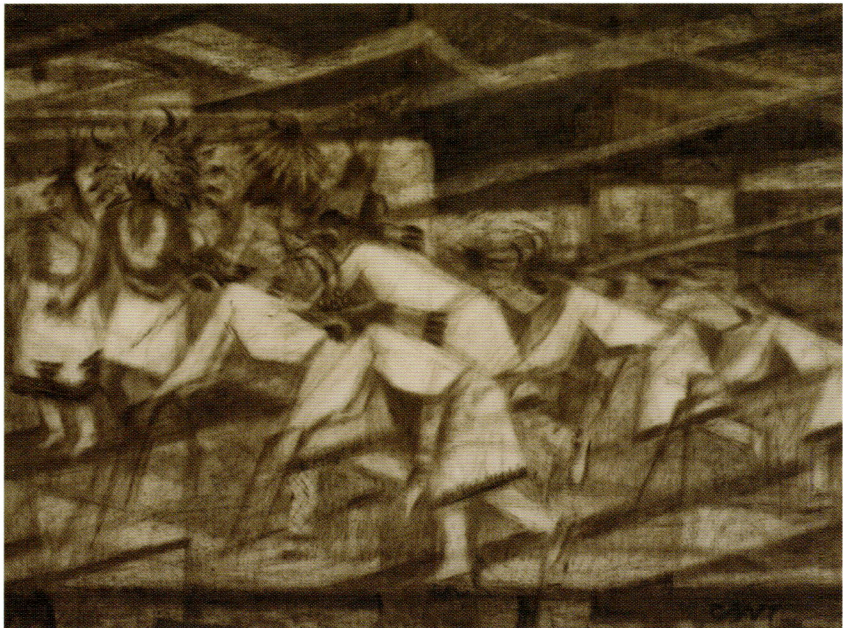

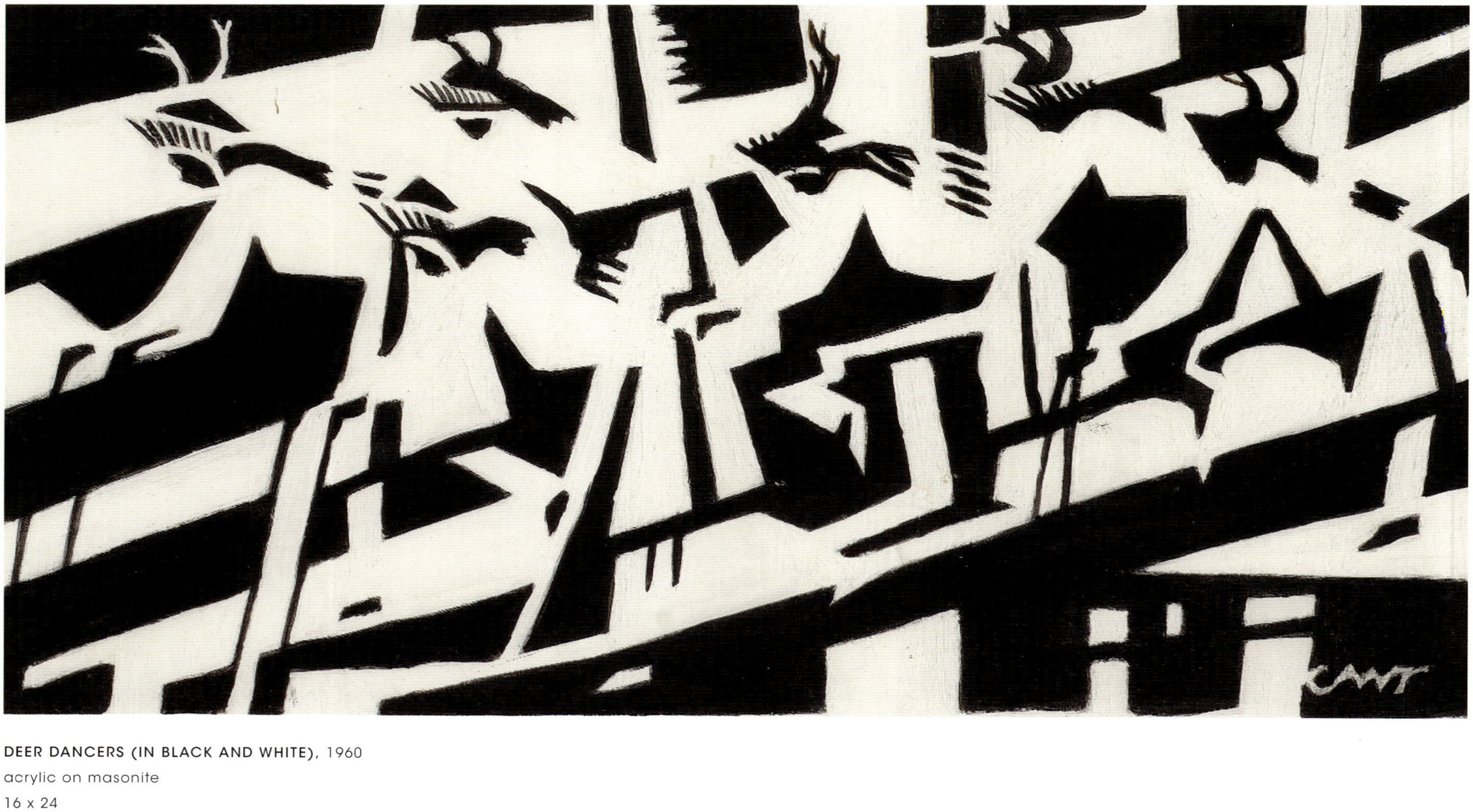

DEER DANCERS (IN BLACK AND WHITE), 1960
acrylic on masonite
16 x 24
private collection; Dennis Wyszynski Photography

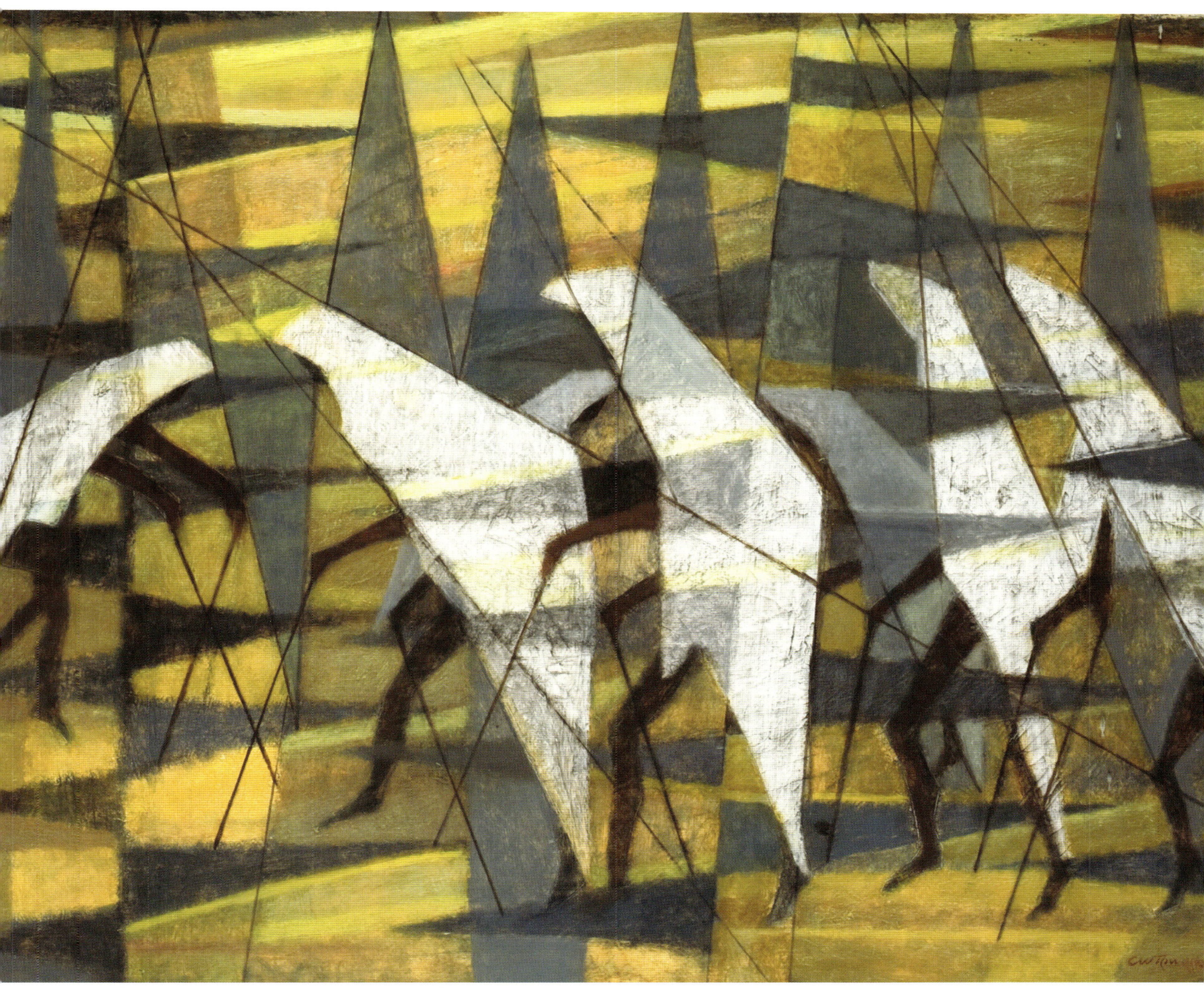

DEER DANCERS (WITH BLANKET MOTIF), 1958
encaustic on paper
17½ x 23
private collection

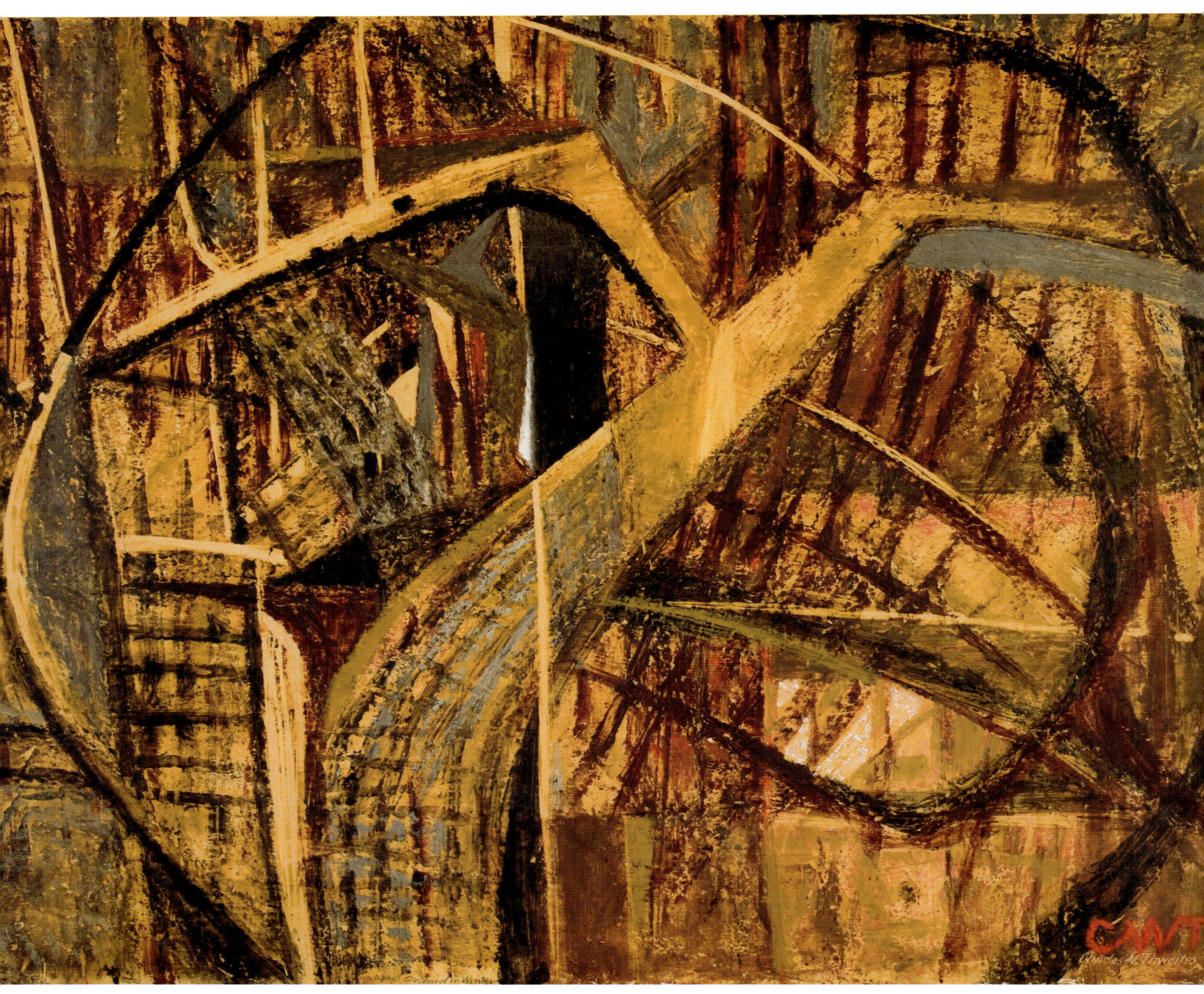

WINTER ORCHARD, 1955
encaustic on paper
17½ x 23

MAN OF MANY COLORS

The thing is that color alone has the capacity of revealing the sensitivity and greatness of a man. By his choice of color and the way he uses it, a man stands revealed. In his ability to make the highest use of color's possibilities lays the artist's function. In his ability to achieve that he equals any other heights achieved by mankind. CWT

From the mid-1950s forward, Thwaites stopped exhibiting in national shows, preferring regional ones. Among them were the 1956 Mid-America Arts Alliance at the Nelson-Atkins Museum, the 1959 Artists West of the Mississippi River organized by the Colorado Springs Fine Arts Center (where he exhibited *Shard and Stone*, see page 39), and the 1968-1969 traveling exhibition of the Federation of Rocky Mountain States.

He also dived into the northern New Mexico art scene, joining the Taos Art Association (TAA) in 1954 and exhibiting at its recently established artists-cooperative Stables Gallery, as well as at the Harwood Gallery and other local galleries. He participated in the juried, open, and invitational shows at the Museum of Fine Arts, Santa Fe, and continued to show at Dord Fitz Gallery, including a September 1954 exhibition of southwestern modernists that also included Charlie Burnell (1897-1968), DeForrest Judd (1916-1993), Oli Sihvonen (1921-1991), and Ward Lockwood (1894-1963).[44]

Recognition was not long in coming. In the 1955 New Mexico Artists juried exhibition at the Museum of Fine Arts, Santa Fe, he exhibited two encaustic paintings, *Winter Orchard* and *Abstraction* (see page 104), the latter of which was illustrated in the catalogue, recommended for museum purchase, and chosen for the out-of-state traveling exhibition. His encaustics from the period are rich tapestries of color and implied textures that fill the paper from edge to edge. Many of them, as with his earlier works on paper, measure 17½ by 23 inches, which, according to Olof Dahlstrand, was a 300-pound watercolor paper Thwaites favored and bought in such large quantity that it lasted him throughout his career. The palette of colors in some of the encaustics is bright, such as *Hollyhocks*. Others are earthier as in *Forest Motif*, *Canyon*, and *Piñons and Arroyos*.

For portraits and major paintings, Thwaites worked on masonite, as is the case in the large encaustic *Sunflower Motif*. Exhibited in 1959 at the Taos Moderns show in Santa Fe, it was a harbinger of things to come, receiving positive critical reviews such as John Skolle's observation that the artist "gives an expert demonstration of spatial relationships ... and *Sunflower Motif* suggests a state of abundance in its imaginative and well-determined intricacy."[45]

The deepest layer of *Sunflower Motif* is a rich blue impression of sunflower heads and stalks. Overlaying that ground is an imaginative sunflower-yellow geometric grid or structure that, while rhomboid, seems to "organize" the chaos peeking through it. The "grid" would become a recurring motif in Thwaites' paintings, and as is the case in *Sunflower Motif*, it occasionally has shadowed planes that give it the illusion of three-dimensions.

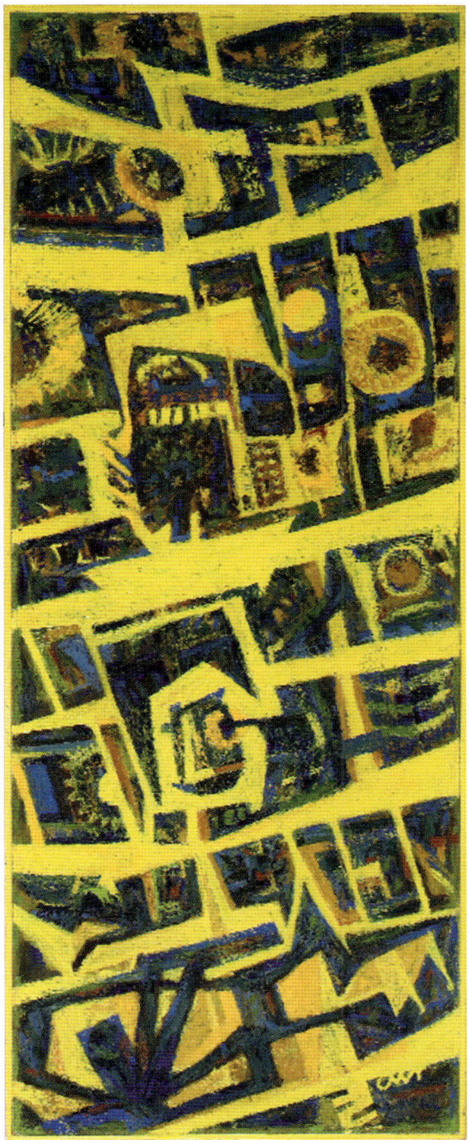

SUNFLOWER MOTIF, 1959
encaustic on masonite
44 x 18½

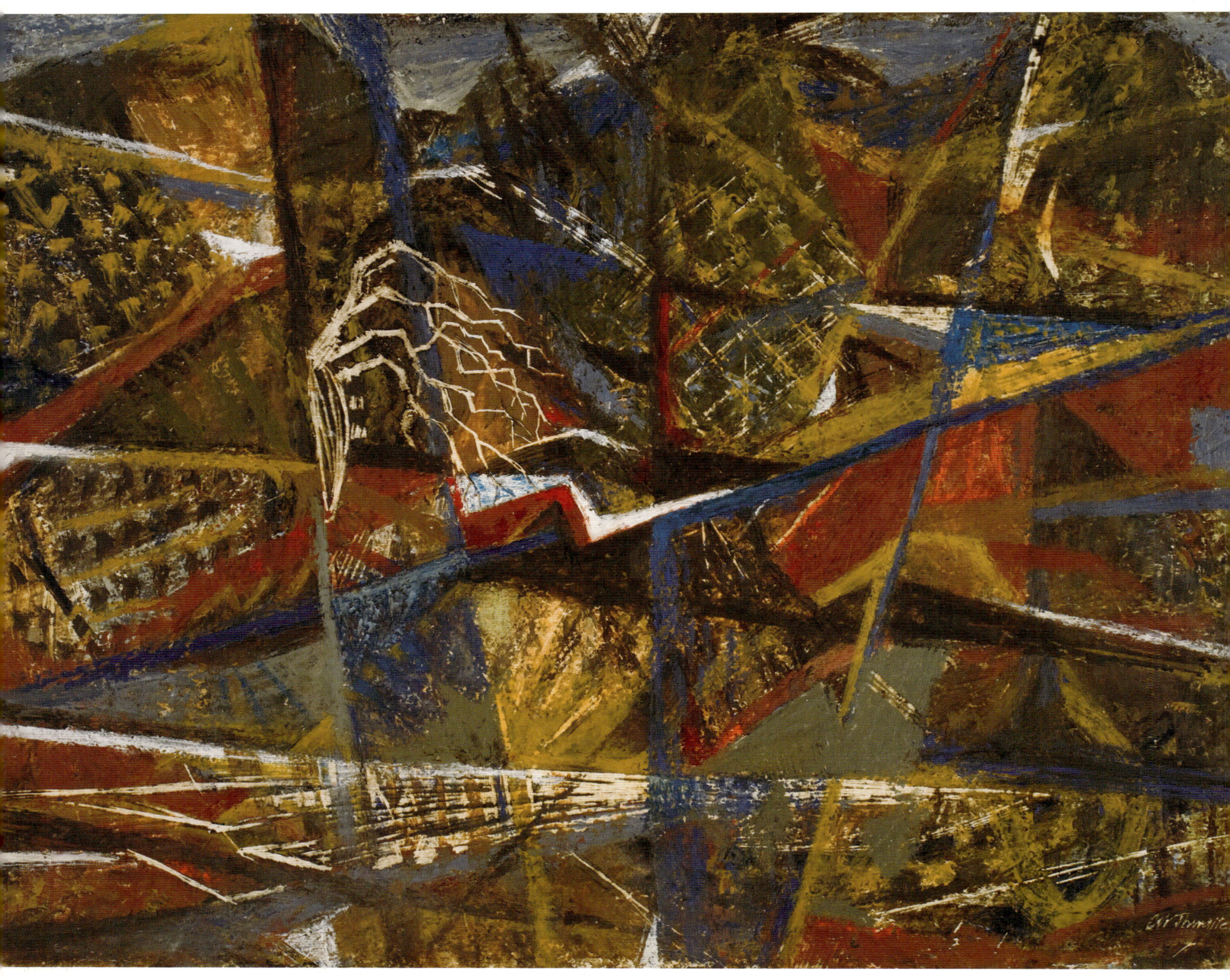

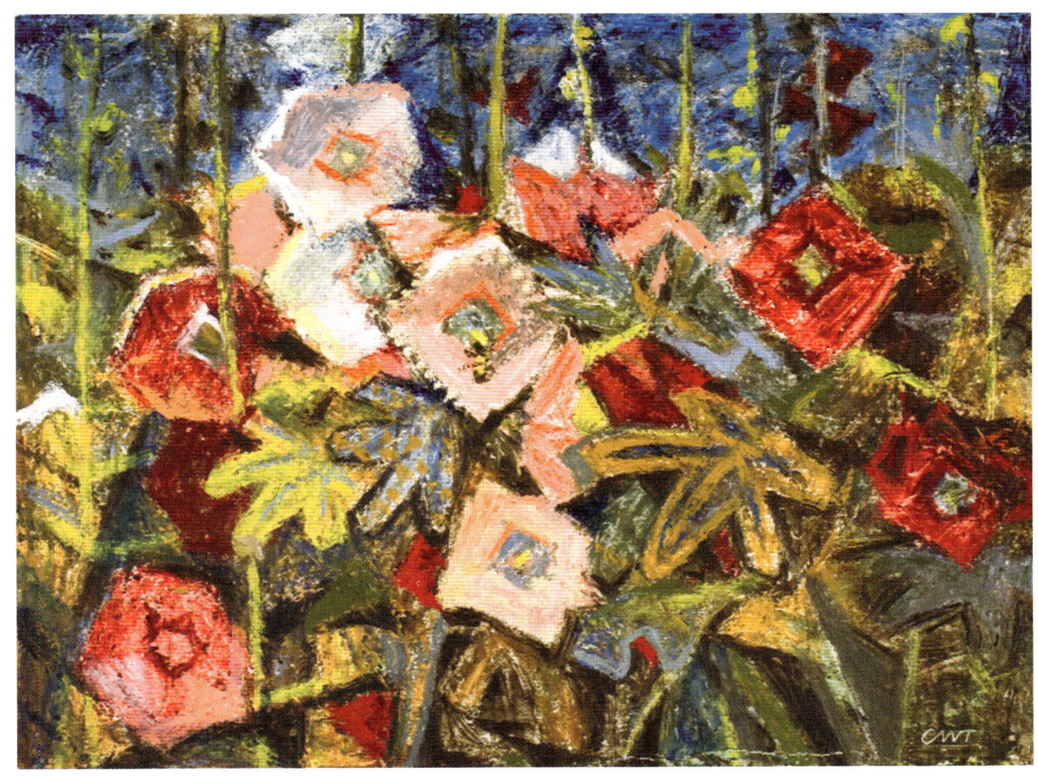

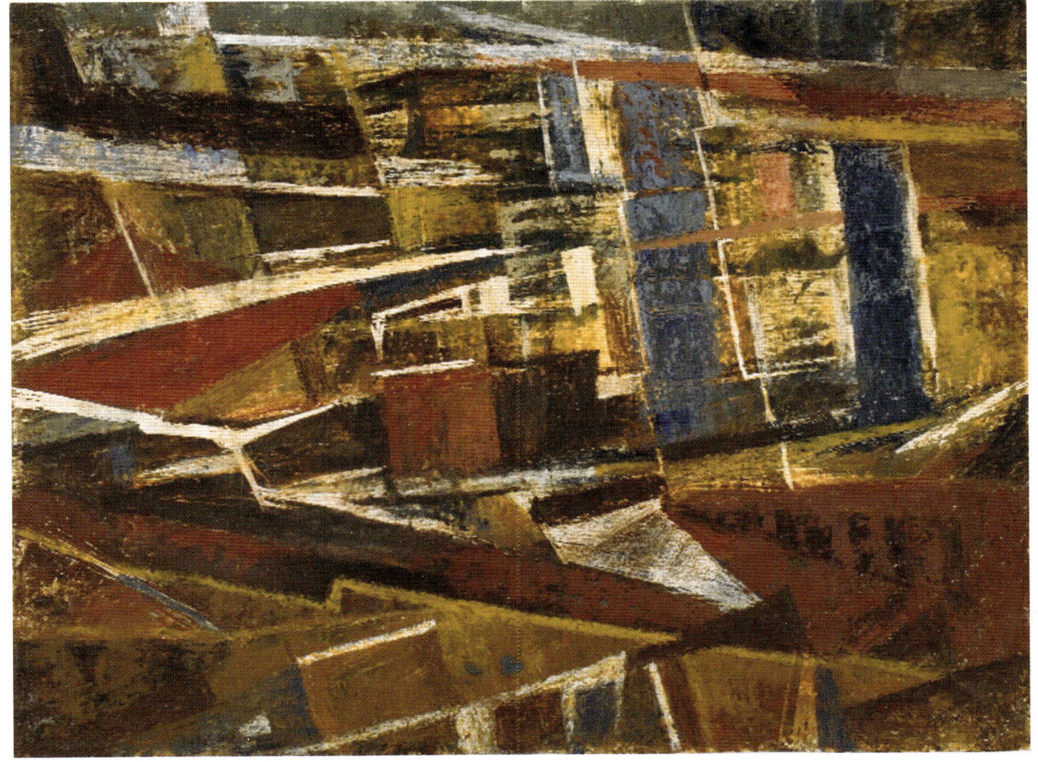

Above:
HOLLYHOCKS, 1953
encaustic on paper
17½ x 23

CANYON, 1956
encaustic on paper
17½ x 23

Opposite:
PIÑONS AND ARROYOS, 1955
encaustic on paper
17½ x 23

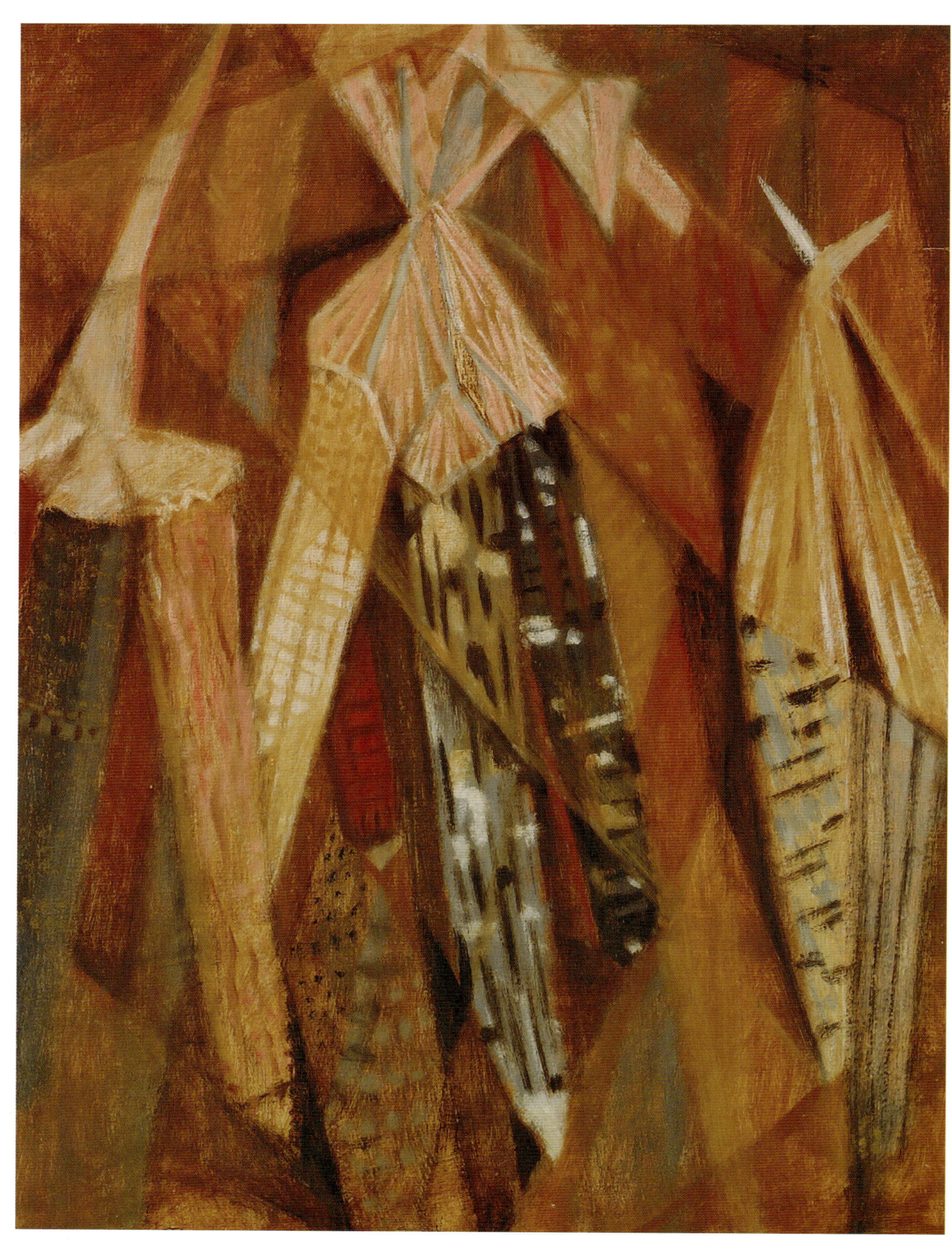

DRYING CORN, 1964
oil on masonite
24 x 18
private collection
Dennis Wyszynski Photography

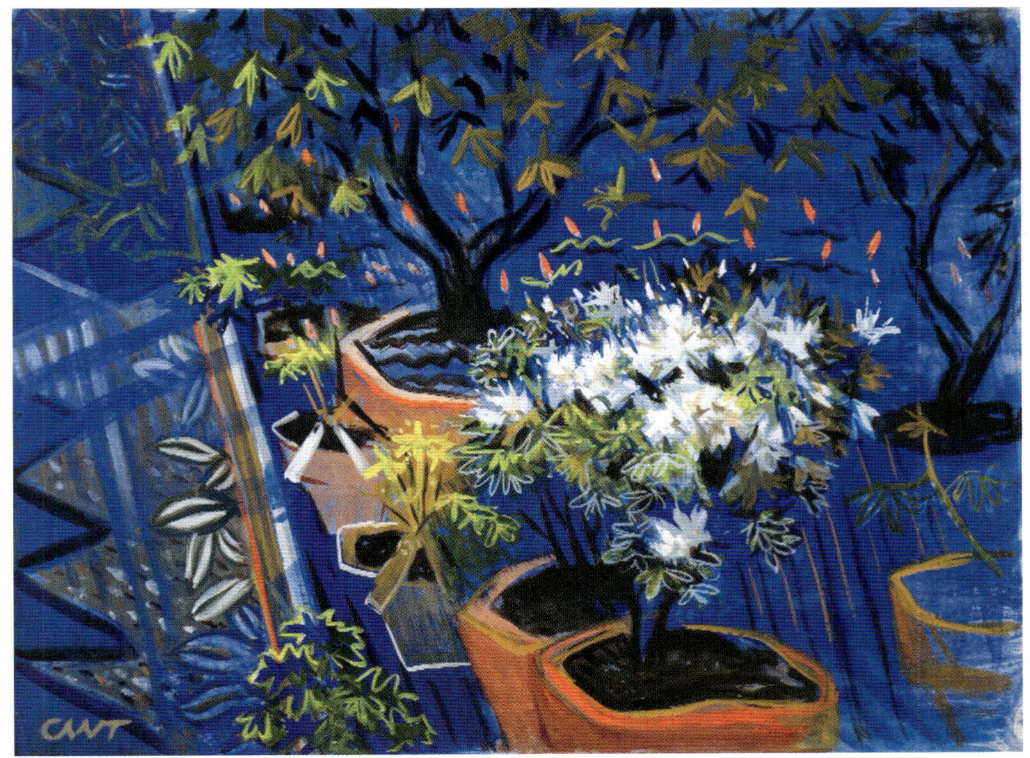

Top:
AZALEA, 1958
egg tempera on paper
17½ x 23

Bottom left:
MASK AND HANDS, 1964
acrylic on paper
17½ x 23
private collection

Bottom right:
LOON, 1955
egg tempera on paper
23 x 17½
private collection
Dennis Wyszynski Photography

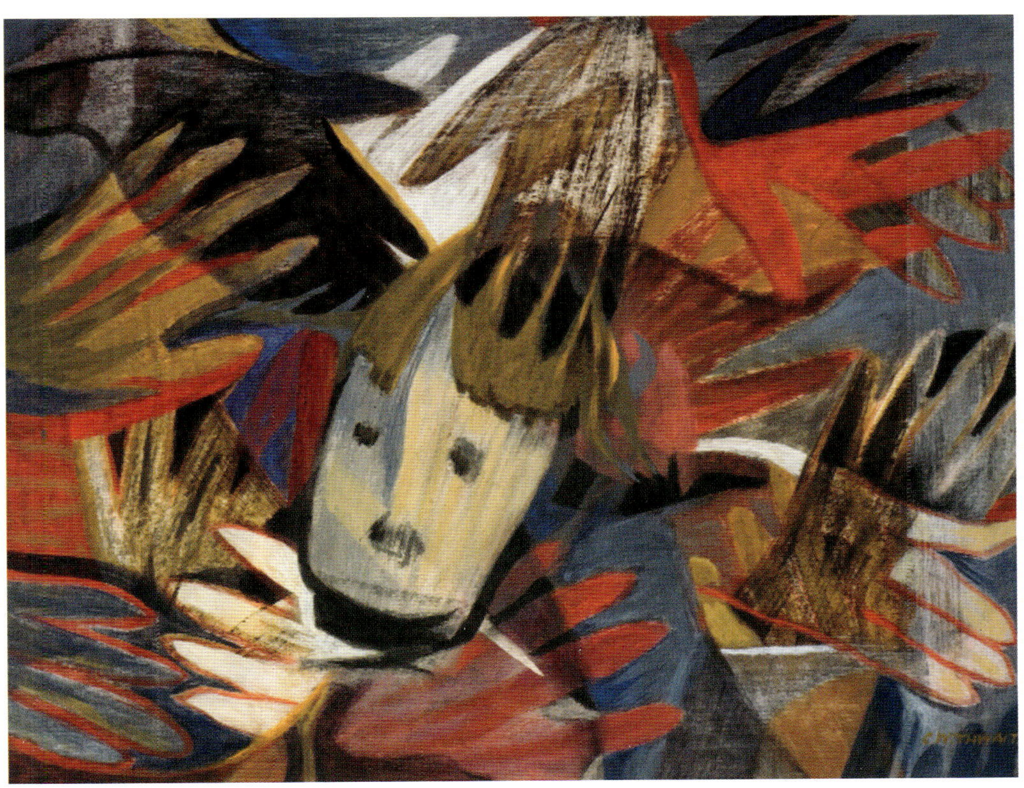

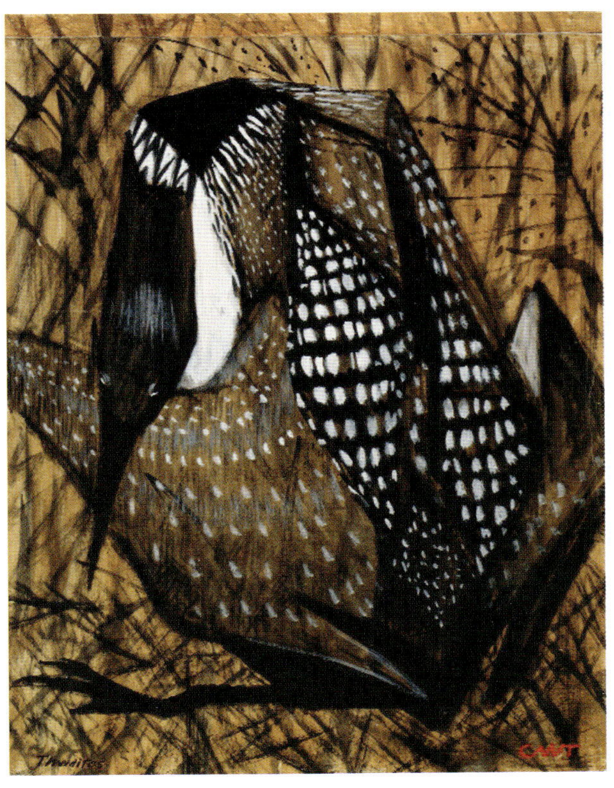

PEARS IN BOWL I, 1952
encaustic on panel
12 x 10

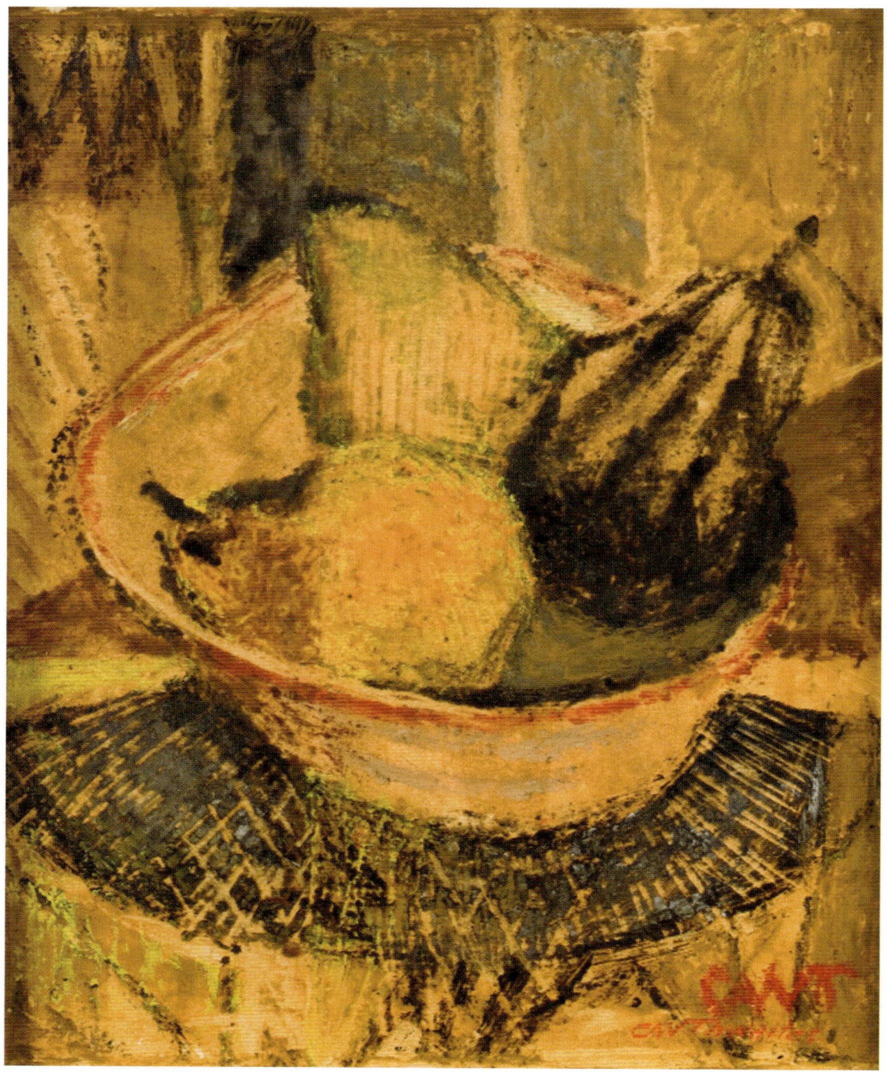

PEARS IN BOWL II, 1952
encaustic on panel
12 x 10

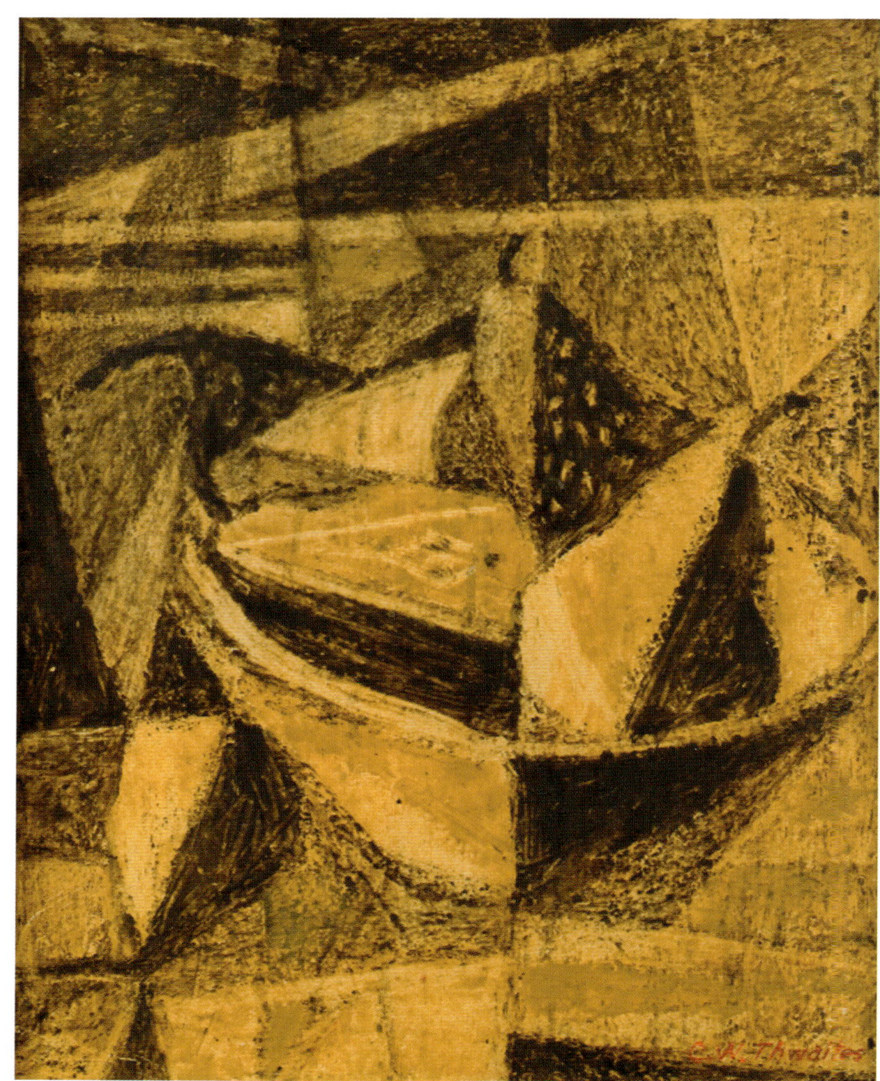

The year 1957 was a banner one for Thwaites. In the spring, he and Antoinette curated a May exhibit of eighteen Taos artists, mostly modernists, at Milwaukee's F.H. Bresler's Gallery.[46] In August, he participated in the TAA Art Week and open studio demonstrations, followed by a September lecture on portraiture delivered to the Los Alamos Art Association. In September, he also had the first of three two-person shows at Stables Gallery, this time with modernist Louise Ganthiers (1907-1982). Thwaites was represented by several encaustic paintings, which reviewer Dave Weber described as a "difficult medium" and

> a method of painting in which colors in wax are fused with hot irons.... [Thwaites] is blessed both with a gift for experimentation and a will to try again and again for the desired effect. He handles the encaustic medium well and there is nothing raucous about his paintings.... He is deeply inspired by nature ... seeing in birds, fish, grasses, and plants a unifying life-force which he nearly always manages to transfer to his canvases.... There is no doubt in this reviewer's mind that Charles Thwaites is an artist to bear in mind.[47]

PUFF BALL MOTIF, 1960
dry oil on paper
$17^1/_2$ x 23
private collection

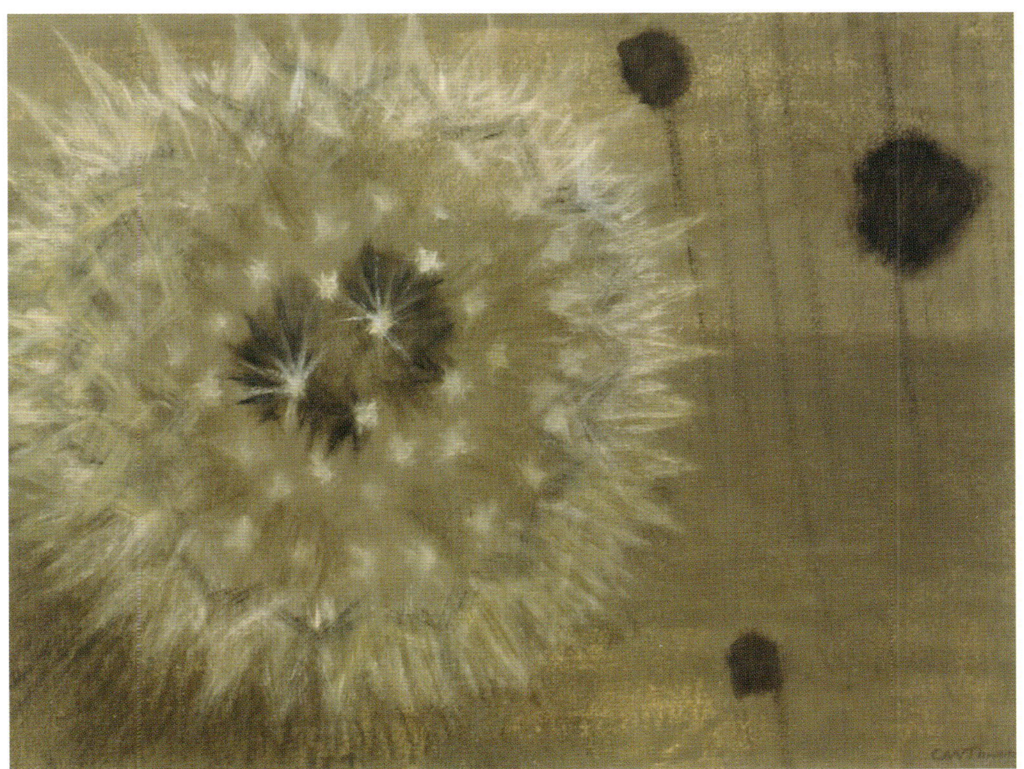

In October, Thwaites was included in the Taos Moderns at the Museum of Fine Arts, Santa Fe, and he had his only one-man exhibition there. Once again Dave Weber applauded Thwaites, noting that he is a

> tasteful and faithful colorist. This is the first—and lasting—impression the viewer gets. *Sunflower Motif*, for instance, shows his impeccable taste in colors, while *Pomegranates* is one of many examples of true color being used. This one-man exhibit is important for the versatility it displays. Thwaites has a sober portrait for a centerpiece; even his signature is formalized. Flanking it are companion studies of a still life—a bowl of pears, in this case. One is done in solid impressionistic fashion and the other steps farther, gets into cubism [*Pears in Bowl I* and *Pears in Bowl II*]. The difference in these three works can be protracted over the whole show. You have to look hard to find two paintings in the same broad style or approach.... The best work ... is *Deer Dance*, a magnificently composed picture the strength of which lies in understatement and graceful restraint.[48]

The following year, Thwaites was listed as teaching portraiture on the roster of instructors at the Taos Institute of Creative Orientation. The school was directed at the time by pioneering modernist, Emil Bisttram, founding member with Raymond Jonson (1891-1982) of the Transcendental Painting Group in 1938. Thwaites' connections to Wisconsin continued. In the fall of 1959, the couple entertained Dr. and Mrs. Farrington Daniels, retiring chairman of the Chemistry Department at the University of Wisconsin, who visited the couple to sit for a portrait Thwaites was painting.

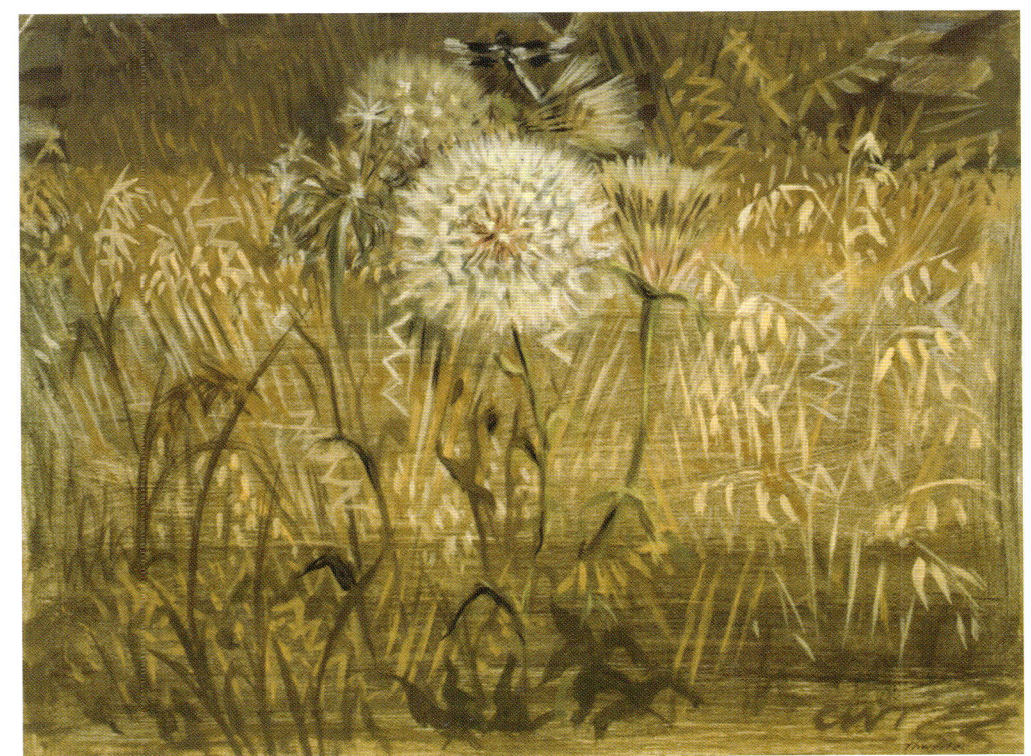

PUFF BALLS, OATS AND DRAGONFLY, 1959
acrylic on paper
$17^1/_2$ x 23

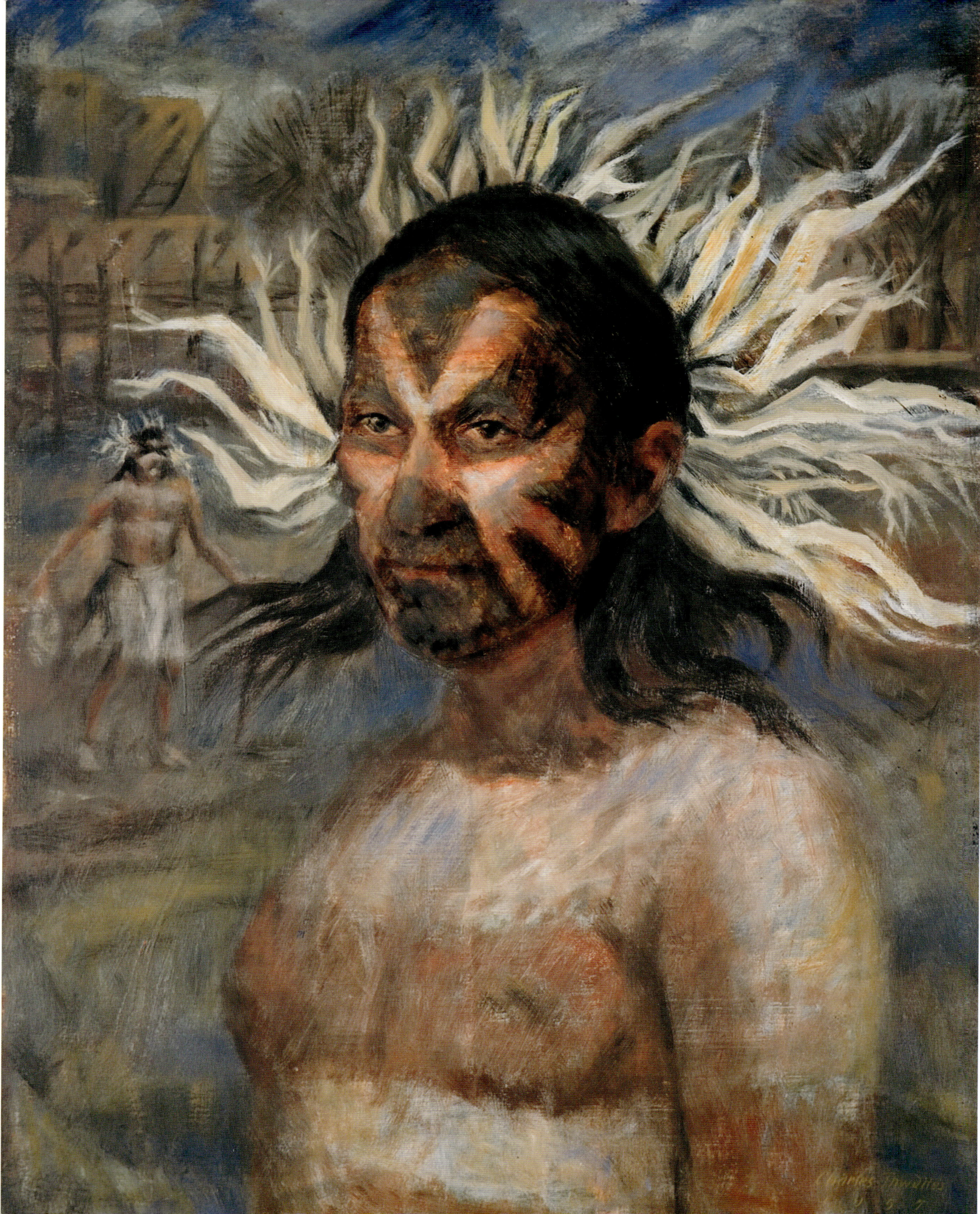

IN LOVE WITH LIFE

Love is a subconscious element. Love precedes academic knowledge. There is no knowledge superior to love. If maximum wisdom is contained in love, the least wisdom is contained in hate. Politics promote hate. Morality begins in knowing that the world is perfect. This law is absolute and also infinitely flexible. Reality is the poetry of perfection. The spirit of painting is in the frame of philosophy and culminates in a synthesis of the universal and the personal. CWT

At the same time he was doing abstract encaustics, Thwaites was also painting representational works in oils and tempera. He was enthralled with the view from the Tony House, documenting it in just about every season. The gardens and grounds of Los Gallos were equally irresistible, as was a passion he developed for dandelion seed heads, which he called puff balls and depicted in *Puff Balls, Oats and Dragonfly* and more abstractly in *Puff Ball Motif*. Dynamic arrangements of objects, color schemes, shapes, and textures include *Drying Corn*, *Mask and Hands*, and *Loon*.[49] Thwaites undoubtedly watched scenes such as *Horses in Snow* throughout the winter, and in the summer, he observed Taos Indians at work, as depicted in *Haying at the Foot of Taos Mountain*.

Shortly after they settled in Taos, Thwaites also embarked on a series of portraits in oil of Taos Pueblo luminaries, many of which are in the estate. A 1955 newspaper article indicates that he exhibited them at Stables Gallery, where he sold a portrait of Ben Couse

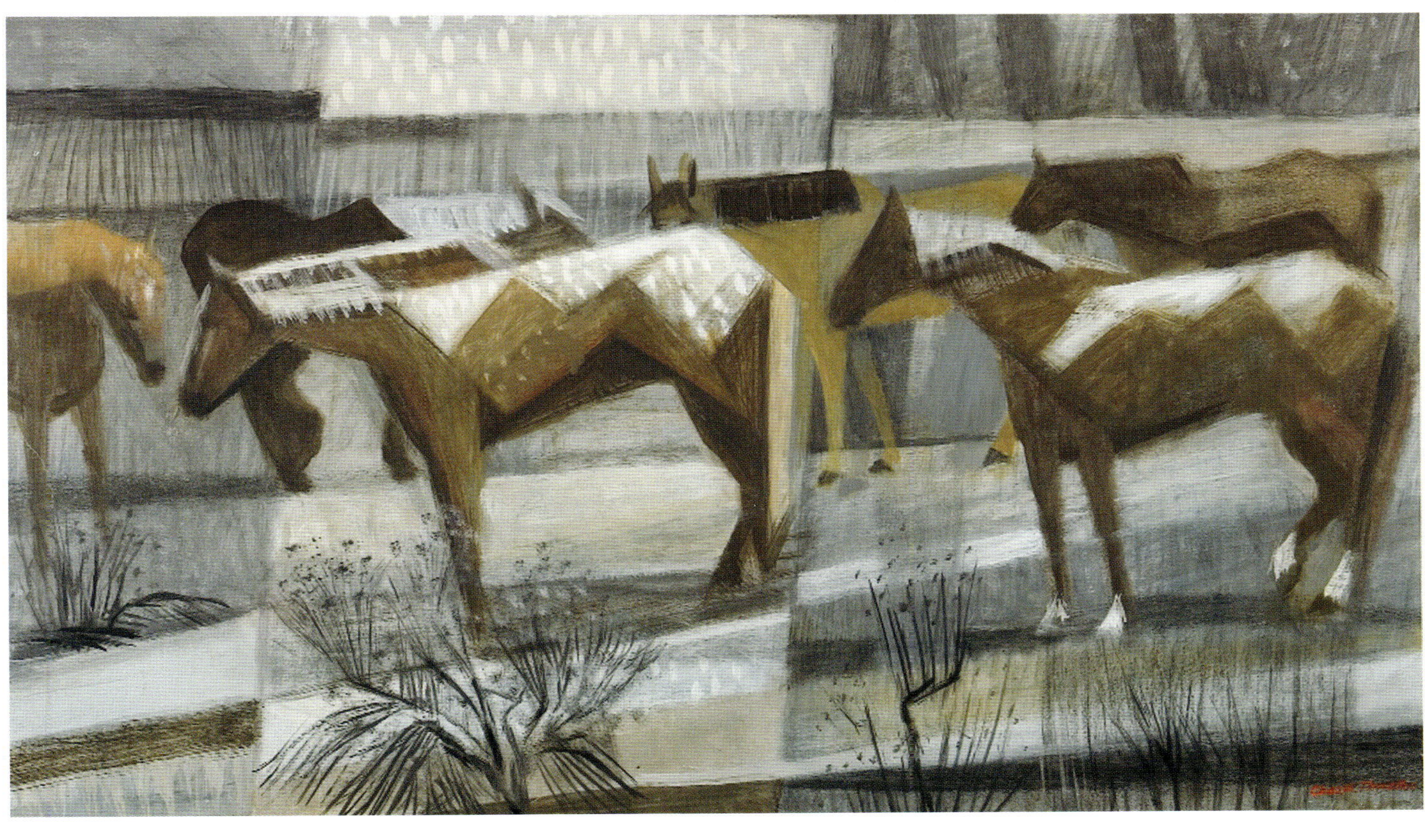

HORSES IN SNOW, 1957
egg tempera on paper
18 x 30
private collection
Alison Dunlap Photography

Opposite:
BLACK EYE, MEMBER OF THE CHIFFONETI, 1957
oil on masonite
24 x 18
private collection
Alison Dunlap Photography

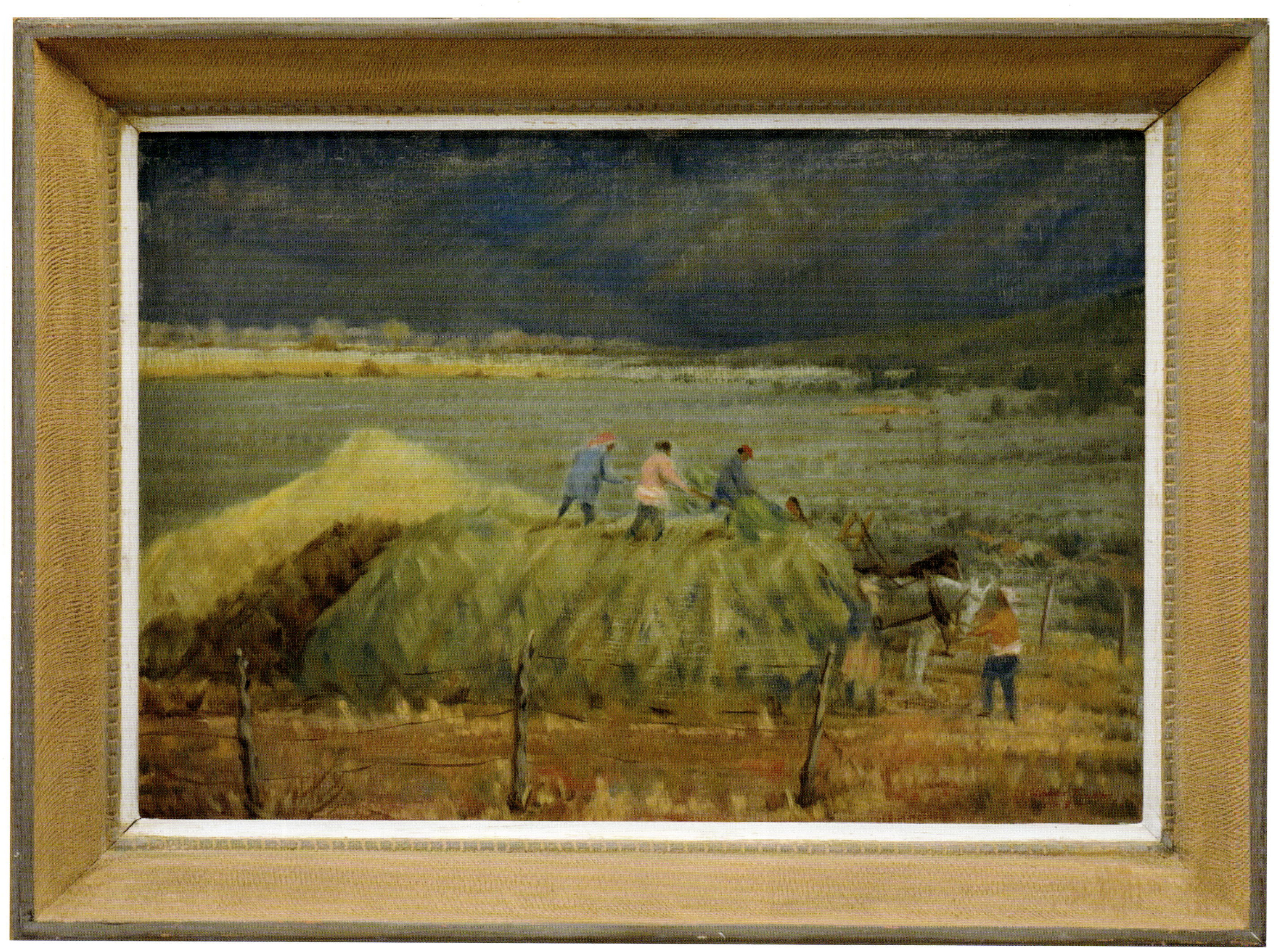

HAYING AT FOOT OF TAOS MOUNTAIN, 1957
oil on masonite
25½ x 33½
From the mid-1930s onward, Thwaites made all of his frames, including the one pictured here.

VIEW OF LOS GALLOS AND GARDENS, 1954
egg tempera on paper
17½ x 23

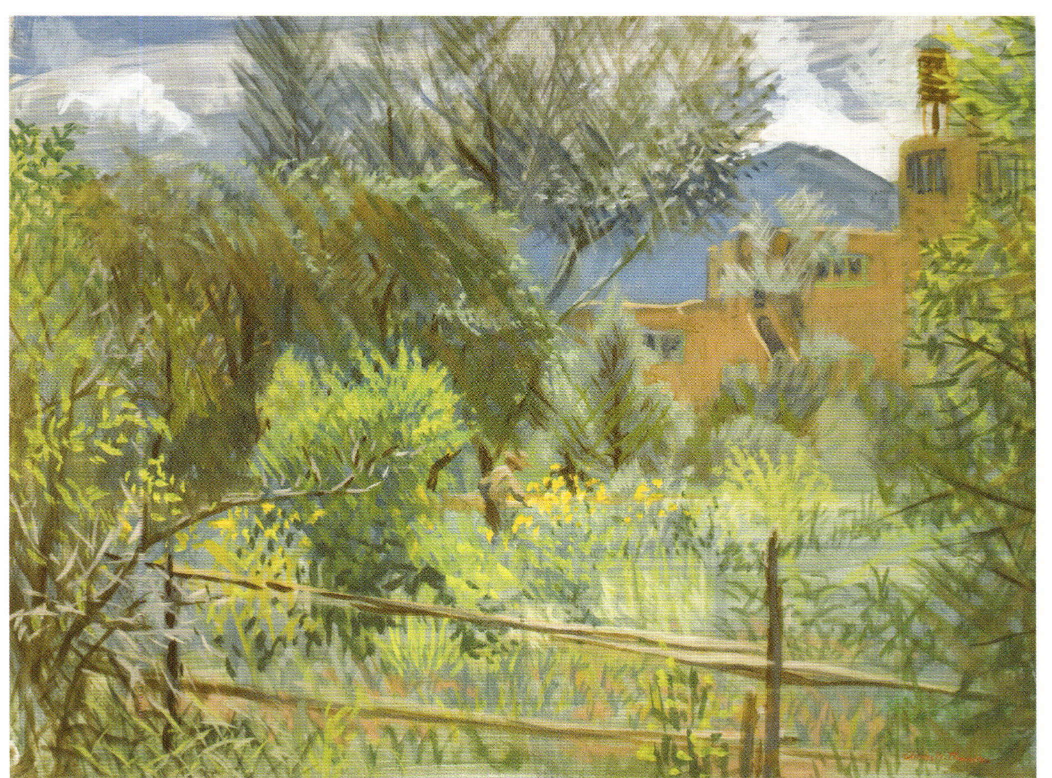

Lujan.[50] He also undoubtedly displayed them at the La Fonda Gallery where in 1956 he was a part of an exhibition, the hanging committee for which included Taos old-timers Leon Gaspard (1882-1964) and E. Martin Hennings (1886-1956).[51]

According to the Dahlstrands, Thwaites' friendship with Tony Luhan gave him access to these people whose countenances he recorded in remarkable detail, surrounded by bold primary colors, notably swathes of red. Thwaites' portraits are neither romantic nor sentimentalized; rather they are aimed at capturing a likeness. Unusual for the artist, he described several of the sitters by their distinctions, including excellence in singing and dancing or membership in important societies, such as the Peyote Cult and Chiffoneti (Clown Society). Of those he identified by name are Pete Suazo, Frank Zamora, Little Joe Gomez, and John Concha, who is also included in a photo of the Thwaiteses from 1956 (see Portrait Subjects).

Whether through their connections with Luhan or as a result of the portrait suite, the Thwaiteses became friends of the Taos Indians. Lucia Dahlstrand remembers visiting the Thwaiteses in the 1950s, meeting Mabel and Tony and being taken to their friends' homes on the reservation, where they commissioned moccasins to be made. Charles and Antoinette also assisted the Pueblo in political and social issues, including a controversy over the Taos bypass going through Pueblo lands. In a 1959 letter from Christino Mirabal, Governor of Taos Pueblo, written on behalf of the council and officers, the Thwaiteses were thanked for their efforts: "There is no word to use to express our hearts' desires in thanking you for your kindness to the Indian race of people.... Not only the bypass controversy, but also many other misunderstandings have been corrected by your help.... We will always remember you as our very best friends who really have sympathy for the Indian race of people."[52]

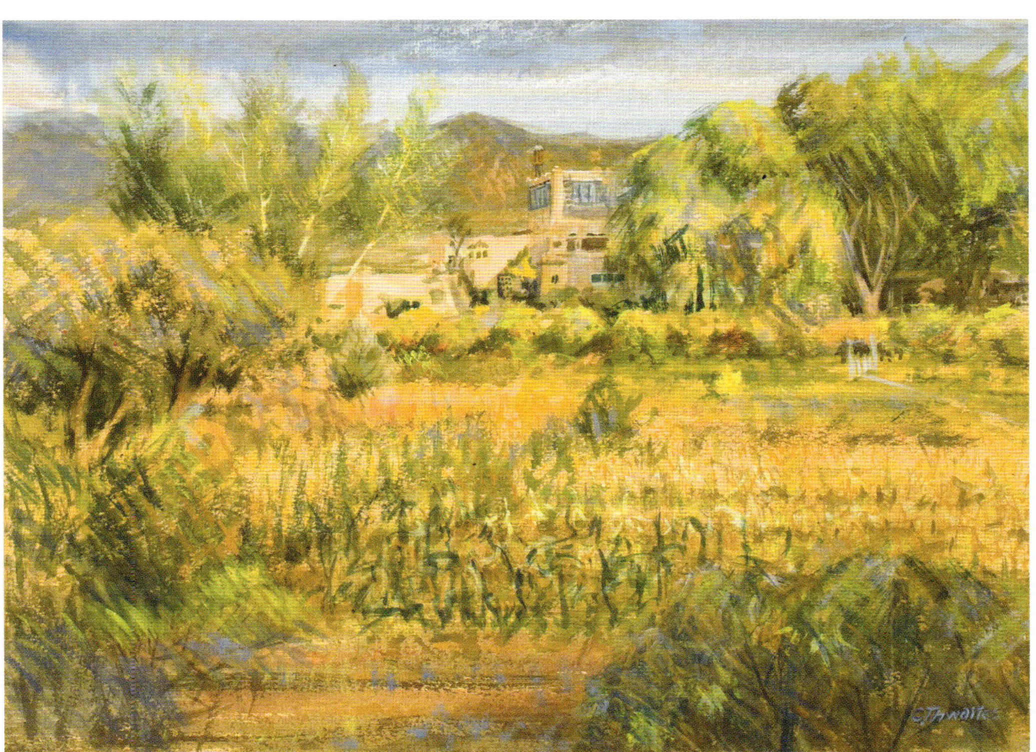

MABEL'S HOUSE, 1959
acrylic on paper
14½ x 20

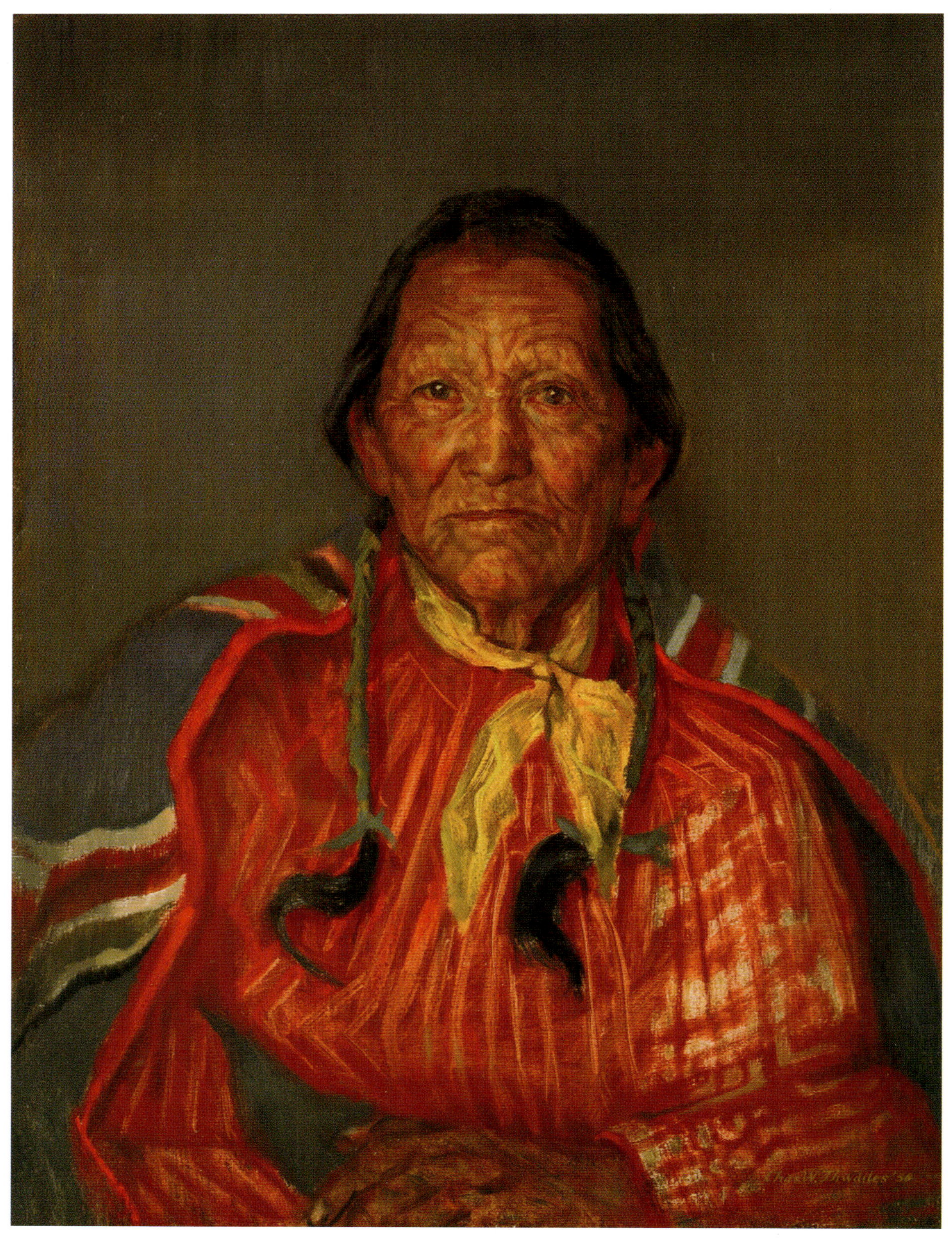

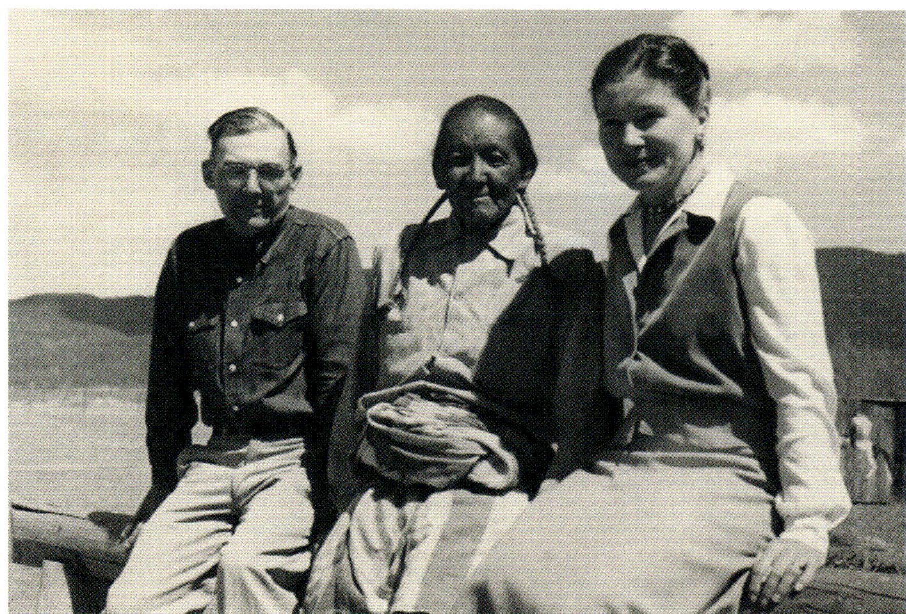

Charles and Antoinette with John Concha at Taos Pueblo in 1956.

INDIANS OF THE BLUE MOUNTAINS— A COUPLE OF SKEPTICS, 1955
oil on masonite
19 x 28
private collection
James Zimmerman Photography

Opposite:
JOHN CONCHA, 1956
oil on masonite
$32\frac{3}{4}$ x $26\frac{1}{2}$
private collection
Phillip Harsh,
Digital Studio Photography

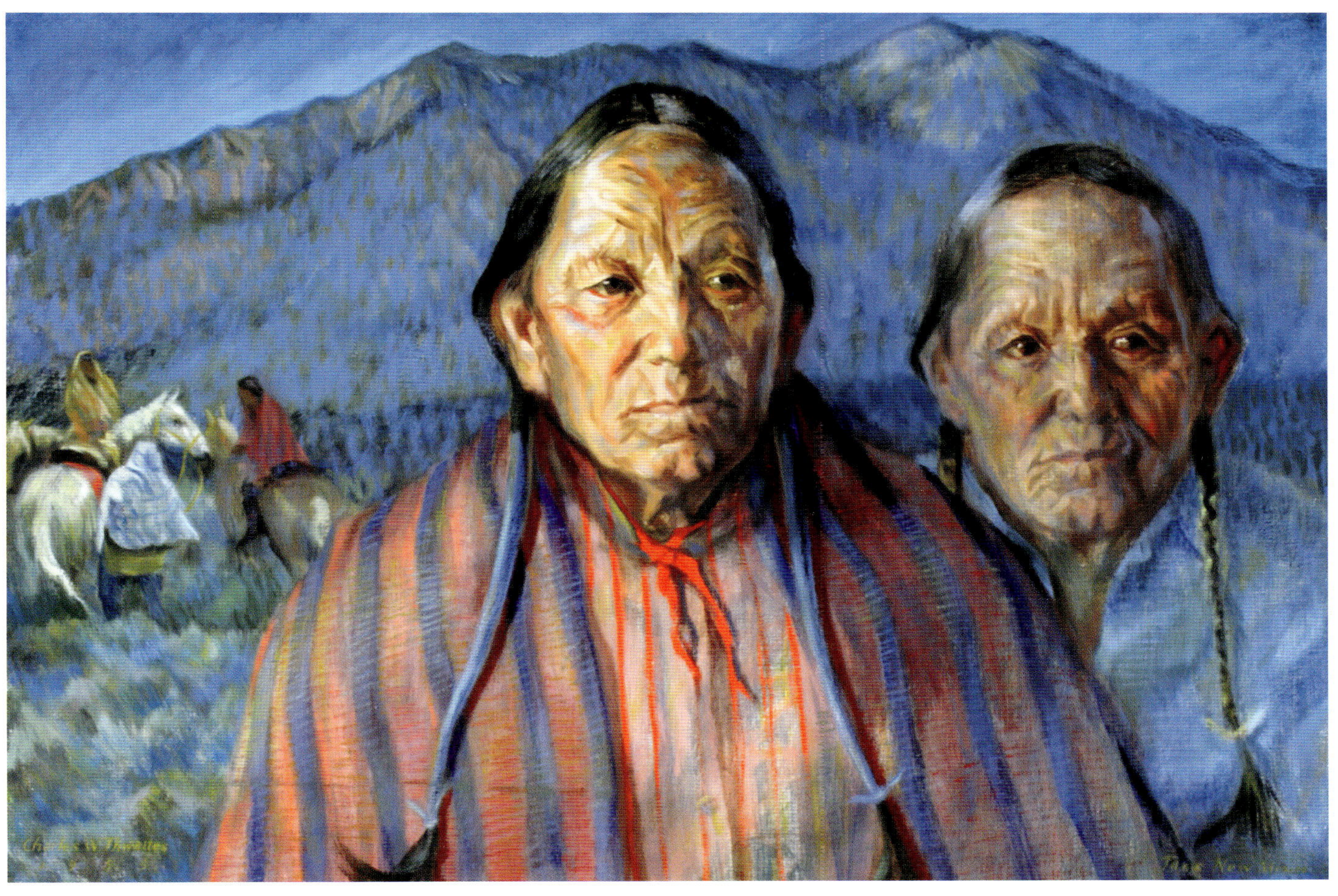

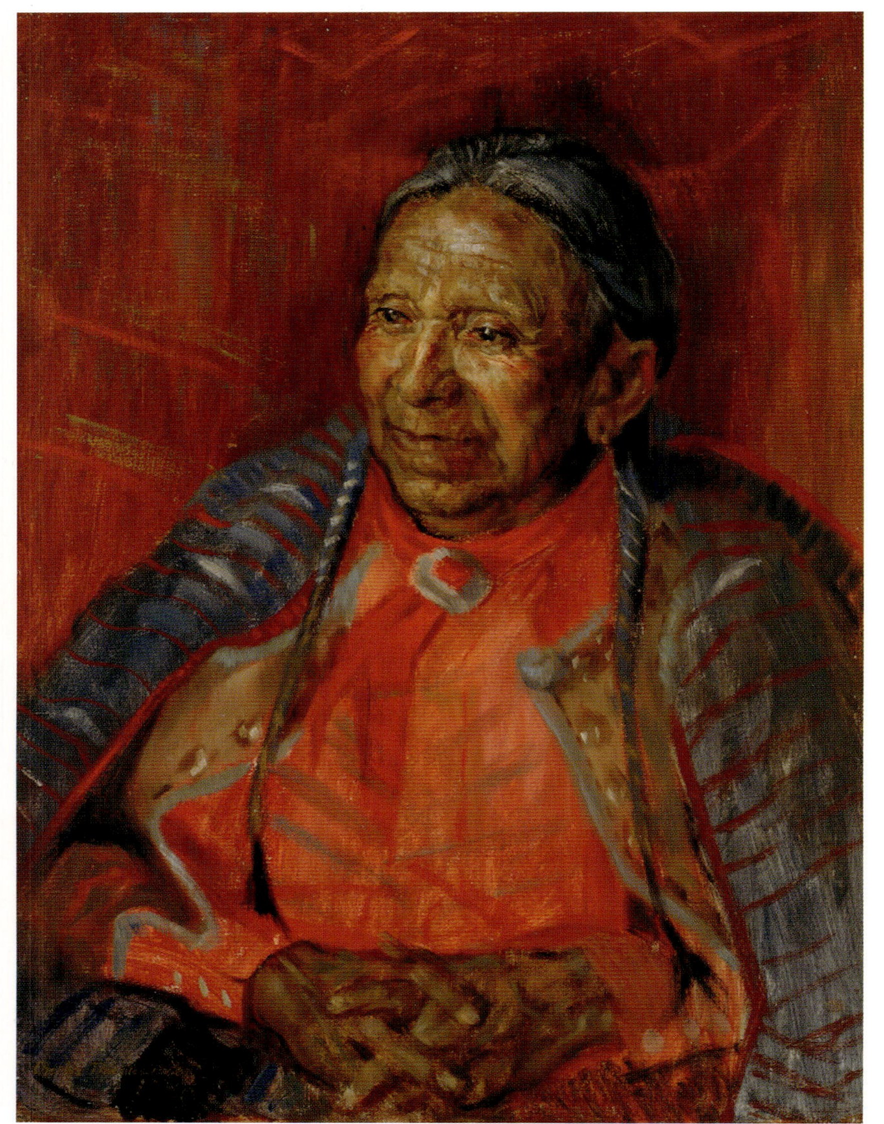

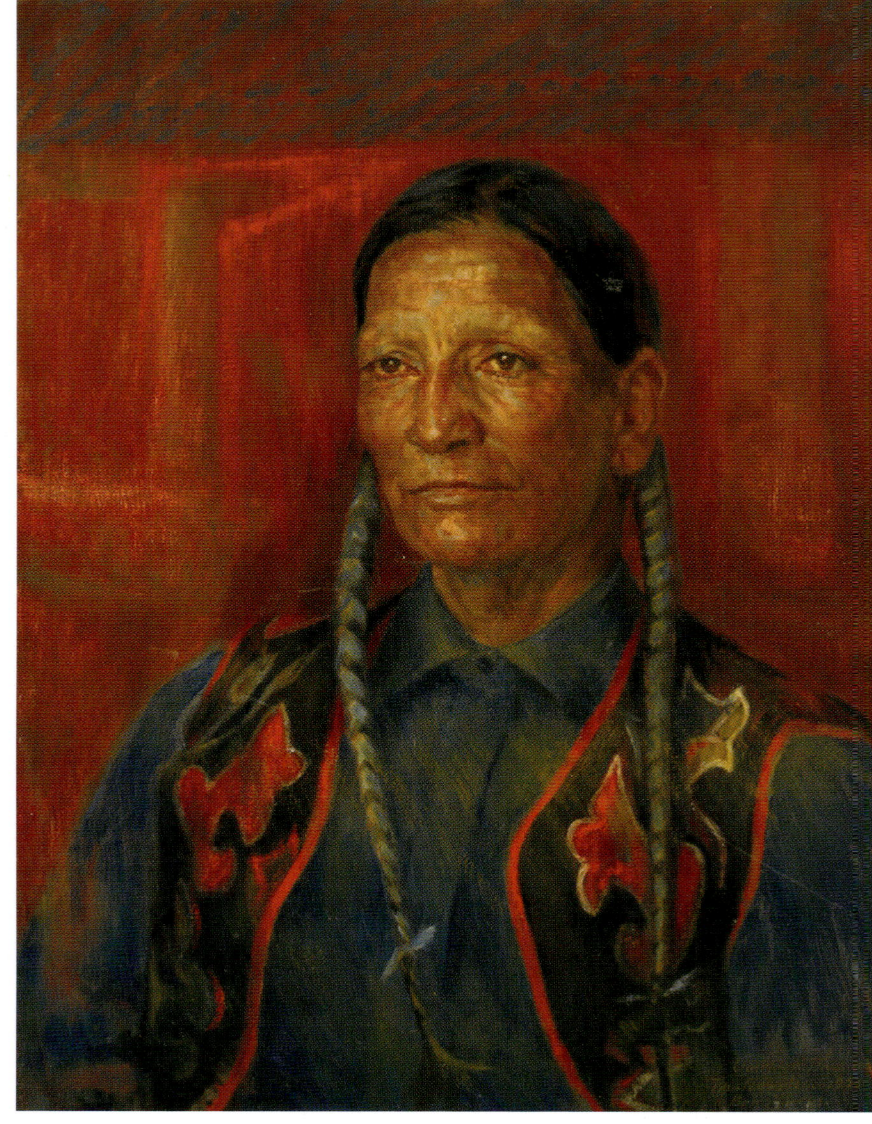

Left: **LITTLE JOE GOMEZ, DANCER AND SINGER OF TAOS,** 1956
oil on masonite
24 x 18
private collection
Dennis Wyszynski Photography

Right: **BEN MARCUS, BEST DANCER IN TAOS,** 1956
oil on masonite
24 x 18
private collection
Phillip Harsh,
Digital Studio Photography

Opposite: **PETE SUAZO,** 1955
oil on masonite
30½ x 24
private collection
Cameron Wittig Photography

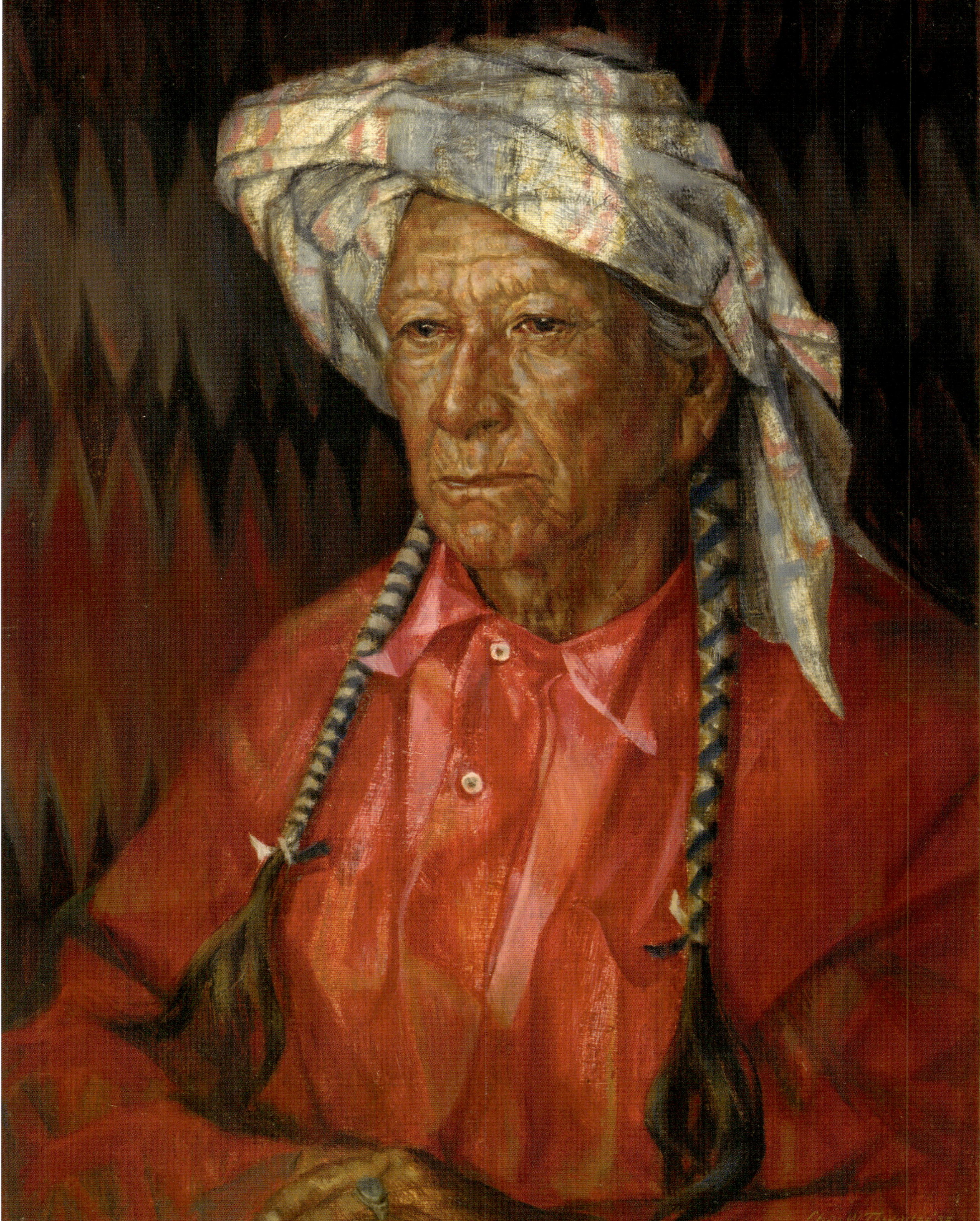

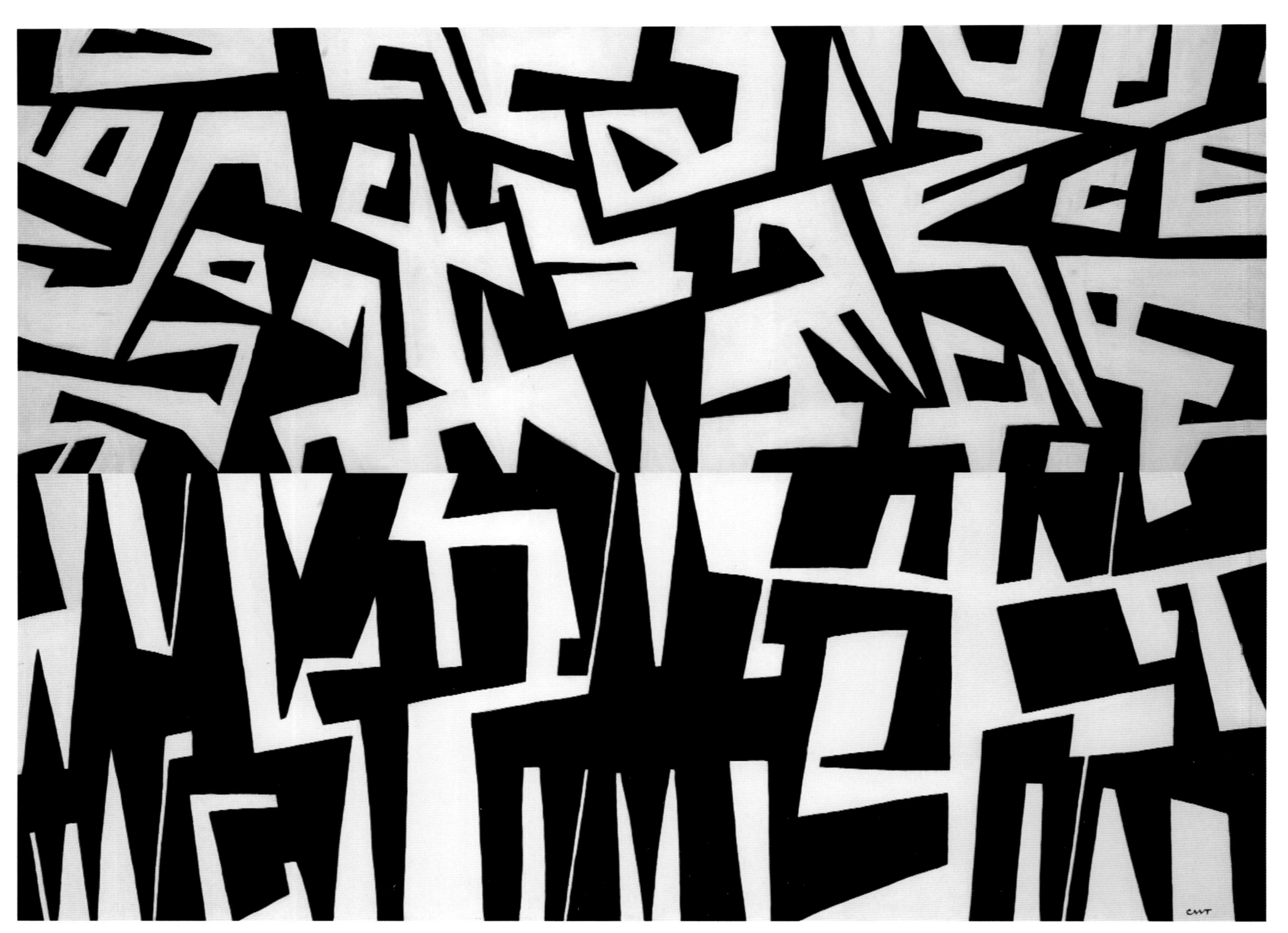

TAOS MODERNS

The abstractionist's biggest complaint with the so-called realists is that they don't begin to use all the wealth of material at their disposal, for if they did and used it as they should, they would be great masters equal to the old masters, which is what we all want. CWT

The phrase "Taos Moderns" recognizing a specific group of artists, according to David L. Witt, did not come into common parlance until 1952, when an exhibition titled *Taos Painting: Yesterday and Today* was organized by the Colorado Springs Fine Arts Center.[53] In 1956, an exhibition organized by Taos artist Ted Egri (1913—) and mounted at the Jonson Gallery at the University of New Mexico, Albuquerque, used the term for the first time in print.[54] Thwaites was included in the 1956 exhibition, in the 1957 through 1960 exhibitions of Taos Moderns at the Museum of Fine Arts, Santa Fe, and the Taos invitational shows in 1961 and 1962 that replaced the moderns show.

In 1958, during the Taos Moderns exhibition in Santa Fe, Thwaites exhibited once again in a two person show at Stables Gallery, this time with modernist Howard Cook (1901-1980). The following year, he showed with modernist Robert D. Ray (1924-2002). Reviewer Bob Lemme, writing in *The New Mexican*, noted of the 1959 show:

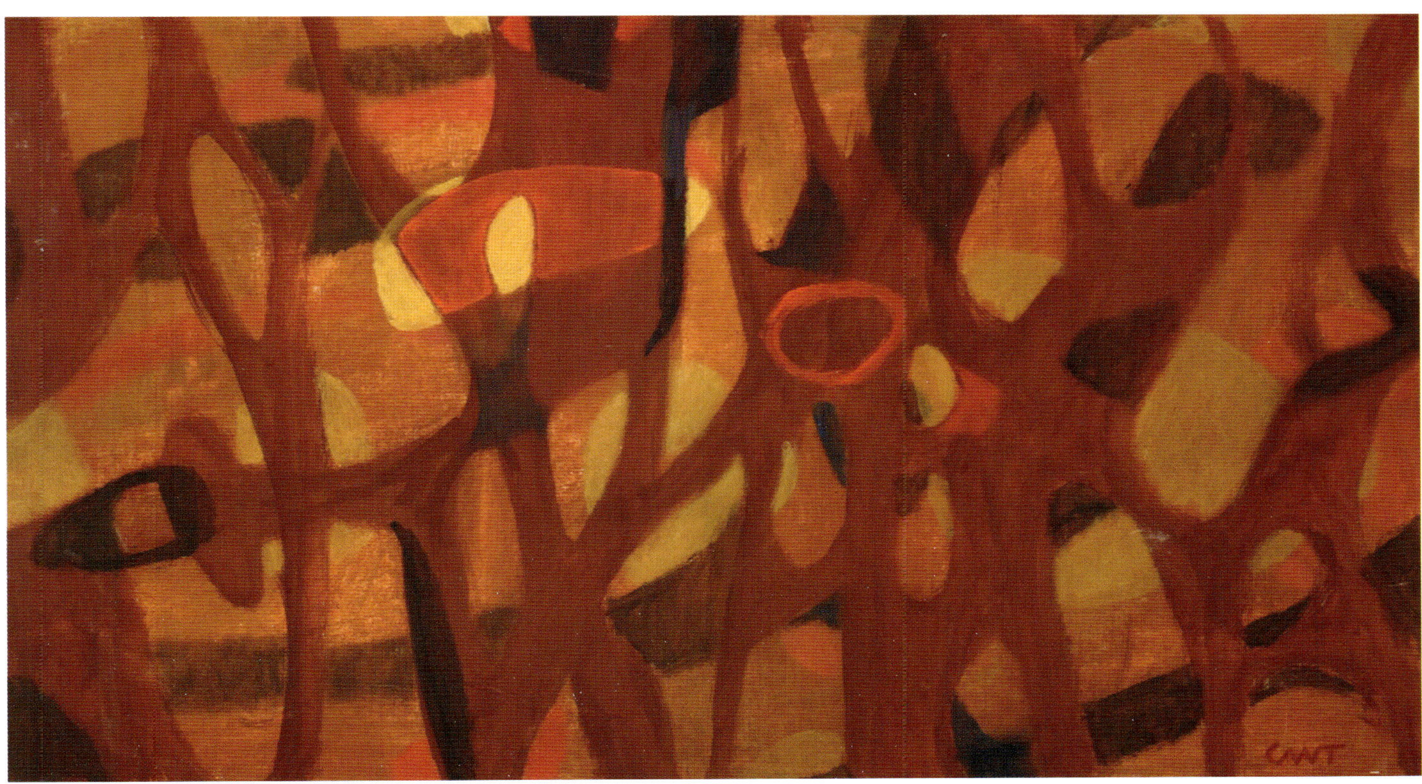

HOT SUMMER NIGHT, 1962
acrylic on masonite
18½ x 32½

Opposite:
PATTERNS IN BLACK AND WHITE, 1961
acrylic on masonite
37 x 45

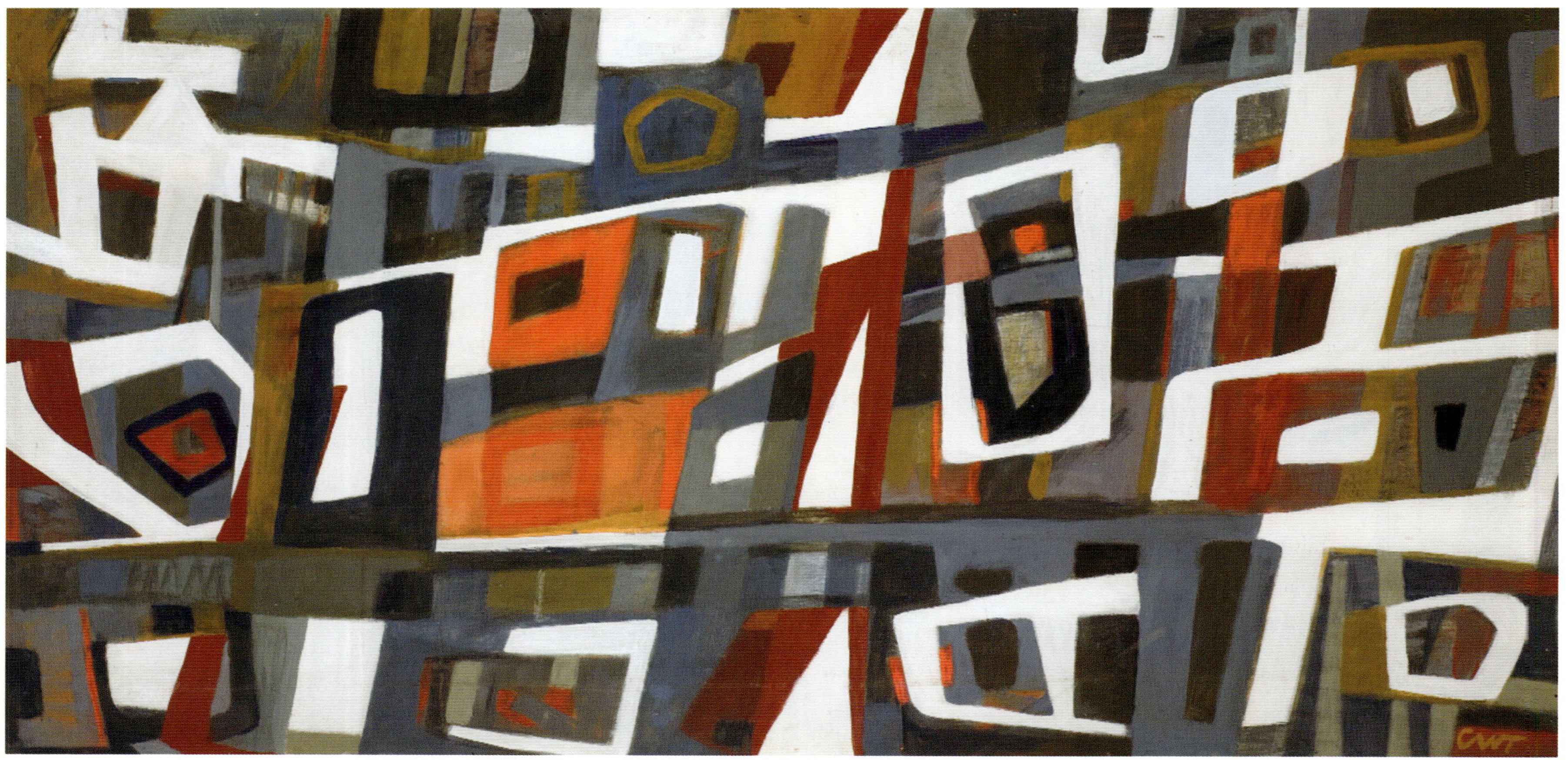

TAOS MODERNS, 1960
acrylic on masonite
24 x 49

> Thwaites' bold, angular treatment of space and shapes often emphasizes pattern and theme repetition. Although springing from nature's organic forms, a synthesis is produced and rendered in bold sharp statements. The severe taming of these turbulent elements appears successful, without muting the tensions within the shapes themselves. Nothing mild mannered about these stark compositions.[55]

Reviewer John Skolle wrote of the same event:

> Thwaites derives his subject matter mainly from the organic aspects of nature, such as the filigree pattern of a piece of bark, the structure of a seed-pod, the weathered face of a rock. In the transformation from an object to the reality of an invented form, he often achieves results more elaborate than the original part which served as a model. His use of color is intuitive and often quite independent from the original object, and yet, it follows a personal kind of logic and becomes the most important factor in the intricate organization of the work.[56]

In 1959, Thwaites joined the selection committee for the Taos Moderns exhibition. With his cohorts, Louise Ganthiers, Beatrice Mandelman (1912-1998), Louis Ribak (1903-1979), Oli Sihvonen, and Andrew Dasburg (1887-1979), the committee wrote the

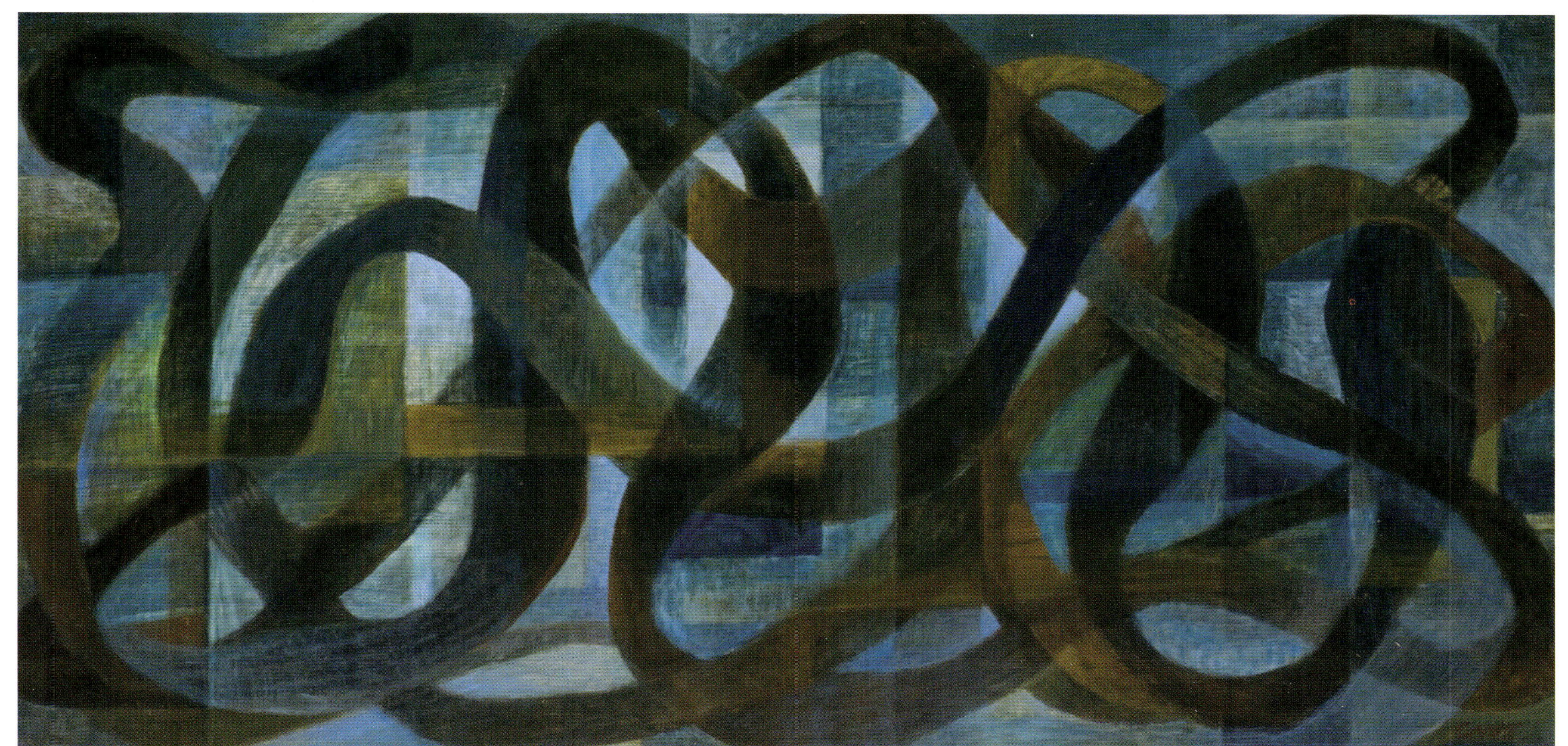

OBSESSION, 1961
acrylic on masonite
24 x 48

following statement, which echoes Thwaites' comments in Notes to Myself: "Each generation finds new freedoms ... to explore creative possibilities for new combinations that bid for our attention and sustain our continued refreshment of spirit."[57]

That same year, Thwaites submitted an abstract work to the Southwestern Artists Biennial Exhibition at the Museum of Fine Arts, Santa Fe. It was chosen out of 400 submissions to be one of 114 artists from the seven-state area.[58] The jurors were Andrew Dasburg from Taos, Vance Kirkland (1904-1981), chair of the Art Department, Denver University, and Everett Spruce (1908-2002), professor of art, University of Texas. The catalogue statements echoed a continuing controversy over modern versus traditional art. Dasburg extolled the "current stimulating vigor of expressionist realism and nonfigurative and enigmatic themes," and Kirkland wrote a warning to viewers expecting to see traditional art: "Much of the new, fresh painting, expressing so much energy, vitality and enthusiasm for living, is thoroughly American but may have a hard time being understood by viewers only conditioned to pictures manufactured for tourists."[59]

Change was on the horizon. In his review of the 1960 Taos Moderns show, Ronald Latimer proclaimed it mediocre, suggesting that many of the participants did not take it seriously. Two exceptions were Ward Lockwood and Thwaites, who submitted *Pomegranate Motif*. "These are the kind of paintings that prove the artists are professionals," Latimer wrote.[60] In 1961 and 1962, the show was controlled by becoming an invitational and Thwaites was included both years.

Thwaites' 1960 painting titled *Taos Moderns* expands upon the geometric grid pattern he used in the encaustic painting *Sunflower Motif*. However, it represents a new medium and a different approach. Water-borne polymer acrylic paints for artists were launched in 1955, and since Thwaites loved materials, he no doubt began experimenting with the quick-drying medium, using it to work on a grander scale. *Taos Moderns* measures 24 by 60 inches, and several subsequent acrylics are large, including *Patterns in Black and White*, a work that measures 37 by 45 inches. Significant in these paintings is an element that is missing—namely, a subject or pictorial reference. While Thwaites continued to do representational paintings and encaustics inspired by nature, many of the acrylics are nonobjective. In them he responded to or interpreted an idea or emotion using purely formal aspects, notably color and shape.

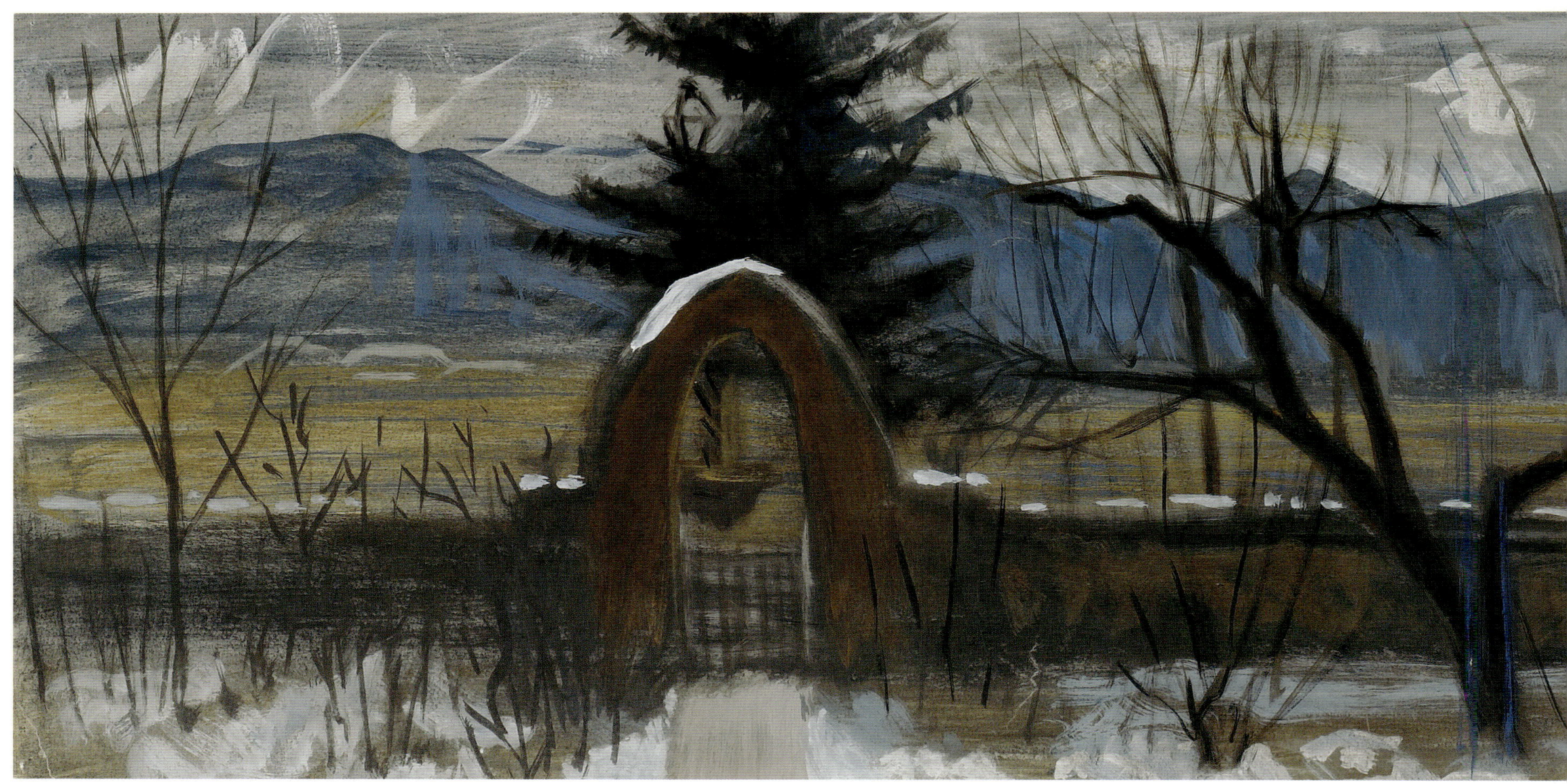

In the 1960s, Thwaites also painted five panoramic views from his studio, including *View from Tony House*, which have a *memento mori* quality about them. Perhaps they were a reaction to Mabel, who was in poor health, having suffered several strokes. In August 1962, she passed away, and a year later, so did her beloved Tony. The property transferred to Mabel's son John Evans, and just as the counter-culture generation began to invade Taos, the Thwaiteses determined it was time to move on.

While attending Pueblo ceremonials throughout northern New Mexico, Charles and Antoinette often encountered a sprightly woman, who they came to know as Sallie R. Wagner (1913-2006) of Santa Fe. Wagner was a champion for and patron of preservation of the land, animals, indigenous cultures, and women's rights. Her colorful past included operating with her ex-husband Bill Lippincott the Wide Ruins Trading Post on the Navajo reservation during the 1940s and later writing about their experiences. Wagner owned a home with a spacious casita near St. John's College in Santa Fe. When she learned that the Thwaiteses were looking for a place in Santa Fe, she offered to rent it to them and to add a skylight to the garage so Thwaites could use it as a studio. It was, the Thwaiteses surmised, yet another synchronistic encounter like the one with Loeffler a decade earlier.

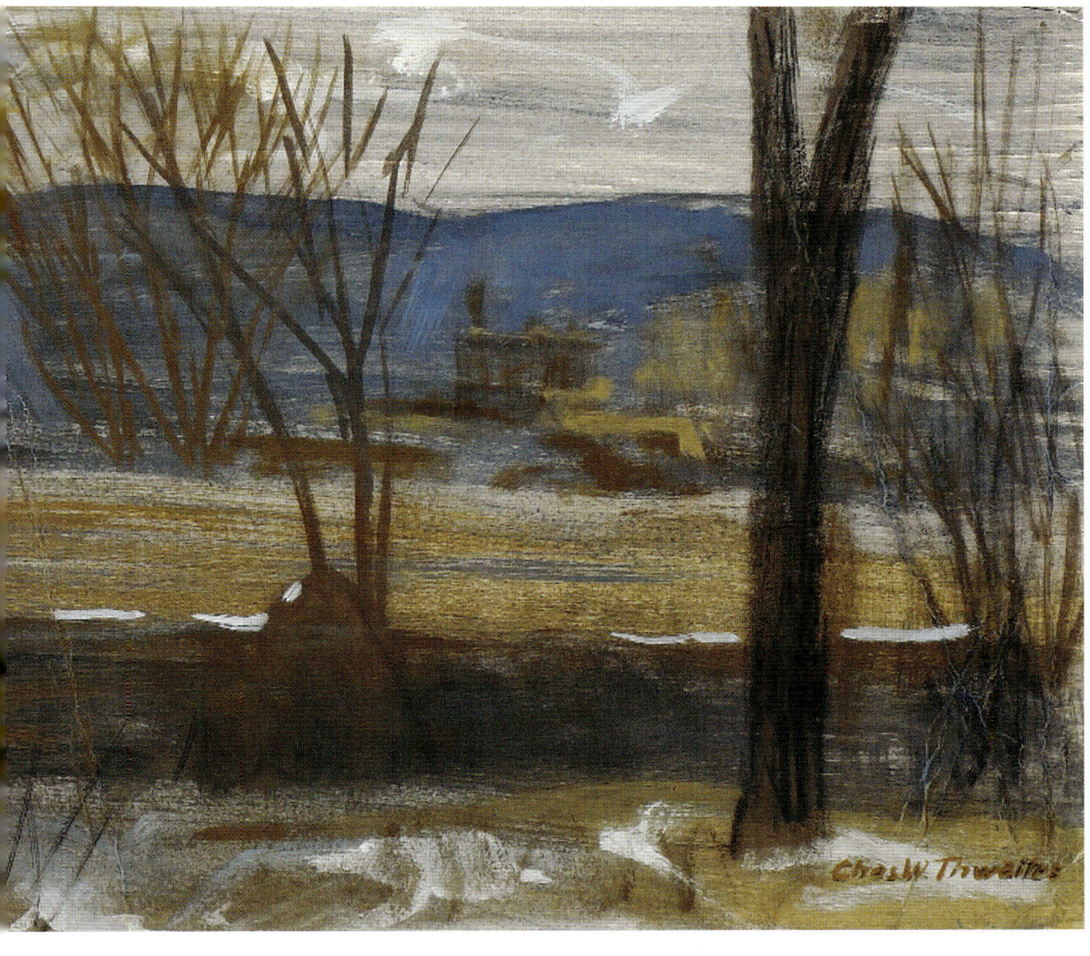

VIEW FROM TONY HOUSE, 1961
acrylic on paper
11 1/4 x 35
private collection
Dennis Wyszynski Photography

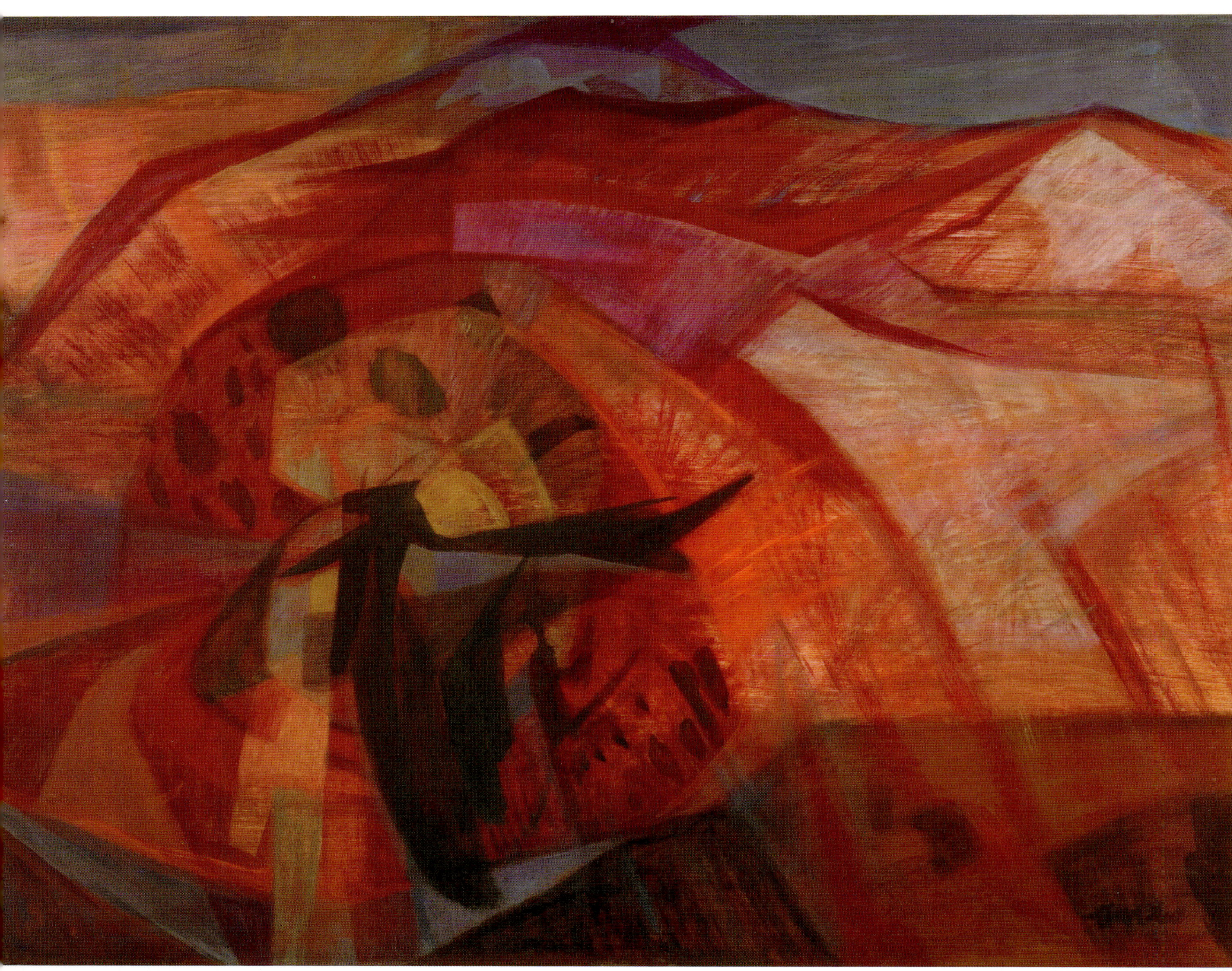

SANGRE DE CRISTOS, 1963
acrylic on masonite
36¾ x 48¾
private collection
Eric Griswold Photography

SANTA FE

So much of our greatest frustrations and anger are in the confrontation with people whose spectrum of ideas is too narrow, stopping them from seeing their real position in the total situation, whether they are right, left or middle, but in any case too limited. CWT

Thwaites exhibited at the Blue Door Gallery and Galeria Escondida, a contemporary Taos gallery, through 1963. Once in Santa Fe, he exhibited at Canyon Road Gallery from 1967 through 1969. For pleasure, he continued painting realistic self-portraits and impressionistic landscapes from his living room window. He memorialized his new home in the large painting *Sangre de Cristos*, which combines a suggestive profile of the mountains with a joyous abstraction of sumptuous colors. The dark figure in the left foreground, which may have been inspired by a flying crow, adds movement and energy to the landscape.

For exhibition purposes, Thwaites' paintings became bolder in complexity and size. His colors and contrasts also became increasingly strident, even though he limited himself to the primaries of red, yellow, and blue, or simply black and white. Some of the paintings have titles indicative of emotions, such as *Fiesta*, *Hot Summer Night*, and *Obsession*, which was submitted to the 1962 Southwestern Biennial. A dynamic painting, *Obsession* well describes a seemingly infinite grid that fades in and out as a serpentine ribbon intertwines throughout it. *Abstractions*, which won an award at a 1965 Museum of Fine Arts, Santa Fe, exhibition, is an imposing work in which the grid structure has become a muscular form barely contained by the surface upon which it is painted.[61]

The confounding optical and mental game of positive and negative space in *Patterns in Black and White* was submitted to the Museum of Fine Arts, Santa Fe, 1966 Biennial and the 1968-1969 Federation of Rocky Mountain States exhibit, where it hung for a month in each of the capitals of the eight western states represented. The latter exhibition was an invitational from the New Mexico Arts Commission, and Thwaites' fellow exhibitors in what was to be his last touring exhibition were Dorothy Brett (1883-1976), Howard Cook, Sam Smith (1918-1999) and Ford Ruthling (1933 —).

In the late-1960s, with the receipt of an inheritance from his uncle, Charles and Antoinette saw an opportunity to open their eyes and minds to places and artworks they had known only in reproductions or in books. They made two trips to Europe, returning with a renewed appreciation for art history and for everything French and Spanish, including the art, language and music.

Perhaps through Sallie Wagner and the proximity of her home to St. John's College, the Thwaiteses came to know Richard Weigle, dean of the college, and his wife. Their friendship deepened, and in

BLUE ABSTRACTION, 1976
acrylic on paper
24½ x 29¼

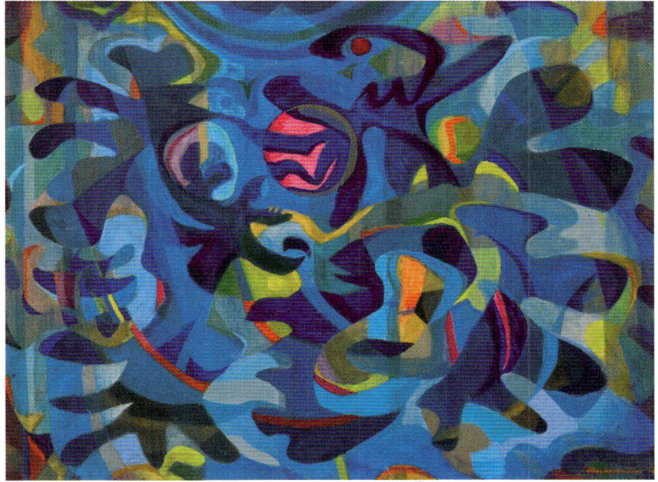

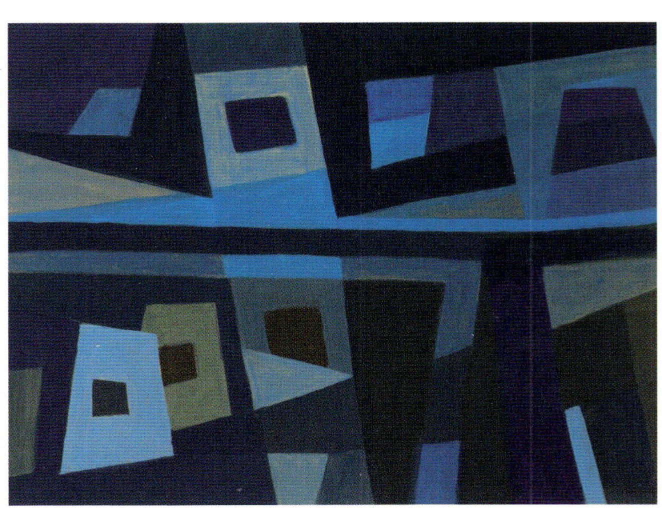

PATTERNS IN BLUE, 1968
acrylic on paper
24 x 29½

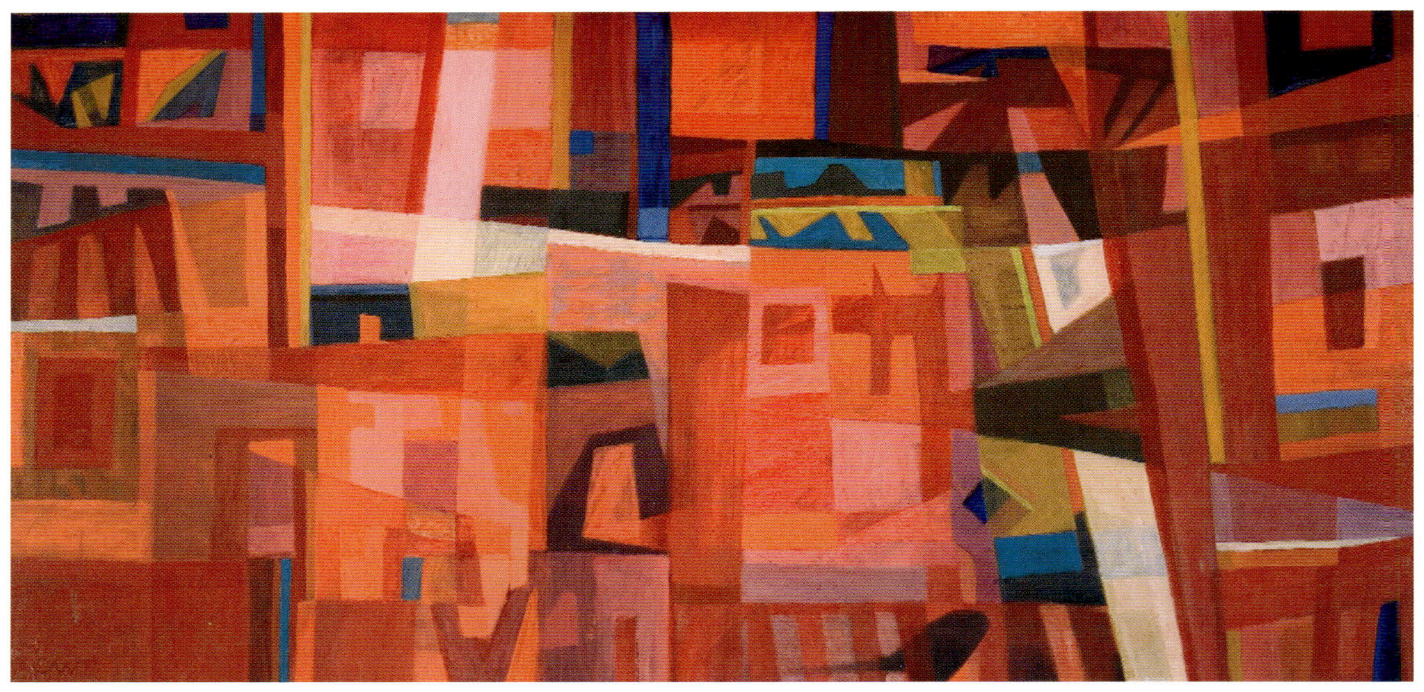

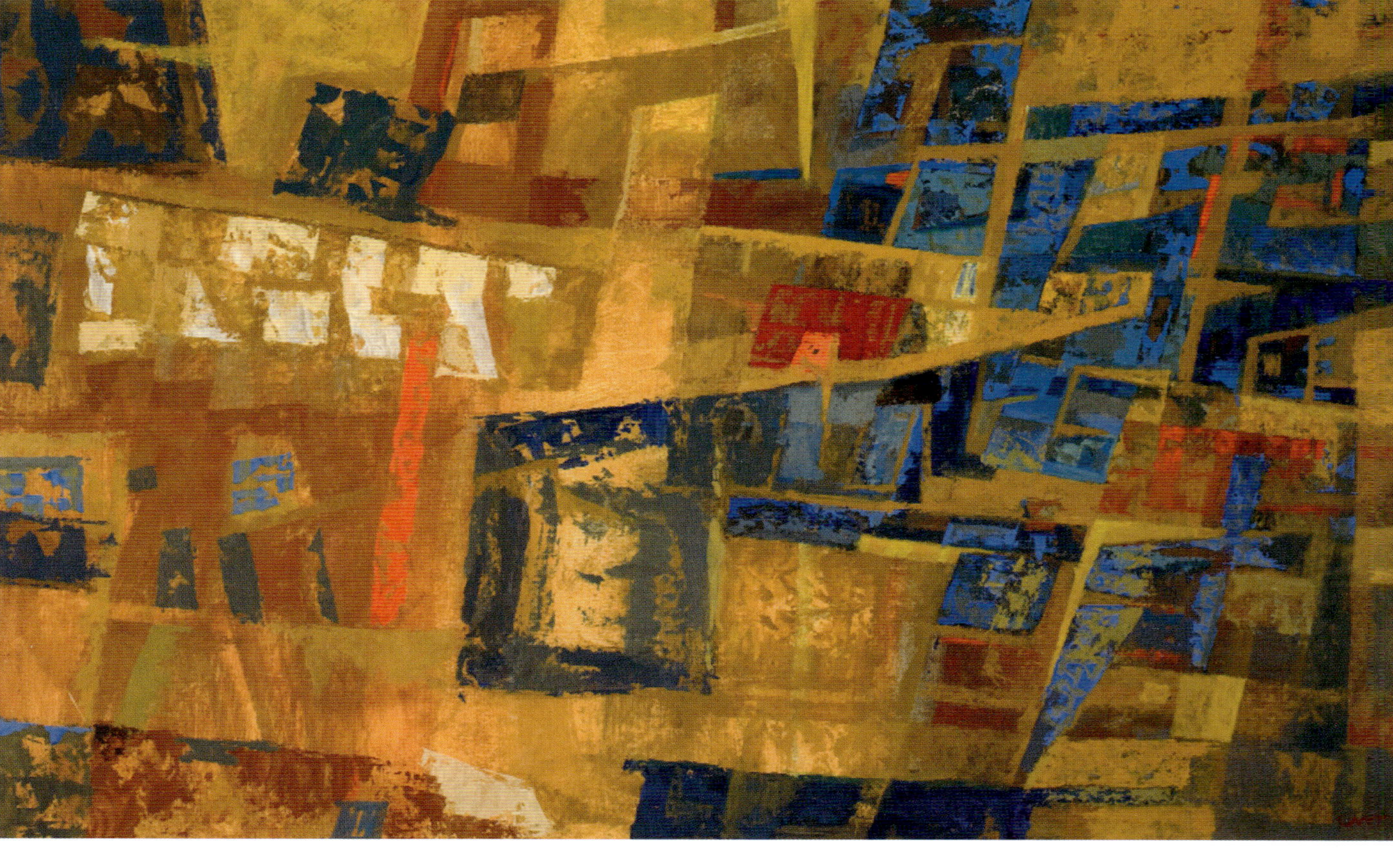

Above:
FIESTA, 1970
acrylic on masonite
$33^{3}/_{4}$ x $47^{1}/_{2}$
private collection
Alison Dunlap Photography

TRANSITION, 1963
acrylic on masonite
$30^{1}/_{2}$ x $48^{1}/_{2}$

Opposite:
PURPLE RAIN, 1963
acrylic on masonite
$16^{3}/_{4}$ x $32^{3}/_{4}$

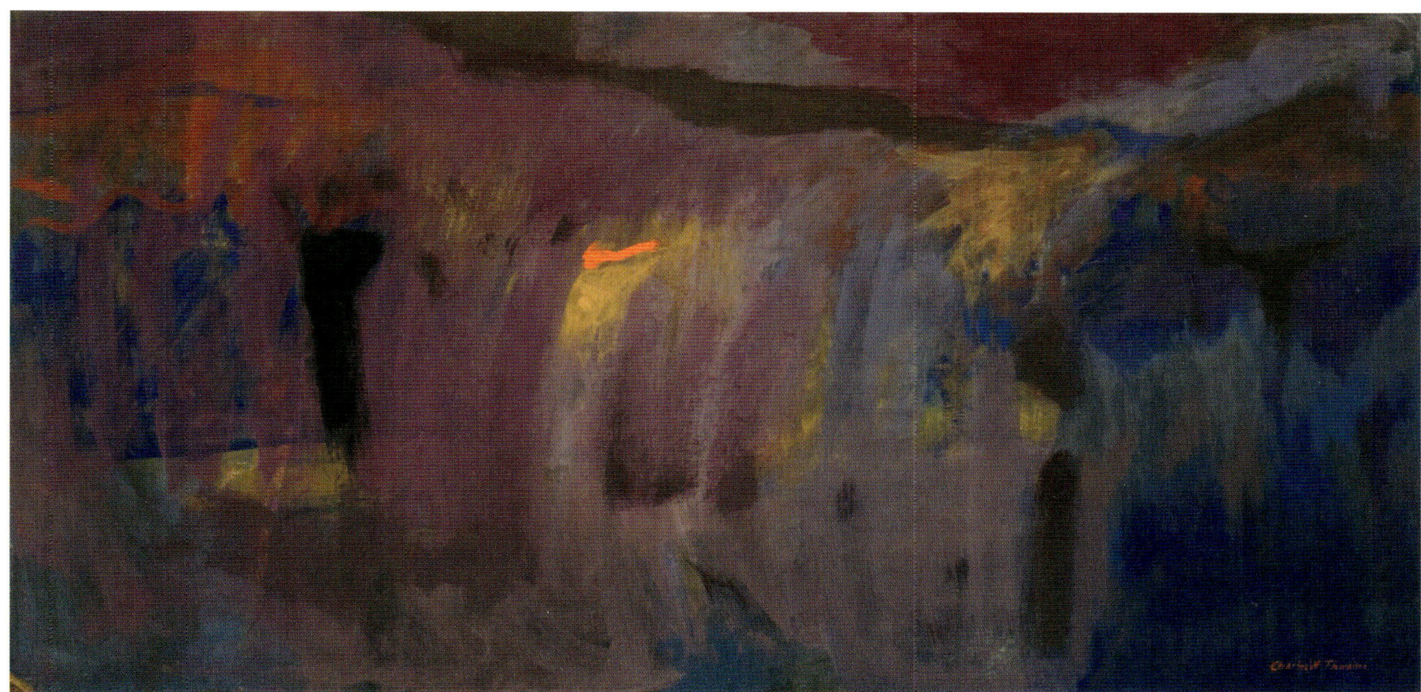

1965, Thwaites was invited to have a one-man exhibition at the college, and in 1969, he was commissioned to paint Weigle's portrait. In correspondence, Weigle relates how much he enjoyed the sittings, which included great conversations during lunch prepared by Antoinette.[62]

In the fall of 1973, Thwaites was appointed artist-in-residence at St. John's, a position he humbly accepted but ultimately found stifling. In his notes, he recounted the ambience of the college, which educates through "the great books," by using Socrates' metaphor of watching the "shadows cast by tutors and students on the wall of my cave" surrounded by the "brilliance and security of the larger, brighter cave, the world of academia ... [which is shrouded in] the murky understanding of another cave. What academia lacks is direct perception, which could destroy it, and [that] is what all the safeguards so precious to it are about."[63]

Thwaites experimented through the 1970s with various print media, including serigraphs of his grid paintings and original prints such as *Strawberry Corn Motif.* He also explored a series of energetic circular abstractions, such as *Imaginative Impulse*, and small, layered collages whose subdued newsprint backgrounds are broken by splashes of red, calligraphic black strokes, and stabilizing blue lines.

In the late 1970s, Antoinette, who had handled the couple's finances and investments throughout their marriage, suffered a stroke, from which she recovered. It was followed in 1981 by a debilitating one. She was hospitalized in Albuquerque and moved to a nursing facility in Santa Fe. Charles visited her daily, becoming increasingly depressed as her health declined. He rarely painted in

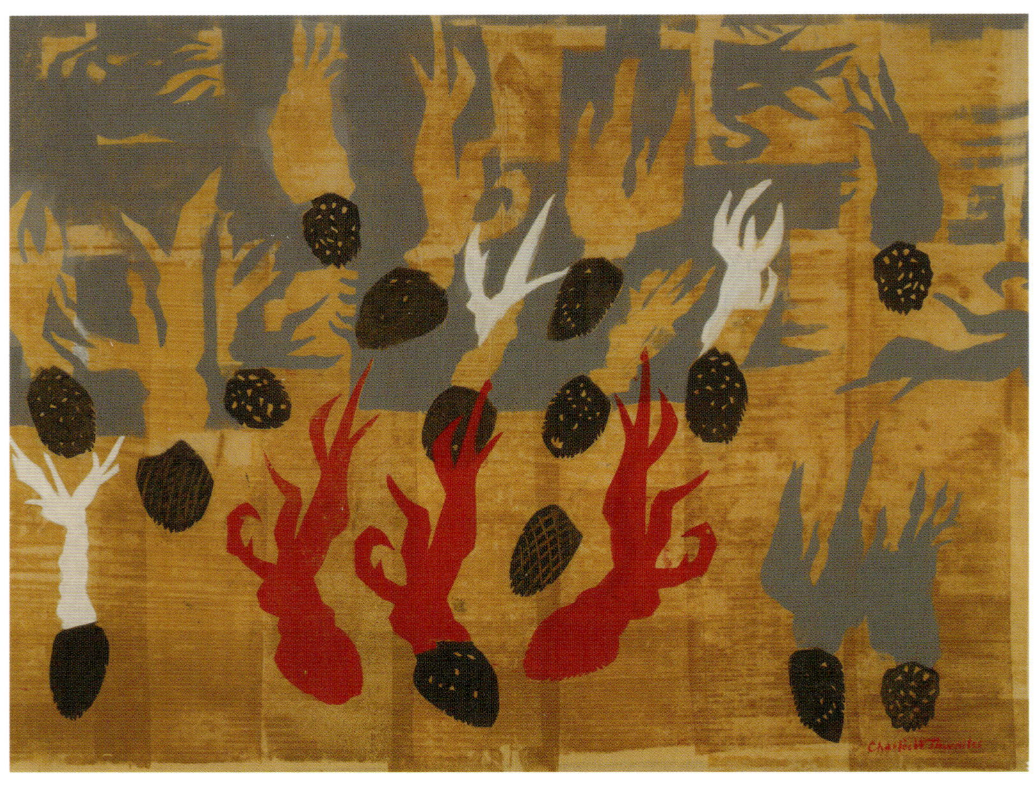

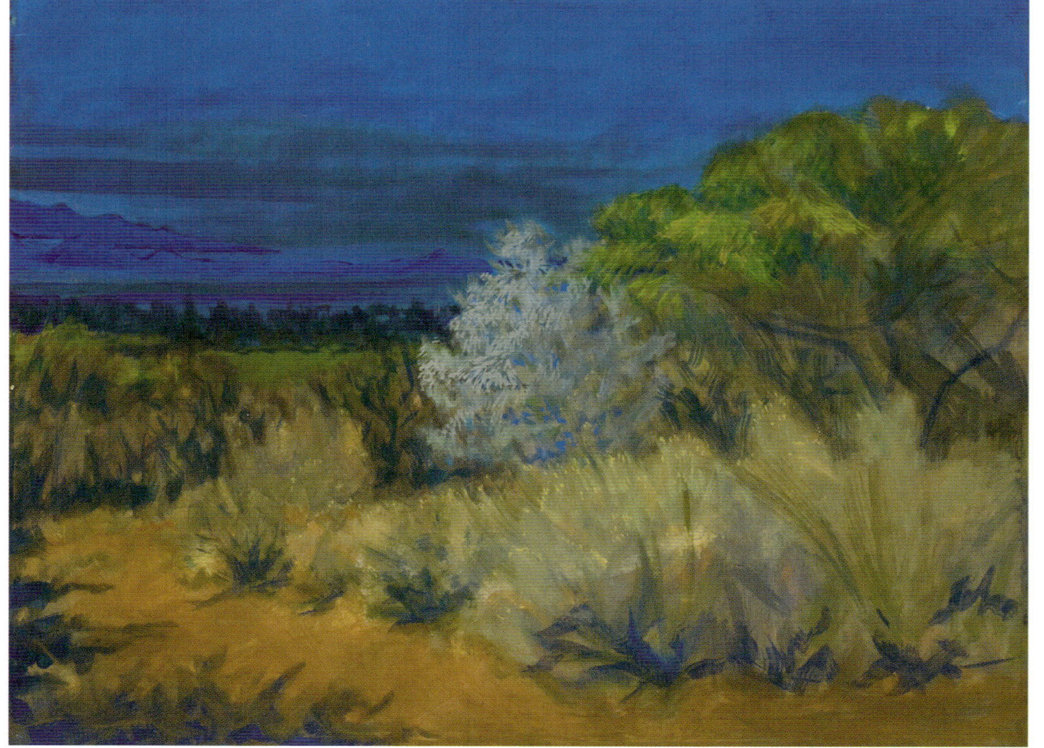

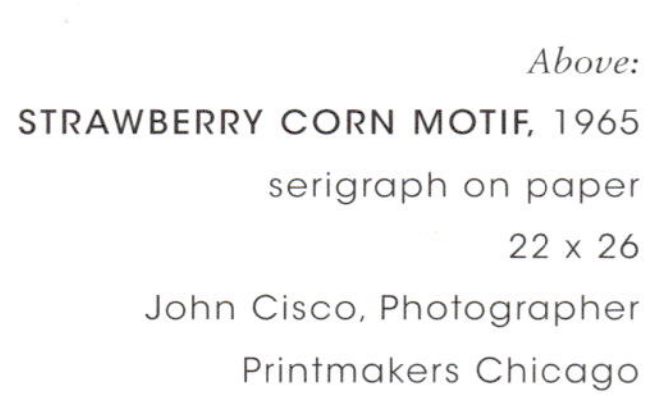

Above:
STRAWBERRY CORN MOTIF, 1965
serigraph on paper
22 x 26
John Cisco, Photographer
Printmakers Chicago

VIEW FROM LIVING ROOM WINDOW, NIGHT, 1975
acrylic on paper
20 x 25

Opposite:
ABSTRACTIONS, 1964
acrylic on masonite
31 x 49

the 1980s, and in October 1991, his partner in art and life passed away. In 1998, Charles entered the same facility in which Antoinette had lived, and in 2002, at age 98, he died in his sleep.

Some of his last paintings were impressionistic views out the living room window of his home looking to the mountains southwest of Santa Fe where blazing sunsets are common. He painted the view in all seasons and times of the day, including moonlit nights such as *View from Living Room Window, Night*. In lieu of painting regularly, Thwaites turned to writing about the process—a somewhat ironic pursuit given his disdain for critics whom he lambasted for their attempts to put into words what art "said" more directly and universally. His commentaries, which were drafted and then meticulously copied using a fountain pen, have been quoted throughout this essay, and additional ones are included in Appendix B, Notes to Myself.

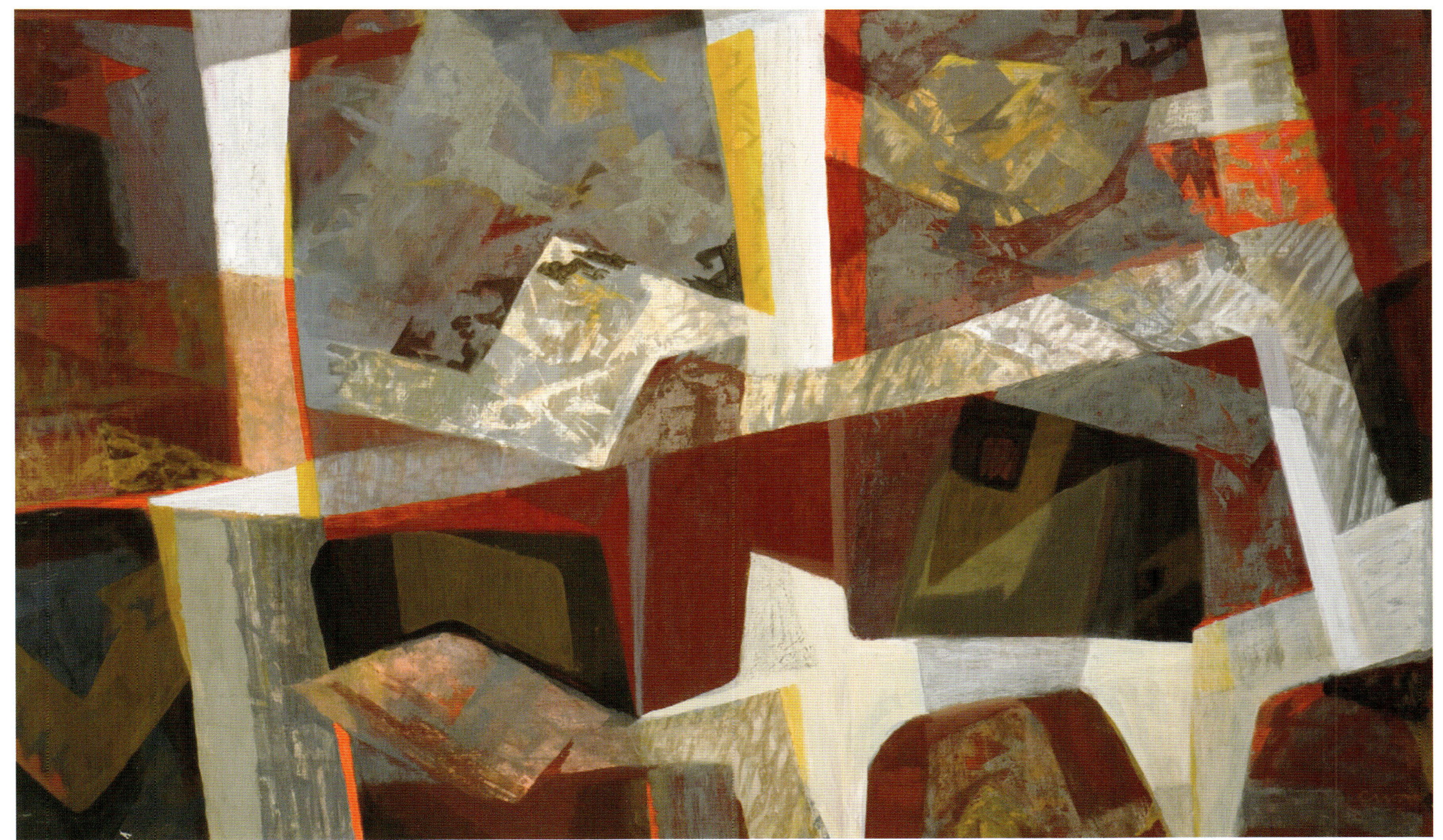

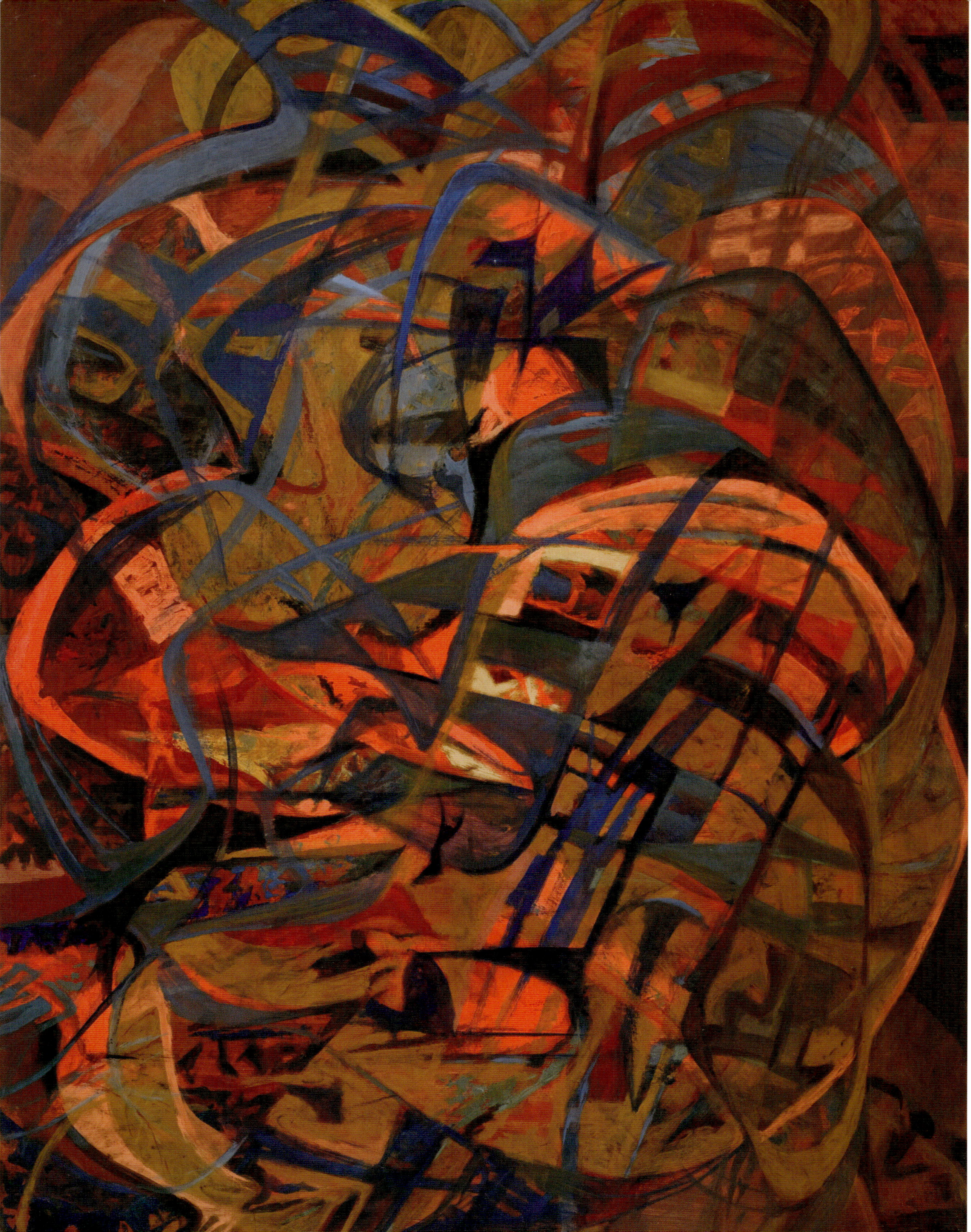

FREEDOM OF EXPRESSION

So time and change keep pace everlastingly and so it has always been that each generation needs new freedoms to explore wider possibilities for less hackneyed combinations to emphasize and test for our continued refreshment of the spiritual, and at the same time to experience and relive the history of great art in our own work. CWT

As his earliest reviewers noted, Thwaites was an introspective artist, examining himself, critiquing his success, and measuring it against the artistic achievements of the past. That self-examination is apparent in his writings, and symbolized in his more than twenty-five known self-portraits done throughout his lifetime.

At the foundation of Thwaites' exploration was the logical, yet mystical act of transforming the three-dimensional world—whether realistically or abstractly—onto a two-dimensional surface, or as Thwaites put it, trying to "organize visual representational material into a little representation of an independent universe."

In responding honestly to what was in his vision, Thwaites was not constrained by a style, medium, or technique. Rather he used what the subject or the emotion demanded, seeking out its universal organizing principles and letting them determine the medium and dominant motif, a word he used often in titling his paintings. As he noted in his writings, his engineering background contributed to his philosophy. "[Engineering] impressed me with the reason and necessity for design in nature, and likewise, in the works of man," he wrote in an essay he titled Plans (see Appendix B).

The Thwaites library is no longer intact; however, a record was made of the magazine titles (such as *Verve* mentioned earlier) and the book titles and/or subjects. The range of cultures and time periods is expansive. Several books covered ancient Egyptian, Greek, Asian, and Persian art, as well as Japanese and Chinese painting. Bosch and the Flemish Primitives up through Renaissance and Baroque artists such as Michelangelo, Titian, Rubens, El Greco, and Goya were represented, followed by Impressionists such as Monet and Toulouse Lautrec, and post-Impressionists van Gogh and Cezanne. The monographs on modernist painters included Modigliani, Soutine, Rivera, Braque, Matisse, and Whistler. There were also numerous books on American Indian art and culture, as well as psychology, archaeology, mathematics, and mythology.

Also included in the library were four books on Rembrandt van Rijn (1606-1669) and six on Pablo Picasso (1881-1973). According to the Dahlstrands, Thwaites studied in depth Rembrandt's compositions, techniques, and materials, becoming a virtual scholar of the artist's oeuvre. In keeping with Thwaites' philosophy that all art is abstract, representational and nonobjective alike, he observed that Rembrandt's portraits are "more than just a picture of a man or woman because of the abstract qualities Rembrandt's genius imparted to the canvas."[64]

IMAGINATIVE IMPULSE, 1968
acrylic on masonite
48½ x 36

Interestingly, Picasso also found Rembrandt to be a profound teacher, especially the psychological implications and physical realism of the Dutchman's sixty self-portraits. One can only speculate on Thwaites' interest in Picasso, who also painted numerous self-portraits. However, in my opinion, Thwaites not only respected Picasso's freedom to paint in any style he wished, but also his genius in organizing a subject on canvas, notably during the cubist period. Several of Picasso's early portraits of women may have inspired Thwaites' compositions. In particular, there are idiosyncratic correspondences between Thwaites' 1941 *Portrait with a Fan* and Picasso's cubistic 1909 *Woman with Fan* (Pushkin Museum). While the styles are dissimilar, both compositions use the fan as a focal point, including the positioning of the sitter's hand (Antoinette's ungloved hand) against the fan, leading to the neck fabric that sets off the face. The backdrop of drapery, geometric patterns, and the sitter's quixotic stare are also similar. Given the Thwaiteses' love of art, it would not be unusual for Charles to pose Antoinette using Picasso's painting, or for Antoinette herself to adopt the pose.

Thwaites did not pursue cubism, per se, however, beginning in the late 1940s he broke up his subjects into planes. In a literal example of cubism's precepts, and perhaps even a pun, Thwaites did companion paintings titled *Floating Cube* and *Exploded Cube*. The former shows the cube intact and the latter displays its planes broken apart and in various perspectives. Other works where he broke the image into planes and reassembled them into dynamic patterns include *Night Patterns*, *Clouds of Lake Michigan*, and *Pomegranates (Fractured)*. In *Piñons and Arroyos* and a number of the encaustics done after he moved to Taos, the landscape is likewise flattened into shapes arranged as quadrants and defined by textures, colors, darks, and lights.

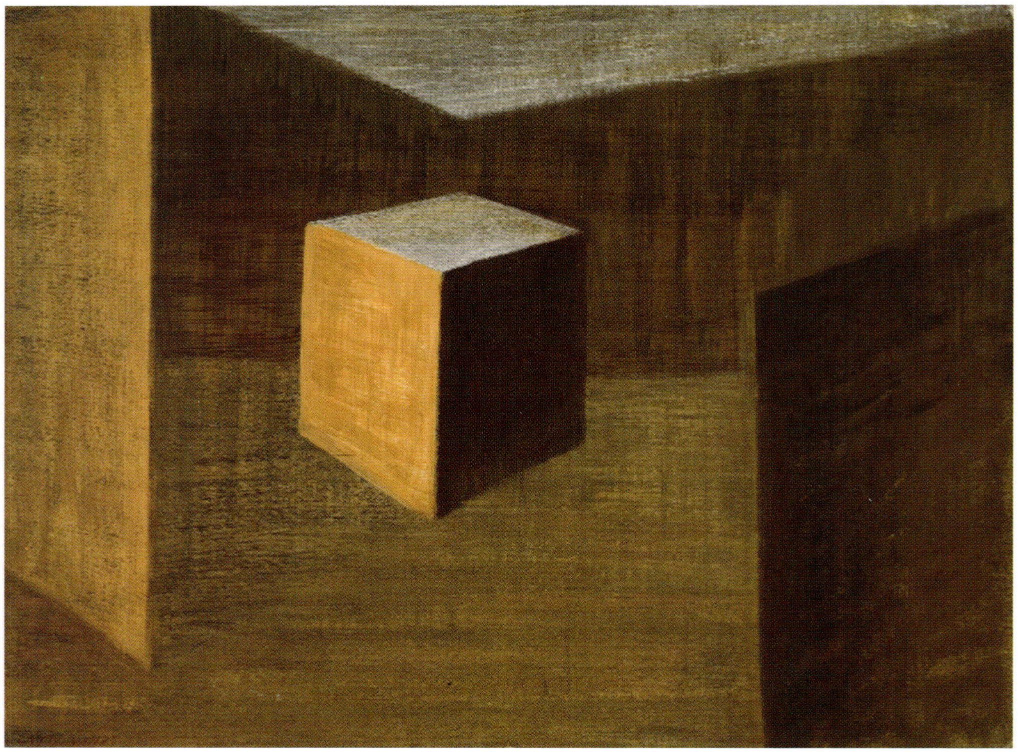

FLOATING CUBE, 1950
egg tempera on paper
17½ x 23

As his writings emphasize, Thwaites was a formalist, believing that all art was the result of designing the formal elements of shape, color, line, form, etc. Throughout his last years in Milwaukee, he also taught design. Undoubtedly, he was familiar with English critic Clive Bell, whose 1913 book *Art* was routinely reprinted and reissued in 1923. Bell was a consummate formalist, judging the value of all artists, past and present, on their ability to organize formal qualities, particularly line and color, or what he called "significant form." Both Picasso and Thwaites paraphrased the following statement by Bell in the design chapter of *Art*, "In art the only important distinction is the distinction between good and bad."[65]

That pattern or "look" Thwaites so often referred to may have been inspired by understanding the mathematical principles of the Golden

Section, utilized throughout art history and taught in most school curricula during the early part of the twentieth century. He also no doubt knew of the Golden Ratio in the human form as described by da Vinci. It is equally probable that Thwaites' penchant for geometry was further stimulated by the theory of Dynamic Symmetry codified in 1920 by Jay Hambridge,[66] and its spiritual extension in the work of Taos Moderns Emil Bisttram and Raymond Jonson.

Born in Iowa, Jonson was widely known in the modernist movement in Chicago, where he had numerous one-man shows while Thwaites was still living in Milwaukee. Once Thwaites settled in New Mexico, Jonson was organizing exhibitions of leading non-objective artists at the University of New Mexico and displaying his works at the University's Jonson Gallery. Like Jonson, Thwaites strove to create paintings that could move viewers esthetically and even spiritually through purely abstract means. Jonson's belief that design is "a way of established order, structure, rhythm, and integration of these elements for the purpose of pure aesthetic enjoyment"[67] is echoed by Thwaites:

> That look which finds sympathetic accord in the deep logic of the emotions, so that you come to know that calm yet exciting, relaxing yet energizing flux of unity with something outside of yourself, that re-creating play upon the nervous system. It is the feeling of living when life is really worthwhile.

Jonson and Thwaites saw their work, media, and styles as evolving meaningfully throughout their lifetimes. So did Picasso, and no doubt Thwaites would have felt comfortable describing himself as a painter without a style as did Picasso who stated:

> "Style" is often something that ties the artist down and makes him look at things in one particular way, the same technique, the same formulas, year after year, sometimes for a whole lifetime. You recognize him immediately, for he is always in the same suit, or a suit of the same cut. There are, of course, great painters who have a certain style. However ... I can never be tied down, and that is why I have no style.[68]

On the scale of "good and bad painting," Thwaites classified as "bad" those uninformed artists who claimed achievements or "revelations" that clearly had, in his estimation, art historical precedents. That kind of hubris perhaps accounted for the bitterness and isolation Thwaites occasionally expressed in Notes to Myself, as in this excerpt from an essay he titled The Dream of Life:

> When one's whole life has been spent being concerned with the value of one's own product, comparing everything one does, not

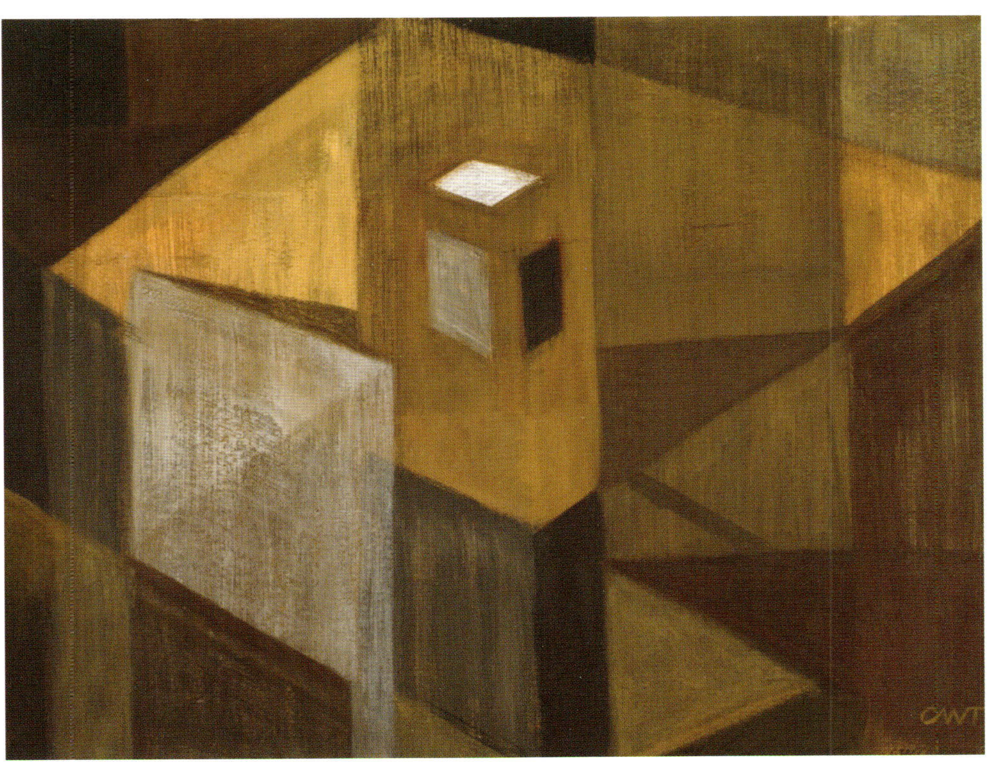

EXPLODED CUBE, 1950
egg tempera on paper
17½ x 23

> only with contemporaries, but the old masters as well, and sharpening one's critical sensitivities to higher appreciation of what is best, only to find that, as far as one's acquaintances and people around us are concerned, your training does not exist, one's best is as one's worst, and anyone's worst is as his best.
>
> A lifetime of spartan self-criticism is no match for the completely uneducated, insensitive opinion. They are jackasses, enamored with all the virtues so beloved by jackasses. Between the small exchanges of ideas when we are together, there are long periods when what might have been a dialogue is only to be continued in solo, as a mythical one.[69]

Throughout his life, Thwaites was process driven, enjoying everything from the analytical to the historical, physical, material, and emotional aspects that brought a two-dimensional surface to life. On a brighter day in his notes, he described the evolution from imitation to creating an authentic response to what the artist was seeing and feeling. It is in informed by manifestos of modern art so prevalent in the second half of the twentieth century. However, Thwaites did not pursue the "new" for the sake of being new and different. Rather, his personal twist on freedom of expression always kept at its foundation the accomplishments of those who came before him—the artists who succeeded in using formal structures to communicate to viewers across time and cultures.

The following statement is a fitting summary and epitaph of Thwaites' more than five decades synthesizing the personal and the universal in art and life.

> Perhaps the primitive urge to imitate—to paint the likeness of things—soon discovers that something can be done to enhance the rendition, making it more forceful and appealing. This something is composition or design. The more we become interested in design, we realize how effective it is in all relationships and possibilities and its essential necessity in every aspect and detail.
>
> By this time the interest becomes so absorbing that we think of the rendition as more of a vehicle and byproduct, instead of the end, which has now become the composition.
>
> Painting directly from things as models is now highly absorbing, because we realize what a gold mine nature is for the visual raw material, such as color, shapes, movements, etc., as the source of our philosophy of organization. From this it is no great step at all to paint from our idea of the organization of the universe itself, which is what we've been trying to do right along anyway—trying to organize visual representational material into a little representation of an independent universe.
>
> Once you attain this attitude of mind, legitimately through your own working experience, it becomes quite clear that a philosophy of organization is the key to understanding many things, and of course, all the arts past, present, and future.[70]

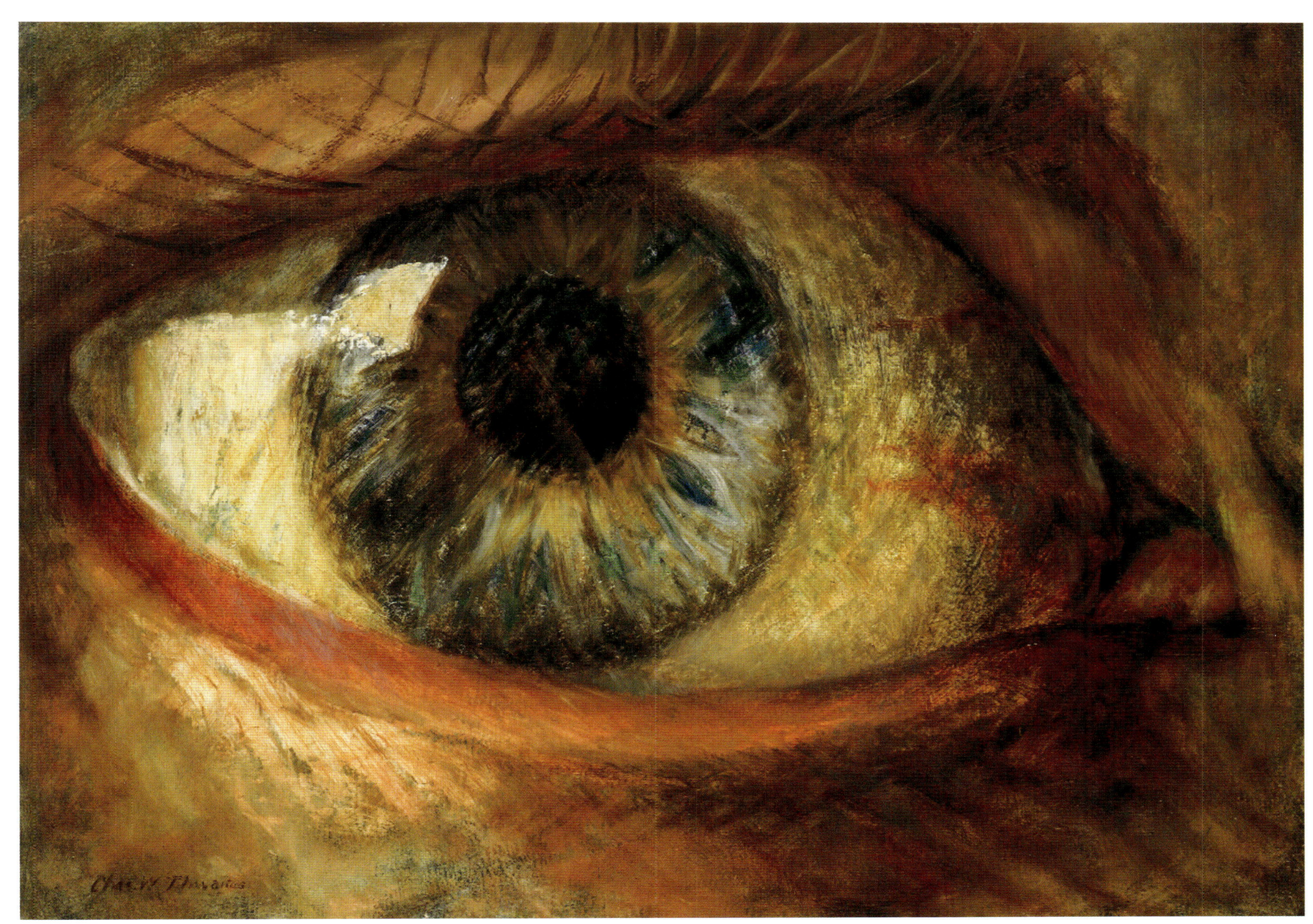

EYE, 1945
oil on masonite
16 x 22
private collection
Dennis Wyszynski Photography

ENDNOTES

Part I, Wisconsin

[1] Fifty-Third Annual Exhibition of American Paintings and Sculpture, The Art Institute of Chicago, October 29 to December 10, 1942. Quite possibly the *Self-Portrait* was the one with a print of *Pieta of Avignon* by Enguerrand Quarton, which won an award in the 1941 Milwaukee Painters and Sculptors Exhibition.
[2] Thwaits added an "e" to the spelling of his birth name in the early1930s.
[3] Handwritten notes, CWT Estate Archives.
[4] Janet Treacy, "The Legacy/Finding a Voice, Gerrit V. Sinclair 1880-1955: A Retrospective," West Bend Art Museum, WI, 2002, reprinted in The Resource Library Magazine, tfaoi.com.
[5] Published in German in 1921 and translated into English in 1934.
[6] Letter to the author from Olof Dahlstrand, July 30, 2007.
[7] Samuel N. Manierre, "Six Wisconsin Painters," *The Studio,* January 1946, Vol. 131, No. 634, pp. 20ff.
[8] Family legend has it that the series of more than ten nudes was done on commission for a bar owner who planned to open his establishment at the end of prohibition in 1933.
[9] *The Milwaukee Journal*, November 19, 1933.
[10] *The Milwaukee Journal*, December 9, 1934.
[11] It is not known exactly when or why Thwaites changed the spelling of his name. His name is spelled variously in early newspaper accounts, however, the 1931 International Watercolor Exhibition catalogue from the Art Institute of Chicago shows it as Thwaites.
[12] In the catalogue for the 1946 Paintings of the Year at the National Academy of Design most of the artworks are priced under a thousand dollars. Thwaites priced his portrait of Antoinette at $2,000.
[13] Letter from Antoinette to Charles, January 10, 1935, CWT Estate Archives.
[14] Letter from Charles to Antoinette, September 5, 1938, CWT Estate Archives.
[15] Letter from Antoinette to Charles, September 1, 1935, CWT Estate Archives.
[16] *The Milwaukee Journal*, March 21, 1937, and *Bulletin of the Milwaukee Art Institute*, April 1937, Vol. 11, No. 8.
[17] The study for the mural is in the collection of the University of Maryland Art Gallery, College Park, MD.
[18] Edward Alden Jewell, "Prize-Winning Designs in Nation-Wide Competition Show at the Corcoran," *New York Times*, November 5, 1939. *Life* magazine, December 4, 1939, pp. 12-13.
[19] Royal Cortissoz, "American Mural Decoration Today," *New York Herald Tribune*, March 3, 1940.
[20] "Mural by Milwaukee Artist is Installed in Post Office Here," *Chilton* (Wis.) *Times-Journal*, August 8, 1940.
[21] The mural was removed from the post office and restored in 1977, joining a University of Minnesota touring exhibition. It is now a part of the Cottonwood County Historical Museum, Windom, Minnesota. It is reminiscent of Grant Wood's agricultural murals (1935-1937) at the Parks Library, Iowa State University. Wood routinely stated, as did Thwaites, that all his paintings began with an abstract design to which he added naturalistic details.
[22] Handwritten notes, CWT Estate Archives.
[23] The image is reversed because Thwaites painted it and himself looking into a mirror; he depicted the painting correctly in *Antoinette in the Studio*.
[24] "Institute Show Stirs Art Row," unknown source, April 13, 1941.
[25] "Prizes Won by State Painters and Sculptors," *The Milwaukee Sentinel*, April 3, 1941.
[26] Handwritten notes, CWT Estate Archives.
[27] Michel Anthonioz (translated by I. Mark Paris), *Verve: The Ultimate Review of Art and Literature (1937-1960)*, H.N Abrams, 1988.
[28] Handwritten notes, CWT Estate Archives.
[29] Ibid.
[30] Thwaites attempted to patent the boat in 1945 but found the process too frustrating to complete.
[31] "Five Showings Open Monday at Art Institute," *The Milwaukee Journal*, November 30, 1947.
[32] *The Milwaukee Journal*, December 16, 1945.
[33] "To Historians' Hall of Fame," *The Milwaukee Journal*, September 1, 1949.
[34] Frances Stover, "Carl Zeidler Portrait on Display in Arena," *The Milwaukee Journal*, April 9, 1950.
[35] Correspondence from October 1939 and January 1940 in the CWT Estate Archive indicates that Thwaites had sent paintings to the C.W. Kraushaar Art Galleries, 730 Fifth St, New York, NY, but it is unclear if he was represented there.
[36] In the Spring 1938 *Verve*, Paul Valery wrote an essay on the nude, describing how the entire attitude toward nudity changed when Adam and Eve were expelled from the garden. In the Fall 1938 issue, an image of Adam and Eve was reproduced from the Les Heures de Rohan.
[37] "Charles W. Thwaites, November 13-December 1, 1944," Contemporary Arts brochure, CWT Estate Archives. A handwritten note in the CWT Estate Archives suggests that Thwaites authored the copy, which was put into the third person by the gallery.

[38] *The Art Digest*, November 15, 1944.
[39] "Five Showings Open Monday at Art Institute," *The Milwaukee Journal*, Sunday, November 30, 1947.
[40] Olof Dahlstrand notes that Thwaites was politically conservative and a staunch anti-communist throughout his life. According to family legend, Thwaites added the red line to this abstraction as a commentary on leftist leaning art juries, which he distrusted.
[41] Karl Zerbe was one of the honored artists in the 1946 AIC Watercolors and Drawings exhibition, which also included "allied mediums." Thwaites was included in the exhibition as well.

Part II, New Mexico

[42] Vogel opened his own space, Valley House Gallery, later in 1954.
[43] David L. Witt, *Taos Moderns—Art of the New*, Santa Fe, NM, Red Crane Books, 1992.
[44] *Amarillo News Globe*, September 1954.
[45] John Skolle, "Taos Moderns Show Diverse and Vigorous," *El Crepusculo*, October 8, 1959.
[46] Artists in the exhibition were Emil Bisttram, Helen Blumenschein, Dorothy Brett, Howard Cook, Ted Egri, Joseph Fleck, John de Puy, Gene Kloss, Michael Klein, Mario Larrinaga, Barbara Latham, Beatrice Mandelman, Louis Ribak, Andrew Rogoway, Joseph Stewart and Thwaites.
[47] Dave Weber, "About the Arts," *The New Mexican*, September 22, 1957.
[48] Dave Weber, "About the Arts," *The New Mexican*, October 20, 1957.
[49] A similar painting done in encaustic won Honorable Mention in the 1956 Annual Exhibition of New Mexico Artists at the Museum of Fine Arts, Santa Fe.
[50] Stables Gallery News, *El Crepusculo*, August 11, 1955. The portrait was purchased by the vice president of the Dallas Republic National Bank.
[51] "La Fonda Gallery Hangs New Exhibit," *El Crepusculo*, April 12, 1956.
[52] Letter from Christino Mirabal to Mr. & Mrs. Charles Thwaites, November 21, 1959, CWT Estate Archives.
[53] Witt, ibid.
[54] Ibid.
[55] Bob Lemme, "TAA Two-Man Show," *The New Mexican*, October 18, 1959.
[56] John Skolle, "Ray and Thwaites Show—Concise, Abstract Realism," *El Crepusculo*, October 1, 1959.
[57] "Taos Moderns Annual to Hang in Santa Fe," source unknown, September 10, 1959.
[58] The seven states were Arizona, Southern California, Colorado, Kansas, New Mexico, Oklahoma, and Texas.
[59] Southwestern Artists Biennial Exhibition catalogue, 1959, Museum of New Mexico Art Gallery, Santa Fe.
[60] Ronald Latimer, "About the Arts," *The New Mexican*, October 9, 1960.
[61] In his 2007 book *Art of New Mexico: How the West is One* (Museum of New Mexico Press), Joseph Traugott asserts that there were two schools of abstraction in New Mexico during the 1960s. The first was more intuitive and poetic, rejecting science, while the second was more structuralist, "focused on geometric shapes and dependent upon the rationality of science and gridded understructures to guide the internal organization." Thwaites falls into the second camp, which Traugott further describes as a "perfect foil for the lingering angst of World War II, as well as the political conflicts of the Cold War."
[62] Letter from Richard D. Weigle to Mr. & Mrs. Charles W. Thwaites, June 6, 1969, CWT Estate Archives.
[63] Letter from Thwaites to Richard Weigle, October 9, 1973, and handwritten note, CWT Estate Archives.
[64] "Charles Thwaites Brush Reflects Candid Manner," *The Milwaukee Journal*, December 23, 1951.
[65] Clive Bell, *Art*, Ballantyne Press, 1923, p. 215. Dore Ashton, *Picasso on Art*, Viking Press, 1972, quote from 1946 on comparing fresco to easel painting, p. 94. Thwaites quote from 1941, see footnote 24.
[66] Jay Hambridge, *Dynamic Symmetry: The Greek Vase*, Yale University Press, 1920.
[67] Van Deren Coke, editor, *Raymond Jonson—A Retrospective Exhibition, University Art Gallery, UNM*, introduction by Ed Garman, UNM Press, 1964.
[68] Dore Ashton, *Picasso on Art*, Viking Press, 1972, pp. 95-96.
[69] Handwritten notes, CWT Estate Archives.
[70] Ibid.

PORTRAIT SUBJECTS

Throughout the 1940s and 1950s, Thwaites was regarded as one of Wisconsin's leading portraitists. His commissions included industrialists, civic leaders, and numerous portraits of retiring professors and deans at the University of Wisconsin, Madison.

While living in Taos, New Mexico, Thwaites made a brief detour to Dallas, Texas, in 1954, where he set up a portrait studio in conjunction with Betty McLean Gallery. It did not live up to expectations, and he returned to Taos, where in the mid-1950s, he did a series of portraits of Taos Pueblo luminaries, apparently as a personal project. Several of the Taos Indian portraits in the estate are not identified by name, although the likenesses are very distinctive. Before he died, Thwaites named some of these sitters, including their accomplishments.

Thwaites taught portraiture in Wisconsin, lectured on the subject, and in the school year of 1958 and 1959, taught it at the Taos Institute of Creative Orientation. In 1969, in Santa Fe, he painted the last of his known portrait commissions of St. John's College president Richard Weigle (1912-1980).

Not included in this listing are portraits of his father and mother, several unidentified sitters, and at least a dozen paintings in which Antoinette modeled. Many of the paintings in which Antoinette posed were not intended as portraits per se and were given identities such as *Rosie* and *Daisy*.

Thwaites also did more than twenty-five self-portraits throughout his lifetime. In many cases they are only partially finished or were done as exercises, sometimes multiples on the same board. Even though he ages in the series, the self-portraits seem to capture more of a persona than a likeness. As in his Notes to Myself, they were undoubtedly a dialogue with his mental and physical frame of reference at the time.

The following list of subjects is in alphabetical order by category, including the date, if known. Those portraits known to have been done after the subject's death are indicated as posthumous.

Government, Civic, Military and Judicial

Abramski, Cyrila (1944), perhaps an American Field Service Volunteer.
Fitch, John Grant (1953, posthumous), army paratrooper killed in World War 11, commissioned by his family (and the widow of Thwaites' uncle) for the Milwaukee Boys Club.
Geiger, F.A. (1943, posthumous), Milwaukee federal judge.
Gregory, John (1946, posthumous), Wisconsin circuit court judge.
Heil, Julius (circa 1944), governor of Wisconsin from 1939 to 1943, and founder of Heil Company.
Mitchell, Mrs. Alexander (1946, posthumous), founder and first president of Women's Club of Wisconsin.
Pfau, George (1946), World War II American Field Service volunteer.
Rogers, Charles B. (1951), former Jefferson County judge.
Ross, Will (1950), chairman of the Board of Trustees, County War Memorial.
Schafer, Joseph (1951, posthumous), University of Wisconsin alumnus and superintendent of the State Historical Society of Wisconsin, 1920 to 1941.
Stevens, E. Ray (1950, posthumous), justice, Wisconsin Supreme Court, 1926 to 1930, Supreme Court Chambers, East Wing, State Capitol.
Wenz, Jean (1944), maybe an American Field Service Volunteer.
Whitnall, Charles B. (1948), founder of the Milwaukee County park system, Milwaukee County Memorial Center.
Zeidler, Carl (1950, posthumous), mayor of Milwaukee, Navy enlistee killed in action in 1942, Milwaukee County Memorial Center.

Higher Education

Banzhaf, Henry L, dean emeritus of Dental School and university business manager, Marquette University, Milwaukee.
Daniels, Farrington (circa 1959), emeritus professor and chairman of the Chemistry Department, University of Wisconsin, Madison.
Dykstra, C.A. (1943), eleventh president of the University of Wisconsin, Madison.
Hart, Fred B. (1945), professor in Biochemistry Department, University of Wisconsin, Madison.
Jackson, Reginald Henry, surgical preceptor and professor of surgery, University of Wisconsin, Madison.
Matthews, Joseph H. (1952), chairman of the Chemistry Department, University of Wisconsin, Madison.
Rasche, William R (1951), director of the Milwaukee Vocational School, WI.
Sanford, Albert H. (1950), professor of history, University of Wisconsin, La Crosse, Wisconsin State Historical Society.

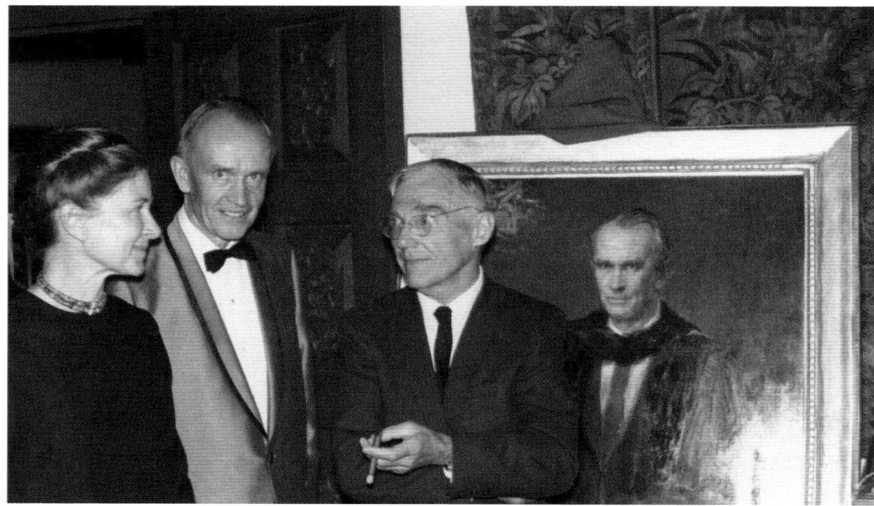

Antoinette and Charles at a reception for Richard Weigle (center) and Thwaites' portrait of the president of St. John's College.

Sellery, George Clarke (1943), retired dean of the College of Letters and Science, University of Wisconsin, Madison, and the unofficial *The Professor*.

Turner, Frederick Jackson (1949, posthumous), alumnus and professor of history, University of Wisconsin, Panamerican Institute, University of Mexico, Mexico City.

Twombly, John H. (1951, posthumous), fourth president of the University of Wisconsin, 1871-1874, Madison.

Weigle, Richard (1969), president of St. John's College, Annapolis, MD, and Santa Fe, NM.

White, William Monroe (1943), president of the Milwaukee Art Institute, WI.

Withey, Morton O. (circa 1953), dean of the College of Engineering, University of Wisconsin, Madison, 1946 to 1953.

Whittaker, Professor (1949), unknown.

Industry, Medicine, Etc.

Bills, Henry, Sr., president of Independent Breweries Company, St. Louis, MO.

Bragarnick, Harry (circa 1940s, posthumous), dry goods retailer and freelance arbitrator.

James, Alfred, president of Northwestern National Insurance Company.

Johnson, Joseph (1945), president and founder of Snap-on Wrench Company, Kenosha, WI.

Kirklin, Byrl Raymond (1954), retiring head of the Radiology Department, Mayo Clinic, Rochester, MN.

McCauley, Mrs. Kennan, Milwaukee, WI.

Pabst, Frederick (1944), chairman of the board, Pabst Brewing Co., Milwaukee, WI.

Reiss, Mrs. William, wife of owner of the Reiss Steamship Co., Sheboygan, WI.

Taos Pueblo

Black Eye (1957), "A member of the Chiffoneti (Clown Society) and a Peyote Boy."

Chalee, Bien (Blue Mountain), "Named after the Sacred Blue Mountain of the Pueblo."

Concha, John (1956), "The spiritual leader of the Pueblo. A former governor and member of the council."

Gomez, Little Joe (1956), "A fine dancer and grandfather who has trained his little grandchildren in the traditional dances of the Pueblo."

Lujan, Ben Couse, Blue Mountain (1955), "A member of the governing council and twice governor of the pueblo. A very influential man. He is also one of the best singers."

Marcus, Ben (1956), "Nationally known as one of the finest dancers in the Southwest. Wins top prizes at the famous Gallup Ceremonial every year."

Suazo, Pete (1955), "A very reserved and conservative Taos Indian. His headdress is one of the typical styles into which their cotton flannel blankets are fashioned in summer. It is used as a protection against the sun."

Zamora, Frank D. (1955), "A member of the Black Eyes, a Chiffoneti (Clown Society) and a member of the Peyote Cult."

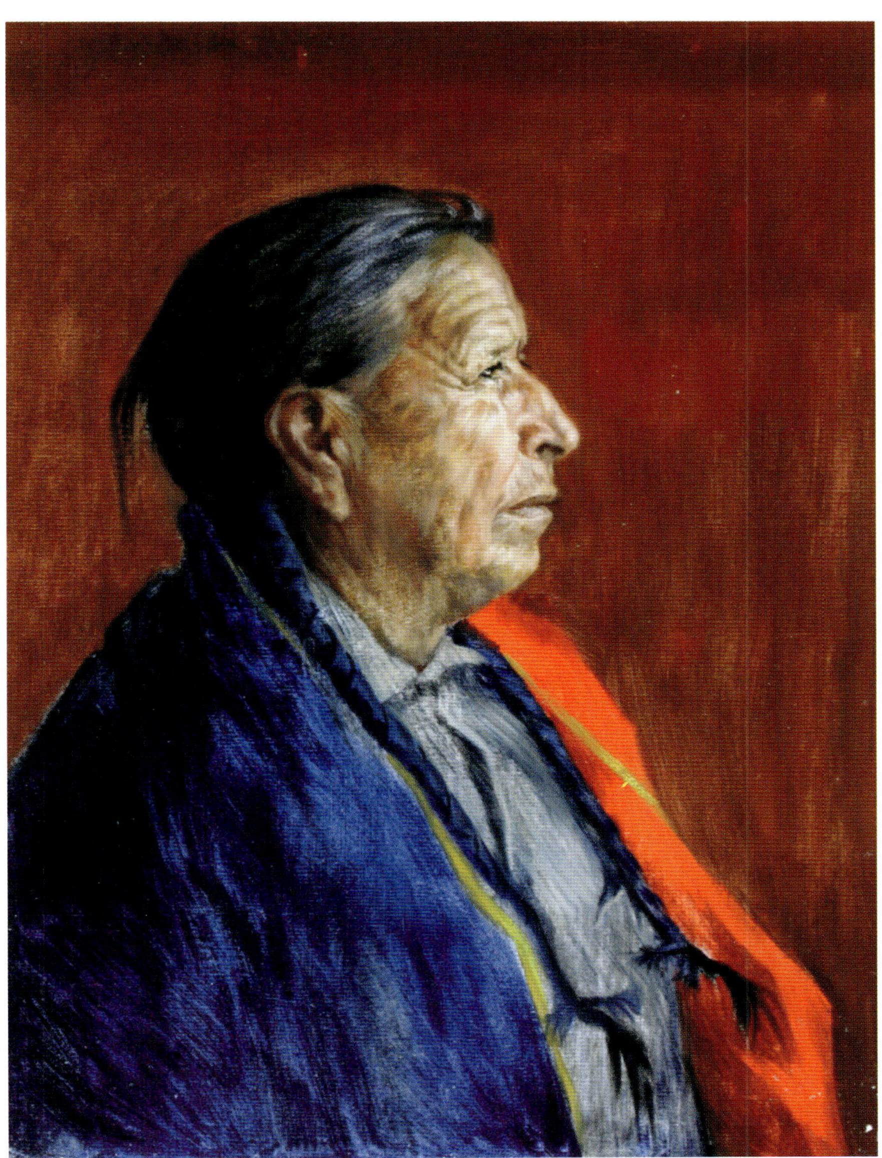

TAOS INDIAN, 1957
oil on masonite
24 x 18
private collection
James Zimmerman Photography

CHRONOLOGY

1904
Charles Winstanley Thwaits born March 4 to Charles H. Thwaits and Nelly Luedecke Thwaits, Milwaukee, WI. Youngest of four boys and one sister. Father manages real-estate investments, as well as working as a bricklayer and building contractor.

1910s-early 1920s
Grows up in an urban environment with summers spent on Cedar Lake northwest of Milwaukee.
Works for his father maintaining rental properties in Milwaukee.
Graduates from Riverside High School, Milwaukee.

1924-1925
Studies engineering at the University of Wisconsin, Madison.
Stumbles on a portrait painting demonstration, purchases materials and does his first self-portrait, taking art classes alongside core subjects.

1926-1929
Switches to art studies at Layton School of Art, Milwaukee.

1927
Applies for his student pilot's license.

1928
Takes painting excursions along the Mississippi River.
Serves briefly as director of the Dubuque Little Institute, IA, including teaching at the Dubuque Art Association.

1930
Teaches at the Layton School of Art.
Begins exhibiting annually in Art Institute of Chicago, IL, juried exhibitions.

1931
Changes spelling of his name from Thwaits to Thwaites.

1933
Joins Wisconsin Painters and Sculptors and shows annually with the group through 1948, winning numerous awards.
Begins dating Antoinette Gruppe (1908-1991), a Milwaukee artist who also studied at the Layton School of Art.

1934
Hired to do easel paintings for the Public Works of Art Project.

1935
Elopes with Antoinette Gruppe. Her family disapproves and her brother kidnaps her, returning her to the family. A week later, Charles steals her back.
Lives briefly in New York, NY, to learn the framing business.
Rents an apartment at 2909 W. Greenfield Avenue, Milwaukee, with a studio at 924 N. Plankinton Avenue, where the couple lives throughout the time in Milwaukee.

1936
Begins exhibiting annually in national exhibitions on the Eastern Seaboard, including Pennsylvania, Virginia, New York, and Washington, DC.

1936-1939
Hired to do easel paintings and supervise Works Progress Administration Federal Art Project.

1937
Juries Wisconsin Painters and Sculptors annual exhibition with John Steuart Curry and Dewey Albinson.

1938
Antoinette is hospitalized for a fistula operation at Worral Hospital (Mayo Clinic) Rochester, MN, staying nearly a month for treatments.

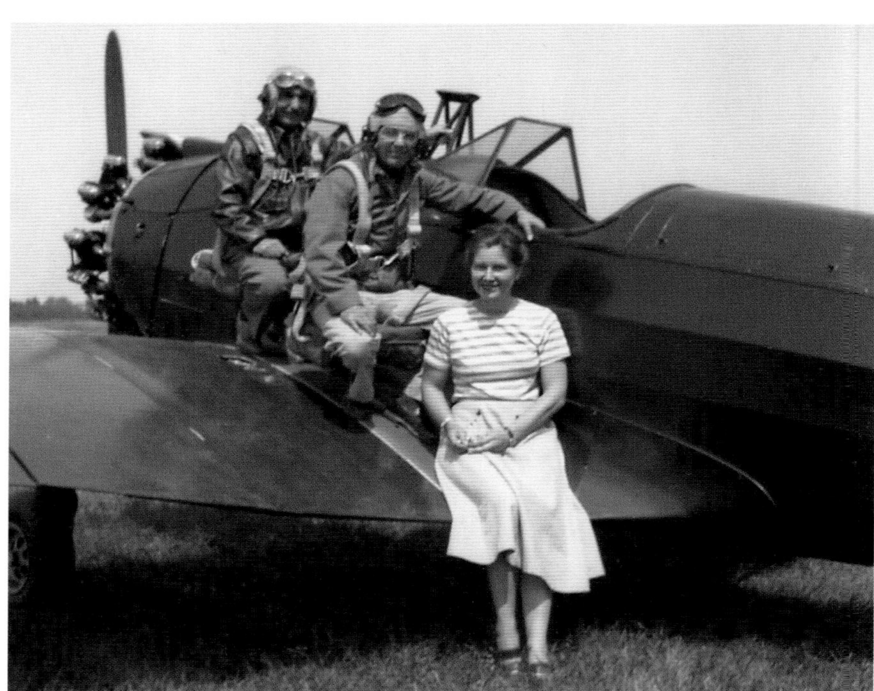

Antoinette and Charles (in the middle) during a flight training session in the late 1930s.

1939
Invited to exhibit at the New York World's Fair, NY.
Wins competition to paint Chilton, WI, post-office murals for the U.S. Treasury Department, Section of Fine Arts. Leads to three additional mural commissions.

1940
Installs *Harvest (Threshing Barley)*, mural in the Chilton, WI, Post Office.
Installs *Lumbering*, mural in the Greenville, MI, Post Office.

1940
Teaches portraiture and design, University of Wisconsin Extension Classes, Milwaukee Art Institute.

1941
Installs mural *Cheese Making* at the Plymouth, WI, Post Office.
Invited to participate in the American Paintings and Sculpture Exhibition, Art Institute of Chicago (AIC), IL.
Designs and builds a collapsible "fold boat" that can be strapped to side of the car during travels to lakes and area waterways.

1941-1942
Spends winter with Antoinette in Tucson, Arizona.

1942
Invited to participate in the AIC Memorial Exhibition for Grant Wood.

1943
Installs mural at the Windom, MN, Post Office.
Paints commissioned portraits of George Clarke Sellery, F.A. Geiger, C.A. Dykstra, and William Monroe White, beginning a significant career as a portraitist that lasts through the 1950s.

1944
Paints commissioned portraits of Julius Heil, Fred Pabst, and Henry L. Banzhaf, and does published pencil portraits of Cyrila Abramski and Jean Wenz, possibly Field Service Volunteers.

1945
Paints commissioned portraits of Fred B. Hart and Joseph Johnson.

1946
Paints commissioned portraits of John Gregory, George Pfau, and Mrs. Alexander Mitchell.

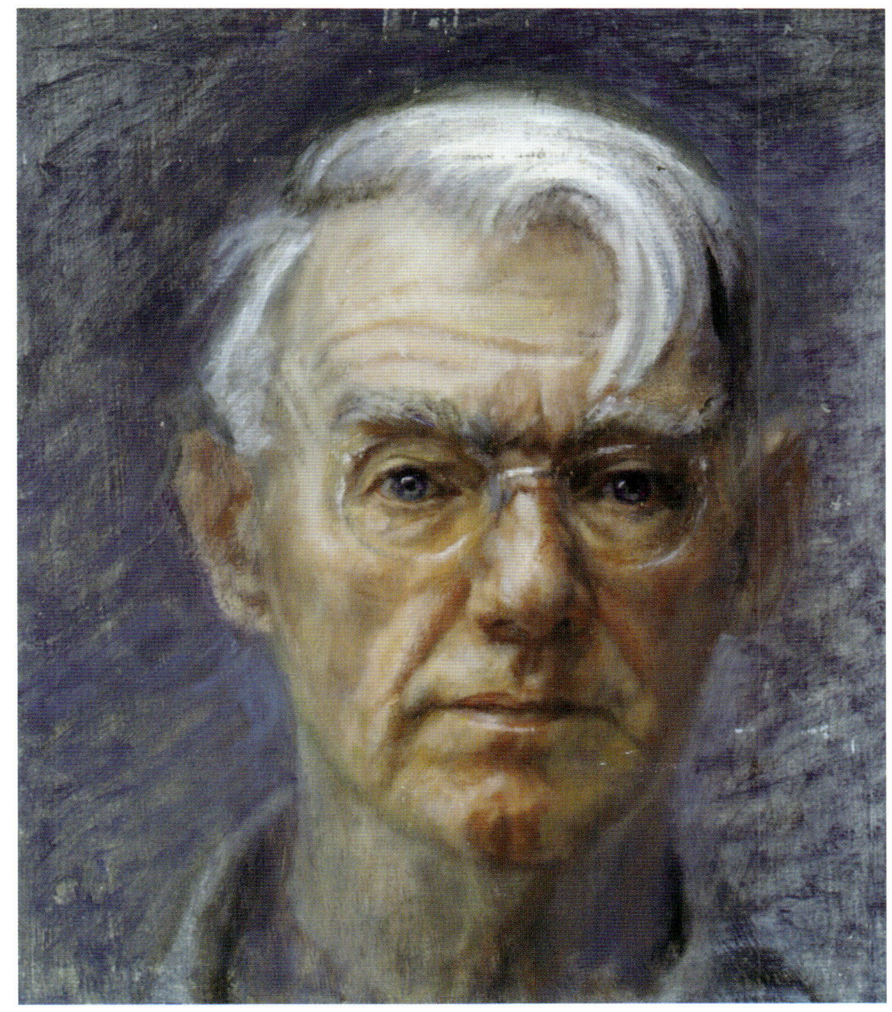

SELF-PORTRAIT (WITH GRAY HAIR), 1975
oil on masonite
12 x 10
private collection
James Zimmerman Photography

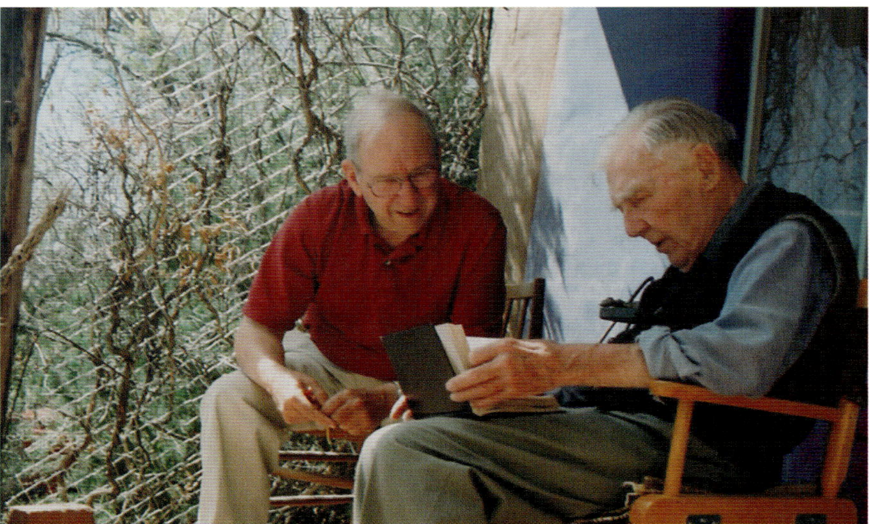

Olof Dahlstrand (left) with Thwaites in 1996 on the porch of his Santa Fe home.

1947-1950

Teaches classes in portraiture and figure painting at the Milwaukee Art Institute, and design classes at the University of Wisconsin Extension

1948

Paints commissioned portrait of Charles B. Whitnall.

1949

Commissioned by American Historical Association, U.S. State Department, to paint the portrait of Frederick Jackson Turner, gifted to Panamerican Institute of Geography and History, University of Mexico.

Paints commissioned portrait of Professor Whittaker.

Judges Wisconsin Painters and Sculptor's impromptu watercolor show with Schomer Lichtner.

1950

Thwaiteses travel throughout the Southwest, tent camping, including a visit to New Mexico.

Begins painting in encaustics.

Paints commissioned portraits of Will Ross, E. Ray Stevens, Carl Zeidler, and Albert H. Sanford.

Judges the Third Annual Ozaukee County Rural Art Show, Mequon, WI, with Helmut Summ.

Speaks on modern art to the Madison branch of the American Association of University Women.

1951

Paints commissioned portraits of John H. Twombly, Joseph Schafer, William Rasche, and Charles B. Rogers.

Judges Wisconsin Painters and Sculptors show with Robert Von Neumann, Lester O. Schwartz, Aaron Bohrod and Rudolph Jegart.

Participates in University of Wisconsin Art Department "Art in the Home" television program, demonstrating how to design a painting and analyzing one of his paintings.

Lectures at the Seven Arts Society, Milwaukee, WI.

Thwaites' father dies in September and his mother in December, freeing him to spend more time in the Southwest.

1952

Takes a two-year lease on the Pink House, formerly in the compound of Mabel Dodge and Tony Luhan.

Antoinette writes about the Taos experience for *The Milwaukee Journal*, Sunday, August 24 (see Appendix A).

Paints commissioned portrait of Joseph H. Mathews.

1953

Spends spring in Arizona, summer and fall in Taos, and winter in Rochester, MN, painting commissioned portrait of Byrl Raymond Kirklin.

Paints commissioned portraits of John Grant Fitch and Morton O. Withey.

1954

Moves to Dallas, TX, and opens a studio at 5722 Forest Park Road, to paint portraits represented by Betty McLean Gallery, Dallas.

Rents the Tony House in the Luhan compound.

Joins Taos Art Association and exhibits at the Stables Gallery and Harwood Gallery.

1955

Starts a series of portraits of Taos Pueblo Indians, through late 1950s.

Begins exhibiting regularly in Museum of Fine Arts, Santa Fe, open and juried exhibitions in which he wins several awards.

Corresponds with Beatrice Van Bergh of New York, who owns Ghost Ranch, which she offers the Thwaiteses for $15,000. They are unable to muster the funds. (See Appendix A.)

1956

Joins La Fonda Gallery, Taos, NM.

Selected by Ted Egri to be included in the Taos Moderns exhibition at the Jonson Gallery, University of New Mexico, Albuquerque.

1957

Exhibits in the Taos Moderns and Taos Invitational at the Museum of Fine Arts, Santa Fe, through 1962.

Addresses Los Alamos Art Association on the topic of portraiture.

Selects fifteen Taos artists for an exhibition at F.H. Bresler Gallery, Milwaukee, WI.

Participates in the Taos Art Association's Taos Art Week studio demonstrations.

1958-1959

Teaches classes in portraiture at the Taos Institute of Creative Orientation.

Gets involved with the Taos bypass controversy, supporting the Pueblo in its refusal to allow passage through their lands.

1959

With Antoinette hosts a tour of Taos for scientists from the Ministry for Atomic Affairs of West Germany and Los Alamos AEC.

Exhibits at the Blue Door, Taos, NM.

Serves on the selection committee for the fourth annual Taos Moderns exhibition, Museum of Fine Arts, Santa Fe.

Paints commissioned portrait of Farrington Daniels.

1960

Thwaiteses spend March in Mexico.

Exhibits at Galeria Escondida, Taos.

Begins painting in acrylics.

1962

Moves to Santa Fe, renting a casita on the property of Sallie R. Wagner.

1967

Following the receipt of an inheritance, Charles and Antoinette take the first of two trips to Europe, concentrating on France and Spain.

1967-1969

Exhibits at the Canyon Road Gallery, Santa Fe.

1969

Paints commissioned portrait of Richard D. Weigle.

1971

Purchases property with a run-down adobe home on the Hakone estate of architect Nathaniel Owings, in Pojoaque, NM. They never live in it.

1973-1974

Appointed artist-in-residence at St. John's College, Santa Fe, NM.

1981

Antoinette hospitalized in October for a second stroke. She lives in various nursing facilities in Albuquerque and Santa Fe, the last being La Residencia, Santa Fe. Charles visits her daily.

Paints only sporadically.

1991

Antoinette passes away October 11.

1998

Moves to La Residencia.

2002

Passes away in his sleep November 21.

2003

CWT Art, LLC, is founded by heirs.

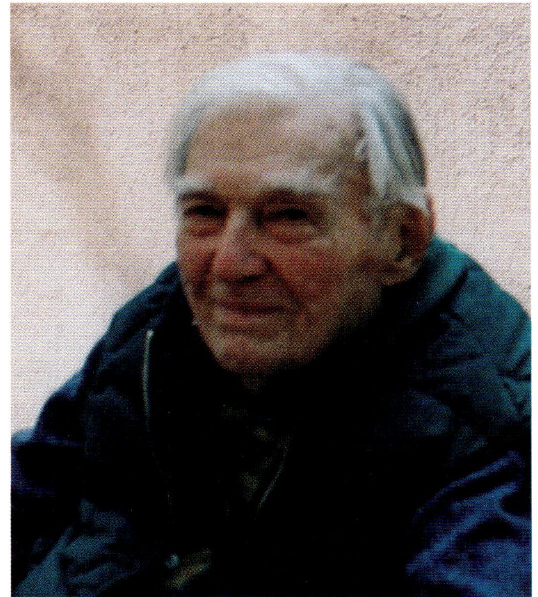

Charles Thwaites in 2000 at La Residencia in Santa Fe.

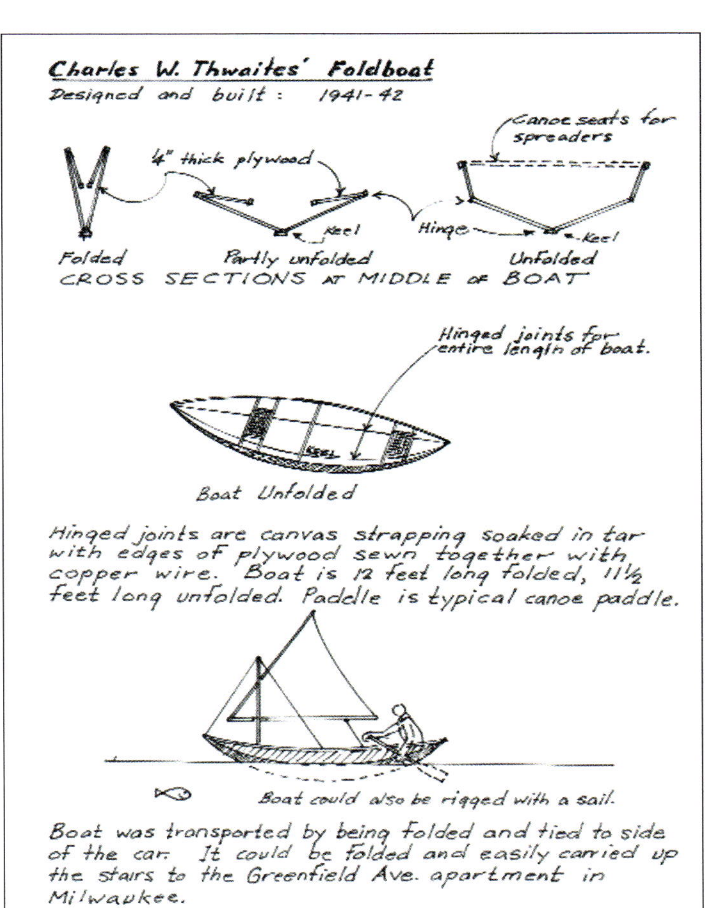

Diagram of Thwaites' "fold boat" by Olof Dahlstrand.

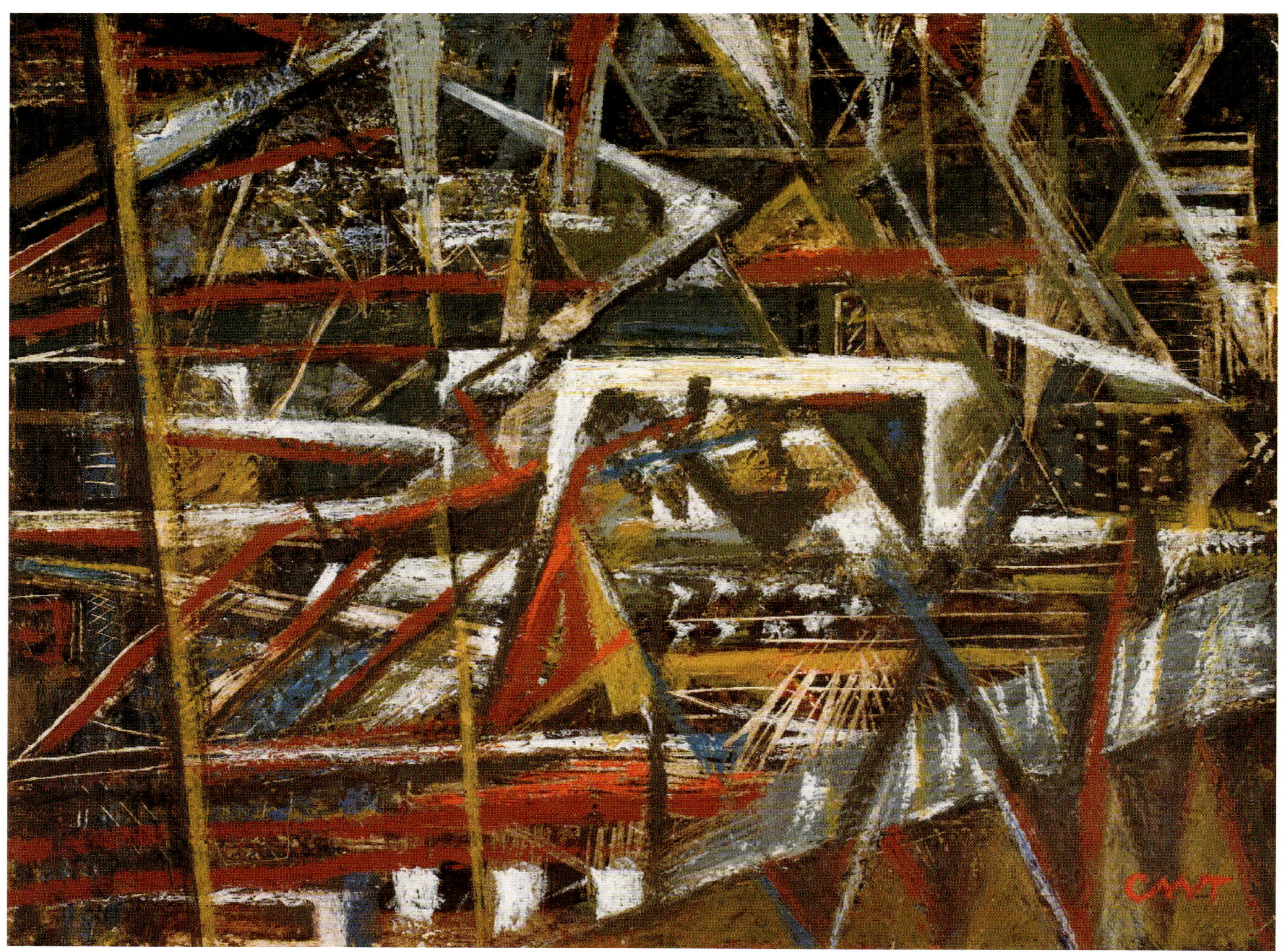

ABSTRACTION, 1955
encaustic on paper
17½ x 23
illustrated in the catalogue and recommended for museum purchase at the 1955 Exhibition for New Mexico Artists, Museum of Fine Arts, Santa Fe.

EXHIBITIONS AND AWARDS

SOLO SHOWS

1937, 1939, 1947, Layton Art Gallery, Milwaukee, WI
1944, Contemporary Arts Gallery, New York, NY
1947, Milwaukee Art Institute, WI
1947, College Women's Club, Milwaukee, WI
1948, Mulvane Museum, Topeka, KS
1957, Alcove Show, Museum of Fine Arts, Santa Fe, NM
1965, St. John's University, Santa Fe, NM

TWO-PERSON SHOWS

1934, with Josephine Wupper, Layton Art Gallery, Milwaukee, WI
1957, with Louise Ganthiers, Stables Art Gallery, Taos, NM
1958, with Howard Cook, Stables Gallery, Taos, NM
1959, with Robert D. Ray, Stables Gallery, Taos, NM

INVITATIONALS, JURIED COMPETITIONS & GROUP EXHIBITIONS

Annotated with artworks exhibited, when known.

1930-1932, 1936, 1937, 1940, 1946, 1948, 1949, International Watercolors and Drawings Exhibition, The Art Institute of Chicago, IL. 1931 *Bathers* and *A Queen*. 1932 *Drawing Z*. 1936 *Composition No. 1—Fox Food*. 1940 *Composition II*. 1946 *Orchard*. 1949 *Composition*.

1933, Three-person Show, Layton Art Gallery, Milwaukee, WI (with Forrest Flower and Richard Jansen).

1934, 1936-1938, 1941, 1943, 1946, 1948, 1950-1952, 1954, Artists of Chicago and Vicinity, The Art Institute of Chicago, IL. 1934 *Gissella*. 1937 *Portrait*. 1941 *Horses at Night*. 1942 *Self-Portrait*. 1946 *Portrait*. 1948 *Composition, Cows*. 1949 *Pomegranate*, illustrated in catalogue. 1950 *The Professor*. 1951 *The Red Line*. 1952 *Desert*. 1954 *Sunflowers*.

1933-1948, Wisconsin Painters and Sculptors Exhibition, Milwaukee Art Institute, WI. 1933 *Yellow House*. 1936 *Summer Evening*. 1943 *Rosie*. 1944 *Portrait (Antoinette)*. 1949 *Nuns* and *Chestnut Tree*.

1936, 1938, Annual Watercolor Exhibition, Pennsylvania Academy of Fine Arts, Philadelphia. 1936 *Fox Food*. 1938 *Cow at Night*.

1936-1938, National Exhibition of American Art, Rockefeller Center, International Building, New York, NY. 1936 *Portrait*. 1937 *Girl in Red*. 1938 *Corn*.

1936-1938, 1945, Wisconsin Salon of Art, Madison. 1938 *Corn* and *Bouquet*. 1945 *Straw Flowers*.

1937-1939, Midwestern Selections from the National Exhibition of American Art Exhibition, Rockefeller Center, shown at the University of Minnesota, Minneapolis. 1937 *Girl in Red*. 1938 *Century Plant*. 1939 *Corn* and *Horses* (traveled to ten venues).

1937, four-person Show, Layton Art Gallery, Milwaukee, WI (with Antoinette Gruppe Thwaites, Margo Miller Flower and Forrest Flower)

1937, group show of Artist Couples, including Antoinette Gruppe Thwaites, College Women's Club, Milwaukee, WI.

1937, 1940-1942, 1945, Annual American Paintings and Sculpture Exhibition, Art Institute of Chicago, IL. 1937 *Corn at Night*. 1940 *Portrait of Antoinette*. 1941 *Portrait with Fan*. 1942 *Self-Portrait*. 1945 *Dad*.

1938-1939, Great Lakes Exhibition, organized by the Albright Art Gallery, Buffalo, traveled to seven venues. *Corn at Night*.

1939, New York World's Fair, NY. *Horses*.

1939, 1941, 1947, Biennial Exhibition of Contemporary American Oil Paintings, Corcoran Gallery of Art, Washington, DC. 1939 *Portrait*, illustrated in catalogue. 1941 *Portrait with Fan*, illustrated in catalogue. 1947 *Summer Nude*.

1939, Forty-eight States Mural Competition, Corcoran Gallery of Art, Washington, DC, traveling exhibition to Whitney Museum of American Art, New York, NY; Cleveland Museum of Art, OH; Layton Art Gallery, Milwaukee, WI.

1939, 1940, 1946, 1947, American Federation of the Arts, New York, NY, traveling exhibitions.

1940, Contemporary Painting in the United States, selected from the Department of Fine Arts, Golden Gate International Exposition, San Francisco, CA, National Gallery, Ottawa, Ontario, Canada. Mural Design.

1940, Rural Wisconsin, Wisconsin State Fair, Milwaukee.

1940, Leading American Watercolorists, curated by Olin Dows, American Federation of the Arts, Washington, DC, traveled to twelve cities.

1940, The Group of 40, selected by Forbes Watson to travel from the 1939 Corcoran Biennial under American Federation for the arts, 18 venues. *Portrait of Antoinette*.

1941, Milwaukee Artists (exchange exhibition), Worcester Art Museum, MA *Self-Portrait*

1941, Two Hundred American Watercolors Competition, National Gallery of Art, Washington DC. *Shocking the Wheat* and *Horses*.

1941, U.S. Marine Hospital Watercolor Competition, Federal Works Agency, Washington, DC. *Landscape* and *Bulls*, *Shocking Wheat* and *Horses*

1941, Directions in American Painting, Carnegie Institute of Fine Arts Annual, Pittsburgh, PA. *Self-Portrait*.

1942, Artists for Victory, Metropolitan Museum, New York, NY. *Pomegranates and Plums*.

1942, Art in War, Art Institute of Chicago, IL, traveled to Layton Art Gallery, Milwaukee, and the Wustum Museum of Fine Arts, Racine , WI. *Steel*.

1942, WPA Mural Designs (not chosen), Milwaukee Institute of Art, WI. *Hickory Rind* (lithograph).

1942, Portraits by Wisconsin Artists, Layton Art Gallery, Milwaukee, *Portrait with Fan* and *Portrait of Antoinette*.

1943, Renaissance Society, University of Chicago, IL

1944, Willmanns Memorial Purchase Exhibit, Milwaukee Art Institute, WI. *Spring Portrait (Whanne That Aprille).*

1945, Pennsylvania Academy of Fine Arts, Philadelphia. *Corn at Night.*

1945, Painting in the United States, Carnegie Institute of Fine Arts Annual, Pittsburgh, PA. *Pomegranates and Navajo Blanket.*

1946, Third Annual Pepsi-Cola Company's Paintings of the Year, National Academy of Design, New York, NY. *Antoinette.*

1946, Contemporary American Paintings Biennial Exhibition, Virginia Museum of Fine Arts, Richmond. *The Professor.*

1946, Kearney Memorial Regional Exhibit, Milwaukee Art Institute, WI. *Portrait.*

1946, First Spring Annual, California Palace of the Legion of Honor, San Francisco, CA. *Self-Portrait*, illustrated in catalogue, and *Composition—Bathers.*

1946, group exhibition, University of Wisconsin, Madison

1947, 1949, 1951, Biennial Exhibition of Paintings and Prints, Walker Art Center, Minneapolis, MN. 1947 *Cows and Sumac* and *Nuns and Street Walker.* 1949 *Pomegranates and Pods.* 1951 *Desert.*

1948-1951, Gimbel Wisconsin Centennial Art Collection Exhibitions, Milwaukee, WI. 1948 *Foundry* and *Corn* (illustrated in catalogue). 1950 *Steel.* 1951 *Flight.*

1948, Wisconsin State Centennial Exhibition of Contemporary Wisconsin Art, Milwaukee Art Institute and Layton Art Gallery, Milwaukee. *Orchard* and *The Professor.*

1948, Selections from the Permanent Collection, Milwaukee Art Institute, WI. *Portrait of Dr. William Monroe White.*

1950, Portrait Exhibition, Layton Art Gallery, Milwaukee, WI. *Dr. Henry L. Banzhaf* and *Antoinette*

1951, Portraits Remembering Mother, Heinemann's Restaurant, Milwaukee, WI. Four paintings of Antoinette.

1953-1957, group exhibitions, Harwood Gallery, Taos, NM. 1953 *Geranium.* 1954 *Abstraction.* 1955 *Winter Orchard.*

1954, group exhibition, Betty McLean Gallery, Dallas, TX

1954, 1961, group exhibition, Dord Fitz Gallery, Amarillo, TX

1955, 1956, Annual Exhibition for New Mexico Artists, Museum of Fine Arts, Santa Fe. 1955 *Abstraction*, illustrated in catalogue, and *Winter Orchard.* 1956 *Abstraction—Loon* and *Pods.*

1956, Taos Moderns, Jonson Gallery, University of New Mexico, Albuquerque. *Abstraction.*

1956, Sixth Annual Mid-America Arts Alliance Exhibition, Nelson-Atkins Museum, Kansas City, MO. *The Red Line.*

1956, group exhibition, La Fonda Gallery, Taos, NM

1957, 1959, 1965, 1967-1969, Fiesta Exhibition, Museum of Fine Arts, Santa Fe, NM. 1957 *The Back Road.* 1959 *Deer and Buffalo Dance.* 1965 *Abstractions* and *Strawberry Corn Motif.* 1969 *Taro.*

1957, 1959, 1962, 1964, 1966, 1970, Southwestern Artists Biennial & Traveling Show, Museum of Fine Arts, Santa Fe, NM. 1959 *Abstraction.* 1962 *Obsession.* 1964 *Silver Puffs.* 1966 *Patterns in Black and White.*

1957-1960, Taos Moderns Exhibition, Museum of Fine Arts, Santa Fe, NM. 1959 *Sunflower Motif.* 1960 *Angular Patterns* and *Pomegranate Motif.*

1957, First Annual Exhibition, New Mexico Highlands University, Las Vegas. *Abstraction.*

1958, First Taos Collectors Exhibit, Stables Gallery, Taos. *Taos Bug.*

1958, 12th Exhibition of Prints and Drawings, Museum of Fine Arts, Santa Fe, NM. *Horses* and *Deer Spirits*, illustrated in catalogue.

1958, 1960, 1963, Biennial Exhibition for New Mexico Artists, Museum of Fine Arts, Santa Fe. 1958 *Composition—Horses in Snow* and *Reticulated Patterns.* 1960 *No. 49.* 1963 *Abstraction* and *Linear Patterns.*

1959, 17th annual Biennial Artists West of the Mississippi River, Colorado Springs Fine Arts Center, CO. *Shard and Stone.*

1959, group exhibition at Realities Gallery (formerly Thayer Gallery), Taos, NM.

1961, 1962, Taos Invitational (replaced Taos Moderns), Museum of Fine Arts, Santa Fe, NM. 1962 *Abstraction.*

1961-1963, group exhibitions at La Galeria Escondida, Taos, NM.

1963, Wisconsin Painters from 1850 until Today, selections from the permanent collection, Milwaukee Art Center, WI.

1965, Small Paintings Traveling Exhibition, Museum of Fine Arts, Santa Fe, NM.

1967-1969, group exhibitions at Canyon Road Art Gallery, Santa Fe, NM.

1968, Invitational, Museum of Fine Arts, Santa Fe, NM.

1969, Second Annual Federation of Rocky Mountain States, Museum of Fine Arts, Santa Fe, NM, traveled to the capitol buildings of eight western states.

1974, Taos Art from the 1940s and 1950s, Stables Gallery, Taos, NM

AWARDS

1933, 1936, 1939, 1941, 1943, 1944, 1949, Wisconsin Painters and Sculptors, Milwaukee Art Institute, Awards. 1936 *Summer Evening*. 1941 two awards *Self-Portrait with Pieta*. 1943 *Rosie*. 1944 *Antoinette in Red Jacket*. 1949 *The Chestnut Tree*.

1938, Wisconsin Salon, Madison, Honorable Mention for *Corn*.

1938, Wisconsin State Fair, First Prize for *Corn*.

1939, Forty-eight State Mural Competition, selection for Chilton, WI, Post Office Mural.

1939, Second Prize, Flag Contest, Wisconsin Colonial Dames, *Steel Mill*.

1940, Rural Wisconsin, Wisconsin State Fair, Milwaukee, three awards.

1944, Wisconsin State Fair for a still-life

1946, Palace of the Legion of Honor, San Francisco, CA, Bronze Medal for *Self-Portrait*.

1948, Wisconsin State Centennial Exhibition Award. *Orchard*.

1948-1951, Gimbel Collection Purchase Awards. 1948 *Foundry*. 1949 *Corn*. 1950 *Steel*. 1951 *Flight*.

1955, Annual Exhibition for New Mexico Artists, Museum of Fine Arts, Santa Fe. *Abstraction* recommended for museum purchase

1956, Museum of New Mexico Annual for New Mexico Artists, Honorable Mention for *Abstraction—Loon*.

1958, Museum of New Mexico, Exhibition of Prints and Drawings, Honorable Mention for *Deer Spirits*.

1963, New Mexico Biennial for New Mexico Artists, Museum of New Mexico, Honorable Mention for *Abstraction*

1965, New Mexico Fiesta Biennial, Museum of New Mexico, Honorable Mention for *Abstractions*.

1969, New Mexico Fiesta Biennial, Museum of New Mexico, Honorable Mention for *Taro*.

1969, Federation of Rocky Mountain States, Honorable Mention for *Patterns in Black and White*.

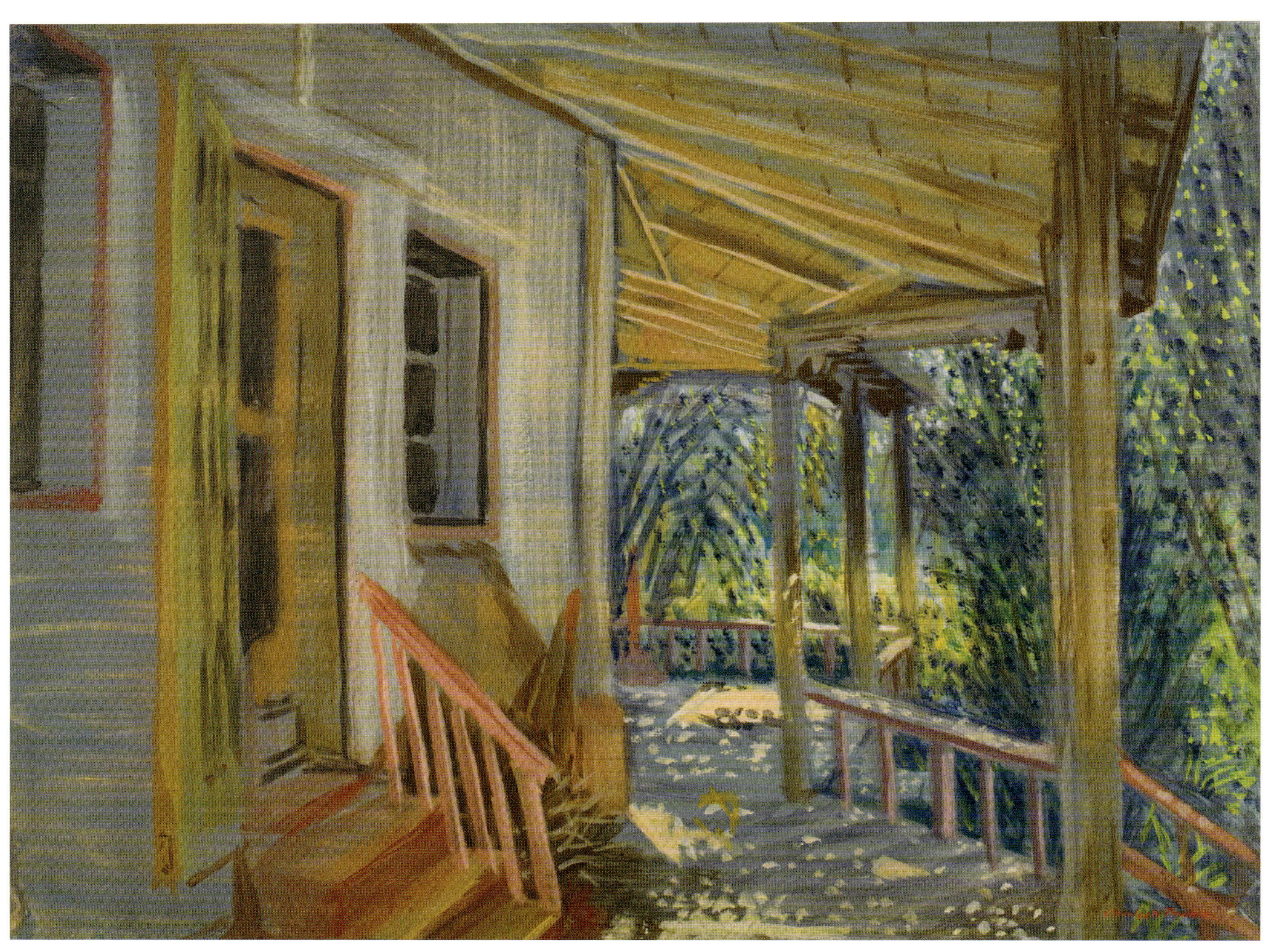

PINK HOUSE PORTAL, 1952
egg tempera on paper
17½ x 23

APPENDIX A: LETTERS

"'Pink House' at Taos is Rented to Local Artists"
The Milwaukee Journal, by Antoinette Thwaites, Sunday, August 1952

Charles Thwaites, Milwaukee, painter of some of the most notable portraits in Wisconsin, and his wife, Antoinette, known for her watercolors, are in New Mexico for the summer, living in the famous "pink house" at Taos, belonging to Mabel Dodge Luhan. In the past, D.H. Lawrence lived there with Frieda. Willa Cather wrote "Death Comes for the Archbishop" while the "pink house" was her home. Georgia O'Keeffe also lived there.

New Mexico is old and familiar painting ground for Charles and Antoinette Thwaites. Each trip finds them more entranced by the southwest. Consider such an experience as this:

They are dinner guests of Mabel Dodge Luhan and her Taos Indian husband, Tony Luhan (lujan) in their retreat from the high altitude at Embudo.

"The house," writes Antoinette, "is on the banks of the Rio Grande at a point where the river is very calm and one can look up its canyon toward distant mountains that are pink and then blue in the sunset."

Flying Saucers
At the dinner, Tony seems grave and sculpturesque, his face framed by two jet black braids. He sits at the head of the table, telling stories of his youth when he delivered the mail between Taos and a remote mountain town, going on foot and using snowshoes in the winter. He tells how he and some of his boyhood friends used to visit Oklahoma, walking the entire distance and giving Indian dances along the way to make expenses.

The talk veers to the beauty of New Mexican skies and then naturally enough someone speaks of "flying saucers."

"We Indians have always known about what you call 'flying saucers,'" says Tony. "We Taos people know that they come from a more powerful tribe—maybe the Hopis or the Navajos. Not so long ago one was seen descending over Taos pueblo."

"What became of it?" asks one of the guests.

Tony smiles. One of those lights, he says, turns into a handsome Indian in ceremonial dress. "The medicine men try to catch him and when they do, he cries for freedom." Tony hesitates a moment and then says, "Sometimes he turns into a coyote."

Doors Too Low
"Mabel Dodge Luhan, 73, leads a quiet life now in contrast to the days of Lawrence, Frieda and Brett," writes Antoinette Thwaites. Mabel has written about her coming to Taos long ago and about the "pink house" in two books, *Lorenzo in Taos* and *Edge of Taos Desert*.

Both Frieda and Brett still live on the edge of Taos and Lawrence's ashes are buried on the little ranch Mabel gave him near San Cristobal, not far from Taos.

"The 'pink house' is situated where the old Taos desert meets the town," writes Antoinette. "The house is adobe with thick walls. The ceilings are of aspen saplings, supported by heavy beams. In the living room a large niche frames the Mexican fireplace, while in turn the niche is framed by hewn beams and corbels from an old Spanish-New Mexican convent. The rambling pink trimmed porch and the outside doors to the house are also parts of the old convent.

"The weathered, hand-carved doors are short to fit the lower doorways which were designed in the style of the very old adobes built when people found it expedient to make it difficult for enemies to enter too easily. People coming in had to bend almost double with the result that a blow on the head was easy to administer. A number of our tall guests have straightened out too quickly, with the result that they have given themselves rather uncomfortable bumps on the head."

Irrigated Gardens
Mrs. Thwaites says that on the little pink door in the bedroom, there is an amusing carving representing Mabel Dodge Luhan and her Taos Indian husband in paradise. The carving was executed by D.H. Lawrence while he lived in the house. Mabel has described this carving in one of her books.

"A few yards to the rear of the house," writes Mrs. Thwaites, "across the main irrigation ditch, begins the desert of sage, pinion and juniper. It stretches to the mountains, miles away. It is also the beginning of the Taos Indian reservation, the pueblo only about two miles from our home.

"From the main irrigation ditch, secondary ditches pattern the land with running water which keeps the gardens and orchards richly green and productive.

"This land of Mabel's is a paradise of tall old cottonwoods, wild plum hedges, fields of corn worked by Indians and every variety of flower. At the moment our house is buried in a mass of giant hollyhocks among which sphinx moths and hummingbirds are having a feast day.

"Taos Indians are farmers and raise handsome horses. They are completely self-supporting except for some medical and school aid. They often pass our house on horseback or in wagons, going to town to do their shopping. The men wear thin cotton blankets over their shirts and trousers and they are ingenious in the ways they drape these cotton blankets. Sometimes the white sheet is worn over the head and shoulders with half the face hidden in an Arab-like fashion. Then again it may be twisted into a turban with only the brow of the head exposed, which gives the Indian the appearance of a Persian on horseback. Another popular style is to wrap it over the hips and tuck it in at the waist.

Full of Artists

"Frequently as an Indian rides by he sings a bit of an old tribal song—beautiful to hear. Since the Taos Indians have no written language, their history, dances, songs are handed down from father to son. The spoken language is extremely musical and pleasant to hear.

"Taos is still the mecca for artists of all descriptions. A number of the old-timers who discovered Taos back in the 1890s, when New Mexico was still a territory, are still painting and reminiscing with visitors.

"There are one man shows opening at the rate of one a week at the numerous galleries. Most of the work is representational, done with an eye to the tourist collector's taste. Some of it is very well done from an illustrative angle.

"Two galleries are devoted to expressionistic and nonrepresentational painting and sculpture, definitely not to the taste of the tourists. We visited with a number of artists in this particular group and have to admire their struggle to exist.

"Most of these artists live here in the summer, building little adobe studios themselves and growing some of their food in irrigated gardens. At Ranchos de Taos four miles from Taos, they have rented an old adobe building to use as their gallery, appropriately called The Ruins Gallery. They have calcimined the walls in interesting colors and put potted plants against the windows, which look over a valley of little Mexican gardens toward the mountains. There, they present their work in little one man shows, usually opening on Sunday afternoons with lemonade.

"In the winter they retreat to Mexico, where in some small town they manage to live for as little as $75 a month per family. It is surprising how non-aggressive they are and how the romantic aspects of the country here and in Mexico appeal them.

"Many of the little Spanish American towns here in New Mexico give the feeling that you are not in America at all. The low rambling adobe buildings with geraniums in every window and ancient wells line the dirt roads.

"Almost always there is the old adobe church with lace curtains in the windows and the early Spanish hand-carved saints dressed by the villagers according to the season and during the cold snugly wrapped in wool. Spanish-Americans love their feast days and the churches are always filled to overflowing, with latecomers kneeling on the steps outside.

"At the moment the sky is overcast and it looks as though the Indians' appeals through the recent corn dance are to be answered with rain for their crops."

Christmas Ceremonies at Taos Pueblo

Draft letter to Dr. Balke, a German scientist who toured Taos with the Thwaiteses, from Charles, Taos, 1961

The holidays this year were graced with sunshine and brilliant blue skies, though quite cold.... We joined in celebrating Christmas Eve at the Pueblo, where our Indian friends light the shepherd's fires, which illuminate their ancient home and the religious procession that winds through the pueblo grounds to the accompaniment of singing, drums and rifle shots. It is brief, but exciting in the dramatic light of the many cedar fires and the great clouds of billowing black smoke. The procession of blanketed Indians carries a beautiful Virgin Mary under a canopy, and this year, the Matachines danced backwards, before the advancing Virgin, in an interpretation of the visit of Montezuma and his young Indian bride. The Matachines' costumes are a strange combination of early Spanish conquerors' helmets, worn with present-day Anglo clothes, the latter consisting of white shirts, a Spanish shawl and an Indian interpretation of the Spanish jewels and long ribbons of many bright colors. Their faces are masked by fringes of black beads over the eyes. An old Spanish fiddler and a guitarist accompany this group. The plaintive melodies they play are in strange contrast to the religious hymns being sung by the bearers of the Virgin. For all the pueblos along the Rio Grande, Christmas is a combination of Christian and pagan ceremonies. One Christmas years ago, we visited San Felipe ... and were quite fascinated by the great buffalo dancers entering the church after midnight mass to do their ritual dance. It was very beautiful. The holidays pass so quickly, it is difficult to let them go and return to normal, which is never quite "normal" in Taos.

Meeting Georgia O'Keeffe

Draft letter to Bettina and George Dietrich from Charles, November 1987, Santa Fe

Thanks for your letter and article on O'Keeffe. Once upon a time, when Antoinette and I were camping in the far West, sleeping in a green tent, we ran out of water, and it so happened that we chanced upon a mail box along a highway where a small road ran down into a valley. And there we found a house. A middle-aged woman appeared in answer to our call and had a younger woman fill our water can. Noticing the Wisconsin license on our car, she said she was from Wisconsin too. And so it came to pass that the water was from the well of Georgia O'Keeffe. It appears that no names were exchanged at the time, but Antoinette told me after we left that she recognized the woman from photos in newspapers. Georgia also told us, because we were so impressed with the beauty of the country, that we should stop in at her only neighbor who owned Ghost Ranch, and was interested in selling her property, a wonderful large house all furnished and 200 acres. We have a letter from the owner, Mrs. Van Bergh of New York, offering it to us special for $15,000, minus 20 acres to keep for her. It is now in the several millions. And so it came to pass, that what's as past is as past can be.

(The CWT Estate Archives contains a series of letters in the hand of Beatrice Van Bergh offering the Thwaiteses the property for $15,000 and finally informing them it had been purchased by the Presbyterian Church.)

APPENDIX B: NOTES TO MYSELF

BY CHARLES WINSTANLEY THWAITES

Thwaites was as "talkative" writer with a command of the language. The estate contains numerous handwritten documents in which he relates personal experiences, tells stories about ghosts and other paranormal experiences, vents opinions about art critics, and expands on his method and the meaning of art. The writing, done in fountain pen, was transcribed from notes (a practice Thwaites also used in his letters), and there are few corrections. Occasionally, he titled the piece. In cases where he did not, I've given them descriptive titles.

According to the Dahlstrands, Thwaites jotted down these ideas as they came to him. Some have references that place them in a rough time period, and a larger group, done on similar paper and identified in the corner with his middle name, Winstanley, were probably written after the Thwaiteses moved to Santa Fe, perhaps in the mid-1970s onward.

Greenville Mural

The cartoon of the mural finished. The photos ready to send to Washington for approval. A knock on the studio door, and as I opened it a little elderly woman asked, "May I come in?" Inside she quickly glanced at the 9½ -by-15-foot wide drawing in black and white on wrapping paper and introduced herself. Her name didn't bring up any associations in the art field to me. She was born and lived in northern Wisconsin most of her life and was very familiar with lumberjacks and lumbering. While she was talking, her eyes were in the cartoon and when she finished she told me that she didn't like the central figure, which I had never felt very happy with either. On her leaving, I saw her to the door and down the stairs to the rough alleyway at the edge of the river, where the road slopes up to the street above.

Back in the studio only a very short time, I looked out to check on her progress. To my great surprise she was gone, never to hear of or see her again. I'd expected to see her about halfway up the street. Evidently I'd waited longer than I'd thought.

Well, I changed the figure entirely, more photos, Washington approval, mural on canvas finally completed and the hanging in the Greenville, Michigan, Post Office.

The mural was too large for me to handle alone. I was able to get a painter boss and his men to put it up with me, and as we were getting it up, everyone as they came in looked up at it and called out to us—"Where did you get hold of old Zeek?" So it turned out that the central figure was a dead ringer for the last of the lumberjacks who still came into town for his supplies.

The postmaster, who happened not to be in town when we left, wrote a very nice letter in which he mentions the strangest thing, or maybe just a coincidence "about old Zeek," elaborating on the particulars of his type and dress he wears.

It has always been a mystery just who the elderly lady was, how she knew about the mural or me, and where the studio was, as there was never any publicity about it, and I never encouraged even friends to the old warehouse room on the river.

Even without the sweet little old lady's visit, I probably would have made small changes, but to change the whole action, pose, type of figure, and likeness that it seems the whole town recognized immediately would have really been a coincidence indeed.

Little did I know that of the myriads of figures and likenesses that might have appeared on the canvas, that the one I painted was the one and only real person in Greenville that qualified perfectly for the place. By what mysterious force was my brush guided?

Plans

I have always thought of painting as design, that is, every move or element in a purposeful relation to everything else. It is a search for organization that we, as humans, need and should expect in art. Perhaps I should list some of the factors which have been my most constant influences, and which might in themselves suggest plans for further study.

Starting as a student of engineering impressed me with the reason and necessity for design in nature, and likewise, in the works of man.

A study of the old masters combined with a study of nature, revealed how close observation, directed by a plan for unity, provided them with the material which was both the means and the end they were seeking.

A certain pursuit of philosophy, or perhaps better, an attempt to make understandable, any and all information that comes to us, molding it into a unitized system or intellectual picture of the universe. This picture of the universe serving as background to the local scene, gives it at once

Winstanley

There seems, for lack of a better way of putting it, that the basic imprint of our understanding is of one physiognomy for art, science, and nature. This might be defined as a unity of abstract relations forming the bases for our own subconscious comprehension, and to which we automatically compare all our experiences. The act of comparison, although it may involves all our senses at the same time, is instantaneous and results in an emotion, either of pleasure, pain, or indifference.

The life of an artist is to cultivate an awareness of this basic look and his reactions to its patterns so that he can play it back in any form his interest dictates.

The life work of such an artist is the graphic history of his endeavors and contains at any one stage all his awareness and lack of it, plus "static," and his ability to unify on canvas his mystic built in knowledge and preferences. This is the esthetic experience in which he realizes his oneness with everything and gratifies all his physical and spiritual yearnings.

Looking back at my own education it was a series of unexpected events which took place physically on my canvas while painting. Some of these relationships were highly pleasing, and then, and perhaps only after that, did I recognize the same organizational design in another's work.

The discovery of the masters is just this discovering in their work of the elements of your own experiences, and the more you discover them in your own work the more you realize that they have tread the same path and have been there long before and usually to a much higher degree.

Lacking this experience may explain why some artists are satisfied with lesser artists instead of only the greatest.

The fact that it is a physical experience is the reason that it cannot be re-experienced by means of words and is therefore not transmitable to word oriented people. This explains the fallacy in writers writing about painting.

P14

One of the pages from Thwaites' handwritten Notes to Myself, and the fountain pen he used to write them (photo of pen by Dennis Wyszynski Photography).

its proper relation and sense of universality, and also supplies a source for purely abstract consideration of relationships.

A Physical Experience

Looking back at my own education it was a series of unexpected events which took place physically in my canvas while painting. Some of these relationships were highly pleasing, and then, and perhaps only after that, did I recognize the same organizational design in another work.

The discovery of the masters is just this discovering in their work of the elements of your own experiences, and the more you discover them in your own work, the more you realize that they have tread the same path and have been there long before and usually to a much higher degree.

Lacking this experience may explain why some artists are satisfied with lesser artists instead of only the greatest.

The fact that it is a physical experience is the reason that it cannot be re-experienced by means of words and is therefore not transmittable to word-oriented people. This explains the fallacy in writers writing about art.

The Look

Have we seen it before—in paintings—in the eye in a Rembrandt portrait—the juxtaposition of color, the ideal in color contrasts, not the trite hackneyed copied but the inspired use of color wedded with equally inspired contrasts of pattern, texture, shapes, sizes, and relation to a greater whole?

It is to be seen in painting from all times and in nature and, looking long at nature, we see it change and vary and reappear in endless succession of emotion satisfying relationships.

It should be drawn to your attention, this phenomenon of organized contrast by singling it out in art and nature so that your deepest needs can find the satisfaction of the senses through the logic of visual relations. These truths find ready reception and swift sensory understanding bypassing the sophisticated acceptance and expected habits of thought. They are natural to a being whose very existence is the all embracing embodiment of parallel truths of organization.

Had you but the interest, you might get to know their look, that look which appeals to the senses without need of any translation whatsoever. That look which finds sympathetic accord in the deep logic of the emotions, so that you come to know that calm yet exciting, relaxing yet energizing flux of unity with something outside of yourself, that re-creating play upon the nervous system. It is the feeling of living when life is really worthwhile. Once you know that feeling your judgment can be relied upon and you are free from depending on others. You have that sense of completeness and are ready to give as well as receive.

Let us admit that intellectually we don't know what it is all about and trust to the intuition through our eye. Let us admit that the elaborate myth we build is really for the purpose of trapping the intellect in an intellectually unsolvable problem so that our emotions can be free to obey the eye.

The Look Again

So as we were saying, Sinclair, artist-teacher at Layton School of Art, knew the look, and Antoinette knew the look from experience of examining the many, many prints which she collected and many paintings in galleries and at exhibitions and her own paintings, comparing, appraising them over and over for years.

Did they need more? Did they need all this philosophy and psychology stuff behind the look? No! No! Not in the conscious mind or in words, but Yes!, deep down in the subconscious. Well, you say so what? And we say this "what what" this "look" has a pattern, and because it is an abstract pattern it exists in many, many forms and not the least important of which is the one imprinted in parallel pattern on your subconscious in the conduct of your own life.

Thus, as we were saying, this "look," this look of the best spot on the canvas is just as valid on the canvas of your life, which you are painting, and when extended to the whole canvas, as we know back then, and realize now, is what really sets some canvases and certain lives .... well, apart and above the many.

It is in silence where the two equal themes of nature meet, the one deep inside of you and the other everywhere outside of you, all the rest of the universe, the total, not one part over accented beyond all the others

Along the Ocean's Shores

Dedication to your eyes, seeing what is there, free from subject matter. Not what the object is, but rather what makes it look the way it looks, is the rich and exciting field of exploration and discovery for the young artist, and is an inexhaustible, endless, lifelong pursuit. As one advances in experience and sensitivity and the growing realization of the limitless richness about us in everything we see, from the simplest exercises in light and shade, to the great masterpieces of paintings, we build up a great awareness of visual images and combinations of color and patterns which are constantly being renewed in infinite variation and greater scope, culminating in a sense of the universal.

To see free, to let the eye tell you what is there, as an instrument free from associations is a very exciting world, but as a human being it is a bit more complex as we advance in experience. There is this thing about philosophy and psychology directing what and how we see and this, of course, makes all the difference, the difference that makes art possible.

And so we find ourselves in that vast sea of possibilities and choices, our conscious selves without sail or rudder, carried on and guided by forces of far deeper persuasion in earthly ties and mystic universal accord.

Yes, all this, all this, to leave our faint footprints in the sands along the ocean's shores, to be washed away by the next tide.

Change

In art we are looking for an echo of our own being and all being at one and the same time. Each painting is a symbol of the universe as an organization and in that spirit is found the guide to great painting, in contrast to the lesser whose authors were less universally inspired.

If we now can imagine building a rather limited but flexible intellectual picture of organization in the background of our mind, we can go about verifying this image with everything we see or indeed are able to apprehend with all senses. You will then find that it is an actual or reciprocal operation. Your preconceived but infinitely flexible intellectual model will serve to direct deeper and broader insight and that in turn will serve to reveal unsuspected relationships that play or feed back, modifying the original pattern and eventually culminating in a greater, immensely richer aesthetic foundation for appreciation. So time and change keep pace everlastingly and so it has always been that each generation needs new freedoms to explore wider possibilities for less hackneyed combinations to emphasize and test for our continued refreshment of spiritual at the same time to experience and relive the history of great art in our own work.

Love

There are many works of art, which at the right time, we could appreciate. That right time being when our experience and needs have sharpened a deeper understanding of the real values mutually in accord—and we fall in love.

Love is seeing a genuine worth and much needed agreement between yourself and something or someone outside yourself.

Love is a subconscious element. Love precedes academic knowledge. There is no knowledge superior to love. If maximum wisdom is contained in love, the least wisdom is contained in hate. Politics promotes hate. Morality begins in knowing that the world is perfect. The germ of the answer lies in the question. The law is absolute and also infinitely flexible. Reality is the poetry of perfection. The spirit of painting is in the frame of philosophy and culminates in a synthesis of the universal and the personal.

To understand yourself—to understand your personal philosophy—is to understand your likes and dislikes in an organized way.

Synthesis of Universal and Personal

Art is stimulated by its own kind, that is to say, the organization of a unit—art, science and nature.

Art, like religion, is always being violated in the name of something else. Usually, art is stimulated by something in that something else. Just how does it work? What happens from the time it receives that outside stimulus and gets on the canvas? The canvas itself makes continued demands and is the object, or to be the object of art which you are making, and it is its success, not the things outside of it, that now take over in importance. It has logic uniquely its own. It is what it says about itself, not something else that we want. It is in silence where the two equal themes of nature meet, the one deep inside of you and the other everywhere outside of you, all the rest of the universe, the total not one part over accented beyond all the others.

There is no greater blindness than lack of interest. The masters always saw the means for a universal statement in the visual aspects of nature. They could pick out those visual aspects which coincided with their inner picture of the universe. Their personal choices represented their built-in attractions and repulsions directed by a highly original philosophy of existence, resulting in a most significant statement of unity.

Perhaps there is such a satisfaction in painting because not only can it be, it must be, all your own, through your own eyes, instead of others, your own selection, reflection, opinion and judgments and above all, your own synthesis, meaning, the formation of a unity of highly disparate parts.

Organization of Color

Color involves everything, all the elements. You cannot put down color without also putting down a value, hue, texture, shape, an area, all contrasting with each other and with the whole and where their tensions produce forces that must be organized.

This is the heart of the organizational material with which visual contrasts are built and is what affects the structure which parallels all other structures.

The fact that any change in any one of the elements cannot help but affect all the others, demonstrates the intimate involvement inherent—especially color change.

The fact that you are never working with any element isolated from the others, such as color or value as such, but areas always involved with all the rest, like it or not, means that the laws governing that factual situation are of first importance.

The fact that it also represents an involvement parallel to all other organizational means and that it is self-sufficient, complete in itself.

The fact that this organizational whole can be mitigated with other organizational entities to form greater productions with farther reaching associations is the reason behind the many diverse ideas on art. The logic of the esthetic pattern (the relation of the contrasts of the specific elements involved) is determined by the organization of each element and of each segment and each segment to the whole.

The Computer

Man, a computer, his product as an image of that computer. Art is evidence of that computer. Many other computers depend on symbols, but painting deals in physical concrete entities that are direct forces.

Its function is to inform through the senses, which employs the total mind in all its possibilities, capable of grasping infinite abstract complexities and relations in visual form as in no other way.

Through this means is grasped the spirit of the philosophy of organization, which gives us an invaluable parallel for understanding everything else. It is the blueprint for idealism, idealism in the means and the end, as against any means to an end, and thus represents the highest morality.

In simple terms it is a common denominator, a yardstick to measure and assess all nature and man's work as a product of it as well.

Yes, the art of painting at its best results ideally in a computer giving you that condensed picture of the entire universe with all its complexities displayed visually as an organization parallel to all other organizations.

It is a graphic physiognomy of the past, present and future.

Painting is a computer keyed to the universe, calculating and recording complex relations beyond our conscious thoughts, transmitting them directly through our nerves to an emotional value. The quality of the emotional value measures the worth of the organization. Because painting is unique in that it is the one form among all others which can be apprehended completely and instantaneously, it gives you the total working of all its parts interacting simultaneously in such a way that its impact is immediate and concentrated in the quality of its unity and purity of its organization. It therefore throws visual organization in the key role it must have over any other subject matter it might contain, and is independent of memory, because the source has been imprinted in our subconscious and is coded in every cell of our being.

It is not subject to, or flawed by the possibility of leaving anything out, with which all other conceivable forms of experiences are plagued.

Thus we have a pattern, a form or configuration accessible and understandable to our senses in visual terms that we can apply and compare to all other forms of organization as a parallel that should be attained and so function as a universal template or paradigm for all other achievements when we reduce them to the same elements and principles.

Literary Minds

The question of the significance of the visual arts as compared to the literary arts is one which has always been answered with great satisfaction by literary persons. It has always been self-evident to them that words come first and because of this very eminence, it is incumbent on the literary to bring all the other arts to everyone's understanding. This point of view has always had such wide acceptance that it has even been quite innocently taken for granted and naturally accounts for its prodigious output and reliance on it that dominates all the other arts.

Now for the Critic

Well, we've all been bored with: He who lives by the sword shall perish by the sword. However, because the critic's sword is a very special double-edge one, he cannot avoid hacking himself along with the object of his criticism, whether favorable or unfavorable, as he gaily chops his way about. This is probably the only excuse for his existence, if it can be excused at all. It is also fortunate because it introduced a bit of sportsmanship into the game, since obviously the critic is not as safe as he generally thinks. Nevertheless, so far it seems, he always lives to chop himself to bits another day, as in Greek mythology. So I expect he'll always just go chippity chopping away.

Final Warning to the Innocent

To the extent to which a man follows only his own choice, without it being absorbed and genuinely integrated in the universal scheme, he is impaled on the wheel of his ego. He is the non-realist, living in a world of make believe, the myth of self, he demands. Let the innocent beware.

A Matter of Conscience

1. Strong is he who can keep his ideas and actions aligned in one definite direction.
2. Strong is he whose conscience has never deviated from the straight and narrow path of serving the self first, last, and always by any means.
3. Strong is he whose conscience from its early childhood shoot has grown to the single tall straight trunk, never having branched out in consideration of others, except when the returns far exceed the service.
4. Strong is he whose conscience makes its owner suffer intolerable agony of unfaithfulness to self when forced to compromise.

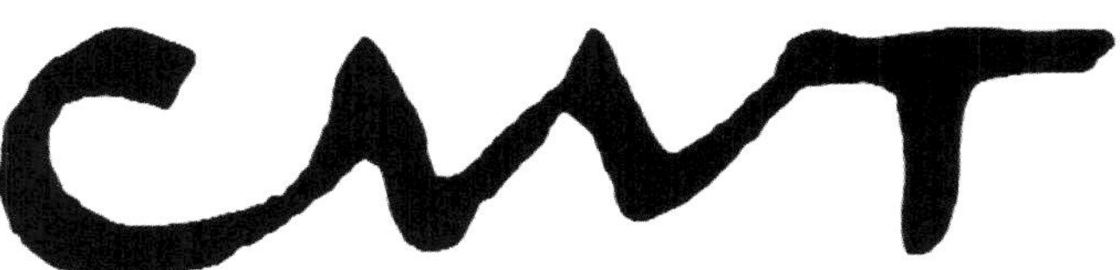

Thwaites was a prolific artist who was constantly at work. In several instances, his paintings on paper have paintings on the backside as well. Some appear experimental, others unfinished. He dated a painting on its front surface only rarely and occasionally ascribed a date on the verso.

His signature is typically printed and comes in a variety of forms, including: Thwaites, C Thwaites, Chas W Thwaites, Charles Thwaites, Charles W Thwaites, CW Thwaites, or just his initials, CWT, with the first two letters and top of the "T" done as one continuous stroke and the descender of the T added (see detail). In many instances he signed the paintings more than once, sometimes joining CWT with Thwaites or a variation thereof beneath it. While he tended to sign in the lower right hand corner, occasionally he signed wherever he could make the signature seen, including in the upper left corner. Several of the paintings are signed in red and some are also signed in script on the verso.

INDEX OF ILLUSTRATIONS